THE EMERGING
MIDWEST

MIDWESTERN HISTORY AND CULTURE

GENERAL EDITORS

James H. Madison & Thomas J. Schlereth

THE
EMERGING
MIDWEST

UPLAND SOUTHERNERS AND THE
POLITICAL CULTURE OF THE
OLD NORTHWEST,
1787–1861

Nicole Etcheson

INDIANA UNIVERSITY PRESS
Bloomington & Indianapolis

Chapter 3 appeared in the spring 1995 issue of the *Journal of the Early Republic* and is reprinted here by permission from the publisher. A portion of chapter 4 was previously published in *The Pursuit of Public Power: Political Culture in Ohio, 1787–1861*, edited by Jeffrey P. Brown and R. L. Canton, and appears here by permission of Kent State University Press.

The paper used in this publication meets the
minimum requirements of American National Standard
for Information Sciences—Permanence of Paper for
Printed Library Materials,
ANSI Z39. 48-1984

Manufactured in the United States of America

Library of Congress Cataloging-in-Publication Data

Etcheson, Nicole.
The emerging midwest : upland Southerners and the political culture of the old
northwest, 1787–1861 / Nicole Etcheson.
p. cm. — (Midwestern history and culture)
Includes bibliographical references and index.
ISBN 0-253-32994-9 (cl : alk. paper)
1. Northwest, Old—Politics and government—1775–1865.
2. Political culture—Northwest, Old—History. 3. Regionalism—
United States—History. I. Title. II. Series.
F484.3.E83 1996
306.2'0976'09034—dc20   95-22704

1 2 3 4 5 01 00 99 98 97 96

FOR ROBERT

CONTENTS

Contents

ACKNOWLEDGMENTS

IT IS IMPOSSIBLE TO REPAY the personal and professional debts incurred while working on this manuscript. As a paltry substitute, I offer these acknowledgments.

James H. Madison, Steven M. Stowe, Maurice Baxter, and Edward G. Carmines saw the manuscript through the dissertation stage. Jim Madison has been a thorough critic and a patient, good-natured mentor. Steve Stowe has read more drafts of this book than he cares to remember but has never failed to provide fresh and insightful comments. Andrew Cayton, Robert Hilderbrand, and Gerald Wolff read later drafts and offered helpful, if often painful, criticism. If their advice went unheeded, only I am to blame.

The history department at Indiana University generously supported this work with fellowships and grants-in-aid. The graduate school of Indiana University provided a grant-in-aid for research travels. The Indiana Historical Society Graduate Fellowship in History enabled me to start work on the dissertation in a timely fashion. The Oscar O. Winther Dissertation Fellowship, awarded by the history department, hastened the completion of the dissertation.

The staffs of the Indiana Historical Society, the Ohio Historical Society, and the Illinois State Historical Library never flinched from any request. The reference librarians at Indiana University unfailingly procured endless reels of microfilm.

My final debts are to my family. My mother, Joy B. Etcheson, encouraged my early love of history and has kept encouraging ever since. Robbie helped hasten the manuscript's completion. It had to be done before he came, because it would never get done afterwards. My husband, Robert J. Williams, did little of the work often demanded of academic spouses. He was neither research assistant nor typist and only a reluctant copy editor. But he has sacrificed and endured much to make this book possible. For that, I dedicate it to him as the small recompense that grubby little scholars can make to those they love.

INTRODUCTION

"THE ENTERPRISING Yankee of Northern Indiana despises the slug-
gish and inaminate [sic] North Carolinian, Virginian, and Kentuckian in
the southern part of the state," wrote Godlove S. Orth, a mid-nineteenth-
century Indiana politician. Southerners, on the other hand, were known
to distrust the Yankee and his penny-pinching, dishonest ways.[1] Such
regional characterizations structured Midwestern politics. As migrants
settled the new region, they created a new identity for themselves as
Westerners. Accommodation with their new neighbors, especially in
politics, required submerging older identifications as Southerners or
Yankees, York State men or Pennsylvanians. Yet those older sectional
loyalties never disappeared; at best they lay quiescent awaiting a political
climate which would stimulate their resurgence.

Upland Southerners can tell the historian something not only of the
culture they helped to create in the new region of the Midwest, but also of
the culture of the South, and of the new nation. Passed from generation to
generation, the customs and ideas which compose a culture shape and
influence the actions of its members. Despite the natural resistance of
individuals and communities to change, new situations arise which alter
these customs and ideas.[2] Political culture is a subset of the larger culture.
It is the "coherent pattern" by which citizens understand their government, political leaders, and themselves.[3] In the Midwest, this "web of
relations," as one political scientist calls it, involved a complex pattern of
regional and political loyalties. Political culture encompasses the shared
assumptions about government and governance.[4] Broadly speaking,
Americans shared an adherence to principles of republican government
best embodied by the Union, and increasingly in the nineteenth century,
loyalty to political parties. Within those shared assumptions lay much
room for differences of emphasis and interpretation.

A region, for the purposes of this work, is more than simply an area
marked by common geographic features. Accidents of history and cultural values also defined it. The South was a region characterized by
slavery, staple-crop agriculture, and membership in the Confederacy.
Section also refers to similarities of culture within a geographic area, and
as such is often used interchangeably with region, but section carries the

added meaning of excessive devotion, so that sectionalism implies deeper loyalties to a place and prejudices against its neighbors.[5]

The Ordinance of 1787, which carved a political jurisdiction out of the American frontier, created the Old Northwest. This region, later part of the Midwest, was thus at first an arbitrarily designated one. Nonetheless, the Midwest came to share commonalities of its own, including commitment to free labor, bourgeois middle-class values, and a sense of itself as the most American of regions.[6] The process of defining the Midwest began when Northern and Southern migrants began to identify themselves more as Westerners than as Southerners or Northerners and continued through much of the nineteenth century as regional and political loyalties pulled people toward or pushed them away from this new identity. This book is about that process.

Historians of the Midwest have long debated the meaning of this mixture of Northern and Southern peoples in the region, usually dwelling on Southern democracy and independence versus Yankee cultural imperialism.[7] That antagonism did exist, but equally important and little studied is the extent to which Southerners and Northerners forged a new regional identity. Upland Southerners who migrated to the Midwest removed themselves from the primary determinants of Southern culture, slavery and the planter elite. In the Midwest, they spent generations in intimate contact, primarily through the political arena, with other cultural groups, especially the New Englanders. Yet the sectional crisis of the 1850s reawakened Upland Southern Midwesterners' fierce identification with the South. Clearly loyalty to the South transcended protection of a plantation system from which Upland Southern Midwesterners had removed.

Unifying forces did exist in the Midwest. Southerners and Northerners alike defined themselves as citizens of the republic, as members of political parties, and as Westerners.[8] While those alternative identities provided a basis for cohesion, they largely disguised rather than replaced sectional differences. All Midwesterners spoke of republicanism, yet Upland Southerners emphasized the manly qualities needed to lead in a republic. All Midwesterners became fierce partisans, but Upland Southerners became so later and with deeper reservations. All Midwesterners called themselves Westerners, and felt superior to Easterners, yet this Western identity faltered during the sectional crisis of the 1850s and 1860s.

The Midwestern pattern mirrored, and provides insight into, the process of nation building and national disintegration which the United States experienced between revolution and civil war. All Americans shared citizenship in the republic and identification with the new nation. By studying the role of regional and sectional loyalties in the Midwest, we can better understand why the new nation faced, and almost dissolved in, bloody civil strife.

In addition, studying the meeting of cultures in the Old Northwest may give pause to historians breathlessly recounting the growth of the new nation. True, the period covered here was one of enormous change. Hierarchical forms of society and government withered, market and transportation revolutions occurred, religious upheaval spread new denominations, and the nation experienced population and territorial growth of an unprecedented scale. For all that, cultural attitudes sometimes change only slowly. So it was in the Old Northwest.

The sources used in this work fall into two categories. One set of documents is persuasive in nature. By means of letters to newspapers and political figures, editorials, petitions, and speeches, Midwesterners attempted to argue others into agreement with their views. Many of these documents follow a formula standard among works of their type. For example, throughout this period, a candidate's announcement of his availability for political office typically included a disclaimer of any desire to obtrude himself on the public notice. Often he pointed out that he had succumbed only to the repeated urgings of friends. This formulaic style of discourse reveals how the writer believed he should communicate his ambitions. Both those ambitions and their phrasing express the political values and expectations of writer and audience. The second set of documents is descriptive in nature. It consists of travelers' accounts, newspaper stories, diaries, memoirs, and private letters, which purported to tell how or why or in what setting particular events occurred. These accounts, of course, were never entirely objective but were colored by the values and beliefs of their authors. These too have their own formulas, although to a lesser extent. Some will quarrel that politicians are notorious dissemblers, at least in their public discourse. Perhaps so. Nonetheless, politicians, at least the successful ones, have to be astutely aware of public sensibilities and community values. They win office by appealing to assumptions shared with the electorate about its institutions and government. In defense of political honesty, however, private political reflections and correspondence revealed the same sentiments as those publicly expressed. For these reasons, historians can depend on politicians to be articulate voices of the political culture.

These Upland Southern Midwesterners shared many beliefs with their fellow Southerners and with other Americans. But their story is nonetheless unique and sheds much light on the meaning of the South for those who left it, on the new republic's ability to overcome sectional loyalties, and on the creation of a new region, the Midwest, which, by the late nineteenth century, many would view as the quintessentially American region.

THE EMERGING
MIDWEST

ONE

❦

North and South in the Midwest

SECTIONAL AND REGIONAL stereotypes have a rich history in the United States. Penny-pinching Yankees, decadent Southern planters, and lazy poor whites populated the antebellum cultural landscape. Upland Southerners frequently gave Northeasterners credit for superior industry and capitalistic virtues, but largely condemned Yankee sharp dealing. The run-down appearance and lackadaisical ways of the hill people appalled immigrants from outside the South. In the Midwest, however, sectional antipathies were muted for a generation as New Englanders, Mid-Atlantic immigrants, and Upland Southerners concentrated on settling a new region. Yet sectionalism did not disappear. Upland Southerners never ceased to grumble about "Yankee imperialism." Sectionalism had merely receded, reaching its lowest point during the Jacksonian period. Two developments explain this easing of antipathy. A sense of being a Westerner grew. This new creature, differing from both Northerner and Southerner, combined, some thought, the best qualities of each region. Also, the second party system subordinated regional loyalties to party loyalties. Democrats or Whigs, whether of Northern or Southern origin, could find common ground by working for the same political principles. Both developments served as unifying ties during the Jacksonian era. These ties were later broken by the sectional forces of the Civil War, which

Table I: Population by Birthplace, 1850
(% of total)

	Ohio	Indiana	Illinois
New England	66,032 (3.3%)	10,646 (1.1%)	36,542 (4.3%)
South	147,006 (7.4%)	173,611 (17.6%)	143,412 (16.8%)
New York	83,979 (4.2%)	24,310 (2.5%)	67,180 (7.9%)
Pennsylvania	200,634 (10.1%)	44,245 (4.5%)	37,979 (4.5%)
Old Northwest*	1,228,224 (62.0%)	665,445 (67.3%)	438,790 (51.5%)
Total Population of State	1,980,329	988,416	851,470

*Ohio, Indiana, and Illinois.
Source: *The Seventh Census of the United States, 1850* (Washington, 1853), ix, xxxvi.

brought back into the forefront previously overlooked distinctions based on regional traits.

Sectionalism, rooted in the differing economies and cultural heritages of New England, the South, and the Mid-Atlantic states, has, of course, long fascinated historians. It has been used to describe the demise of the Articles of Confederation, the coming of the Civil War, and much of what lay between the two. The discussion has included endless argument about what the differences between North and South mean. To what extent did slavery, a peculiarly Southern institution, break down national feelings? Inside the South, did differences between black belt plantation society and Upland Southern yeomen weaken the sense of Southern identity?[1] To answer these questions, few have looked at the place where these cultural streams met, the Midwest, and those few have concentrated on the struggle between traditionalist Southerners and Yankee cultural imperialists.[2]

The Yankees, whom Godlove Orth held up as the embodiment of virtue and enterprise, were relative latecomers to the Midwest. Southerners arrived first, crossing the Ohio River in the years after the American Revolution, usually ahead of government surveyors. They came from the Upland South, the interior border region of the Old South which includes piedmont Virginia, Maryland, North Carolina, Kentucky, and Tennessee.

North and South in the Midwest

Table II: Population Growth
(% increase over previous census)

	Ohio	Indiana	Illinois
1800	45,365	4,875	NA
1810	230,760 (408.7%)	24,520 (403.0%)	12,282
1820	581,434 (152.0%)	147,178 (500.2%)	55,211 (349.5%)
1830	937,903 (61.3%)	343,031 (133.1%)	157,445 (185.2%)
1840	1,519,467 (62.0%)	685,866 (99.9%)	476,183 (202.4%)
1850	1,980,329 (30.3%)	988,416 (44.1%)	851,470 (78.8%)
1860*	2,339,481 (18.1%)	1,350,138 (36.6%)	1,711,919 (101.1%)

*White and black population.
Source: *The Seventh Census of the United States, 1850* (Washington, 1853), ix, and
Population of the United States in 1860 (Washington, 1864), 598.

These five states provided the bulk of the immigrants to the Old Northwest. The census of 1850, the first to list places of birth, reveals that 16.8
percent of Illinois's population had been born in the South. The figures for
Indiana and Ohio were 17.6 percent and 7.4 percent. Although the census
listed residents in those states born in such deep South states as Georgia,
Louisiana, or Florida, the Upland South states accounted for the vast
majority of Midwesterners of Southern nativity: 97.3 percent in Ohio,
95.9 percent in Indiana, and 88.8 percent in Illinois. Furthermore, the
majority of each state's residents had been born in that state or one of the
other two. (See Table I.) That fact obscures somewhat the actual Southern
presence, for those Midwesterners counted as born in their respective
states were often the children and grandchildren of Southern immigrants,
the earliest settlers in the region.[3]

Although some New Englanders had entered the Midwest in the years
after the Revolution, notably the Ohio Company settlement by New
England Revolutionary War veterans and the Western Reserve of Ohio
claimed by Connecticut, Yankees did not arrive in the Midwest in
significant numbers until the 1820s and 1830s. The first half of the

nineteenth century was a time of explosive growth in which populations frequently doubled and even quadrupled or quintupled over previous censuses. (See Table II.) The years of greatest growth, the first two decades of the nineteenth century, were also the years when immigration was heavily from the Upland South. The Ohio River was the Southerners' path to the Midwest, and they crossed it or came down it as soon as the Revolution ended. In southern Ohio, they occupied the Virginia Military District, the Symmes Purchase, and the Congress lands in central and western southern Ohio. In Indiana, the boundary between North and South was believed to lie along the route of the National Road, which bisected the state at Indianapolis. Illinoisans called the Southern-dominated section of their state Egypt. Although Egypt lay in the far southern counties, the Upland South stretched into north central Illinois, including the Sangamon River country familiar to the Lincoln family and other Kentucky immigrants.[4]

Nineteenth-century Midwesterners were keenly aware of these settlement patterns and of cultural differences apparent in food, speech, architecture, and religion—factors today used by cultural geographers to distinguish cultural regions. A New Englander on the Illinois prairie commented that her Southern neighbors disagreed on the preparation of what both called a "boiled dinner." The New Englanders who settled Ohio's Western Reserve divided the land into geometric patterns and re-created their familiar township organization. In the Virginia Military District, a part of Ohio settled by Southerners, tracts were shaped irregularly so as to take the best advantage of natural resources. Patterns of land division were rooted in the colonial past of the two regions. Three streams of log construction converged in the Midwest. The Tennessee and Kentucky preference for half-dovetailing corner timbers moved north of the Ohio River; Pennsylvanians brought V-notching westward. New Englanders used false-corner timbering and the setting of horizontal timbers into corner posts in northern Indiana, Illinois, and Ohio. Even the simple chore of milking the cows had cultural significance. For the New Englanders, milking was a man's task; but for the Southerners, milking was very much a woman's job. It was considered degrading for a man to do such work. In central Illinois, Southerners considered a man milking the cows a "Yankee innovation." If a hired man was asked to milk the cows, he would either quit or demand more money. A correspondent of the *Scioto Gazette* suspected his neighbor was a Yankee, "for he brings water from the spring, and sometimes helps his wife milk the cows on a rainy day."[5] Gender divisions, among other things, differed from Southern culture to Northern.

Southerners and Northerners also noted differences between the "temperaments" of the peoples of the two sections. Thomas Jefferson called

Northerners "laborious," "independent," "jealous of their own liberties and just to those of others"; Southerners were "indolent," "unsteady," and "zealous for their own liberties, but trampling on those of others." Jefferson, however, wrote of the influence a plantation-based Southern society had on its free population. Most of the Southern settlers in the Midwest came from the upcountry yeomanry. They were variously called backcountrymen, backwoodsmen, or frontiersmen. They were, for the most part, small subsistence farmers who lacked slaves or the means to acquire them, lived on the outskirts of settled areas, possessed limited access to markets, and lacked the wealth and refinement of the plantation elite. Looked down upon by the planters, they in turn were deeply suspicious of plantation society, fearing its tendency to subjugate poor whites as well as blacks. Reverend James B. Finley looked back on the Kentucky backwoodsmen of the 1790s as a "hardy race of men and women" who possessed "more common sense and enterprise" than their more privileged cousins. The nineteenth-century image of the two sections saw the Yankee as thrifty and industrious, and the Southerner as pleasure-loving, generous, and unaffected by monetary considerations. The other side of those characteristics, however, was that the New Englanders were "mercenary, hypocritical and Philistine," while Southerners were "self-indulgent" or "self-destructive."[6] Although often described in unflattering terms, the Southerner was thought to be self-reliant, independent, uninterested in economic advancement, and content to get by from day to day.

Even among many Southerners, the backcountry people who migrated to Ohio, Indiana, and Illinois had a poor reputation. One account of the origin of the nickname "Hoosier" attributes it to the Southern slang for hayseed or rube applied to the mountain residents of Tennessee, Virginia, and North and South Carolina, many of whom settled in Indiana.[7] George Washington described the backcountry people of Virginia as "a parcel of barbarians and an uncouth set of people." Examples of their vulgarity included a local justice of the peace who served dinner without table cloth or knife.[8]

Historians have followed the lead of contemporary accounts in depicting the Southern frontiersman as less interested in fine manners, self-improvement, or economic return beyond self-sufficiency. Whether the culprit was lack of access to markets, the effects of plantation slavery on nonslaveholders, or a Celtic ethnic heritage, the Southern backwoodsman possessed both an enviable reputation for independent spirit and self-sufficiency and an unenviable one for sloth and dirt.[9]

In politics, Southern backcountrymen were notorious for lack of deference. Historians of the South have long noted the paradox that Southerners developed a fierce attachment to liberty out of their close acquaintance with chattel slavery and fought a civil war to protect that liberty, as they defined it, and slavery. Historians of the Southern backcountry, however, have noted the uneasy relationship between planters and yeomen farmers. The latter deferred to the former yet resented them. The planters, in turn, remained uneasy about that grudging deference and about nonslaveholding whites' allegiance to the slave system. Planters might develop an ideology that saw black slavery as necessary to white egalitarianism and democracy; the backcountrymen who migrated into the Old Northwest did not. They saw themselves as dispossessed by the expanding plantation system. In the Midwest, they no longer needed to be deferential, but they continued to be resentful.[10]

If even cultured, aristocratic Southerners such as Washington found the life and manners of the backcountrymen wanting, it is not surprising that Northerners had even more averse reactions. The Ohio Company offered its colony as a model, contrasting its "regular and judicious" settlement of federal lands with the erratic settlement by squatters from the South. Among the political benefits potentially accruing to the United States would be the shining examples of "government, science, and regular industry" which the new settlement would present to the people of Kentucky and the Illinois country who, far from the established states and evidently lacking these virtues themselves, were in danger of losing altogether "their habits of government" and, more important, their allegiance to the federal government. Generously, the New Englanders offered to "revive the ideas of order, citizenship, and the useful sciences" among the backcountrymen. The Ohio Company offered to ensure that worthy settlers, the kinds who would promote rapid economic growth, would settle the Northwest.[11]

Even though the Ohio Company succeeded in transplanting the New England village to the Ohio wilderness, its paternalistic aspects, which included overseeing the planting of shade trees and the proper observance of the Fourth of July, were not appealing to the backcountrymen. Thaddeus Mason Harris found many examples of their "degrading character" in their neglect of farming, their "rough and savage manners," and their "miserable cabins." He contrasted the Virginia side of the Ohio River with the "industrious habits and neat improvements" on the Ohio side at Marietta. "Sloth and independence are prominent traits in their character," he wrote; "to indulge the former is their principal enjoyment, and to protect the latter their chief ambition." John Cleves Symmes, the New Jersey land speculator, was another who commented on the independence of the Kentuckians he hired to escort him down the Miami River. After they deserted him forty miles up the river, he condemned them as "very ungovernable and seditious; not to be awed or persuaded."[12] Symmes, like the New Englanders at Marietta, had profound doubts

about the "governability" of these Southerners. They were too independent for civil life and too lazy for economic progress.

In turn, Southerners had their own prejudices about Yankees. "A
Kentuckian suspects nothing but a Yankee," advised traveler Elias Pym
Fordham, "whom he considers as a sort of Jesuit." An English traveler
noted that in Illinois, "If any one has been cheated, he is said to have been
'yankeed,' and any worthless thing, which is tinselled and varnished, is
said to be 'yankeed over.'" In traveling through the Western country,
George Ogden noted that in the Western and Southern states Yankees
were held in low repute. One Virginian, who was considering emigrating
to Ohio, wrote that he had received a "very unfavourable account of the
people of that Country." He had been told that the residents were "a very
unhospitable, unsociable set of folks and that a man raised in this part of
the country would hardly ever be able to conform to their manners and
customs."[13]

A shrewd young Virginian, at college in Ohio, played upon cultural
prejudice when asking for money—again—from an uncle back in Virginia. He refused to continue to account for the money spent, "Because I
presume no one of the family, much less yourself, can indulge the idea, or
even imagine that we can live here without spending some money—
Recollect that we are living among a tight set of Yankys, and consequently
have to pay a high price for everything we get."[14] Southerners in the
Midwest saw their Yankee neighbors as not only tight fisted but also
downright sneaky. Yankees were not to be trusted in money matters, as
their excessive concern with finances made them grasping. The young
Virginian avoided haggling over money by taking the high ground on the
assumption that his honesty was above reproach and all unpleasant
expenditures could be blamed on Yankee sharpers.

When more Northerners moved to the Midwest, political accommoda-
tions had to be made to attract the support of the new settlers. In running
for governor of Illinois, William Kinney was forced to deny "the stale and
nonsensical charge of being inimical to the immigration to our state of the
valuable and industrious population of New England, whom I have been
made to designate as 'blue-bellied Yankees.'" While admitting he might
once have used the term "blue-light Yankees" to refer to New Englanders
who had engaged in illegal trade with the British during the War of 1812,
Kinney maintained that all patriotic citizens would join him in condemning those who threw obstacles in the way of winning that war. Nevertheless, Kinney had been forced by political circumstances to avoid sectional
criticisms, even to retract sectional slurs that had once been permissible.
Richard Douglas of Chillicothe took Kinney one step further and vowed
that, although a Yankee by birth, he could give a stump speech "whole
hog" like a Kentuckian. Feeling that Southerners had gone too far in

accommodating Northerners, one Illinoisan complained that place of birth was being made a qualification for political office so that Western and Southern men could be turned out to make room for a "*virtuous* and *industrious* northern population." He did not call, however, for a return to anti-Northern prejudice, but urged that all unite for the common good.[15]

Another story reveals hostility to the influx of New Englanders. A Yankee newly arrived from Connecticut asked the price of a shave. When the barber said a shilling, the Yankee protested loud and long that back home it would only be three cents. Even after the barber agreed to shave him for that price, the Yankee refused to pay until the job was done. The barber did the job with a rusty razor, full of nicks, which left tufts of hair on the pained newcomer's face. The Yankee refused to pay at all, and the barber coolly replied, "I've had more than a shillings worth of *fun,* and I think you have suffered more than a shillings worth of *pain,* so you may keep your three cents, and we'll quit even, if you say so." The author called this the Yankee's first lesson in the high prices of the West, but it was also a look at Northern values from non-Northern eyes. What New Englanders saw as praiseworthy frugality, others saw as refusing to pay full value. The shifty Connecticut Yankee first quarreled about the price, then refused to pay until after he was shaved, and finally refused to pay at all. The barber, on the other hand, insisted on his rights and refused to be moved by the Yankee's attempts to bargain. The reader, anticipating from the Yankee's demeanor that he will never pay for the shave, can only congratulate the barber on his shrewdness and willingness to stand up for himself.[16]

Two Fourth of July toasts indicate the realization by the Jacksonian period that the Midwest was now both Southern and Northern in origin: From Virginia, "one of the parents of Ohio," celebrants in Chillicothe hoped to inherit "her open candor, noble generosity and unshaken patriotism"; from Connecticut, "Ohio's other parent," they claimed to have gotten "the heads that could think, and the hands that can do—and the hearts that can go ahead." But formal occasions and their accompanying oratory did not entirely replace the old suspicions or change the cultural dominance of the Southerners. Sent to Illinois to save residents from ignorance and profanity, a New England missionary found in a St. Louis paper an article warning the public to be on guard against Northern missionaries. Stephen A. Douglas discovered that being Southern had advantages for a young man beginning his political career in Illinois. His opponent for First Judicial Circuit State's Attorney, John J. Hardin, had not only held the office for two years, but also was a member of an old Kentucky family, which, Douglas noted, "in this country is the strongest recommendation a man can have for Office." By arriving first and in large numbers, Southerners in the Midwest created a local culture which Northern and Middle State immigrants could only hope to modify.[17] One such hope, never entirely realized by Midwesterners, was to overcome sectional prejudices.

Some unifying forces did exist in the Old Northwest. As a new region distinct from New England and the South, the West inspired its residents with a loyalty to its own needs and institutions. Political candidates such as William Henry Harrison, Henry Clay, and Andrew Jackson attempted to exploit that loyalty by running as Westerners. In politics, the West became conscious of its separate interests. A minister appealed to Congressman John G. Davis of Indiana for help gaining election as chaplain of the U.S. Senate. The reverend gentleman felt the strongest argument in his favor was the *"claims of the West"*:

> *The Great West* has never had the Chaplain to the Senate. . . . *Eastern* men, who could afford to be on the ground, by hanging around the Senators have succeeded—while more modest Western men, at a distance, have been overlooked. Now tell them to try for once a *Western man— Western born—Western raised—Western educated,* and see if he can make a mark. It is due to the West.[18]

Although a correspondent of Indiana politician John Tipton argued that Martin Van Buren was the most capable candidate for president, he hastened to add that Richard Johnson "is a *Western man.*"[19]

Midwesterners were self-conscious in their awareness that they were forming a new man, the Westerner. Before one New Englander emigrated to Ohio it was his impression that although the land was fruitful, the people were "a set of half savages, and in fact *a nation of drunkards.*" He acknowledged that the state was still "a motley mixture of all nations, kindreds and tongues," but was "fast amalgamating to form a national character." He believed the ignorance caused by the dangerous and unsettled hunting life was giving way to manners that were "more enlightened and refined." In encouraging New Englanders to come to Ohio rather than to Maine, he doubtless felt their presence would tilt the balance from ignorance toward enlightenment. Nevertheless he was describing the formation of a new man, a man who was neither a refined New Englander nor entirely a frontier savage. "D.," a Cincinnatian, commented on the prejudices that immigrant groups and current residents held about each other. He argued that people now in Cincinnati should judge immigrants on the basis of individual merit, not place of origin, and should remember that they too were once new immigrants. The newcomers should also put aside their local prejudices and try to cultivate an identity as citizens of Cincinnati. D.'s emphasis throughout was on creating a new Western, Cincinnati identity which all groups could share. Even foreign immigrants contributed their part to the amalgamation. An 1817 Fourth of July oration in Cincinnati spoke of "the interesting spectacle of persons assembled from the four corners of the globe—educated under different governments; & yet all adopting the same political principles and wonderfully harmonizing in favor of our constitution." If peoples of such different nationalities could "forget their national feuds and prejudices, shake hands in peace, and become fellow republicans!" it was not surprising that Southerners and Northerners might feel caught up in the great experiment of creating a new country and a new identity.[20]

The Westerner was a different creature from the Easterner. Westerners described themselves as manly, politically astute, and egalitarian. Unlike the Eastern coquettes, Western women were straightforward. Yet foolish Easterners persisted in the belief that they were somehow superior to the Westerner. "The man of the East is but an inert biped—a mere baby in comparison [with the Westerner]. Yet strange as it may seem, these beings, whose senses are as obtuse as a pumpkin, whose dialecticks are of the dandy-obscure, and who have 'no more talents than a turnip,' are self-class'd as the first order of men! Let them enjoy the illusion."[21]

Party politics, as well as Western identity, often required a conscious effort to submerge regional loyalties. The Illinois Democratic newspaper became angry with a Chicago paper that had tried to stir up sectional animosity against John A. McClernand, a candidate for the Senate. Calling McClernand "the prince of 'Egypt,'" the Chicago *Tribune* wrote that he ruled *the poor ignorant people of that region* as thoroughly as Mr. Calhoun does those of South Carolina." The *Tribune* called the Kentucky settlers of Illinois "a set of Yahoos" and was grateful that the population of the Southern counties, which were dominated by "ignorance and barbarism," was decreasing, making way for "a new and better population" that could "make 'Egypt' as rich in intelligence and enterprise as it is now ignorant and barbarous." The Chicago paper concluded by urging legislators from northern and central Illinois to vote against McClernand. The Democratic paper dismissed these as the beliefs of "men who but yesterday became citizens of the state." They maintained that although most Northerners did not feel such sectional hatred, "tricksters and demagogues" nevertheless tried to create sectional feeling to further their cause.[22] While sectional loyalties underlay political life, parties strenuously tried to unite voters on behalf of party candidates and policies and to mute sectional appeals that damaged party loyalty.

The Indiana Whig Godlove S. Orth phrased his description of Indiana in the same terms, laziness versus enterprise, that were familiar to the founders of the Ohio Company and to other observers of the Old Northwest. Orth believed that the Southerner,

> regarding the "patriarchal institution" as the direct gift of God to man, looks upon the freeman who toils with his own hands and proclaims a belief in the patriotic sentiments of his fathers, as a fanatic and a fool. So on the question of State policy, one section is Improvement, the other is Anti—one portion is willing and able to submit to a taxation sufficient to redeem our ruined credit—another portion, who have no avenue to market for their produce, will not yet submit to anything of the kind. In fact they are unable to bear their present burthen.

Orth clearly seethed with anti-Southern sentiments, yet his recommendation for campaigning in the 1840s was to "carry on the battle, without reference to any other portion of the State, every local prejudice or sectional jealousy must be appeased and brought to operate in our favor."[23] Sectional animosities had to be subordinated and channeled to the needs of the party. Although sectionalism had not been eliminated, it had been forced into the background by the emergence of national parties in the 1820s.

Even in personal matters, politics could overcome sectional tensions. When Oliver Johnson, a young Democrat of Southern background, fell in love with the daughter of his family's new Yankee neighbors, the Howlands, he was concerned with how his father would view the romance. Fortunately the elder Johnson had a good impression of Mr. Howland: "Mr. Howland was a college man but not a bit stuck up. Pap had maneuvered around until he found that Mr. Howland's politics was the same as his. That made a clincher to a finish with Pap."[24] Prejudiced against the Eastern background of their new neighbors, the Johnsons nonetheless found a basis for friendship in agreement on political matters and shared party loyalty.

As this review of the intersection between partisanship and sectionalism makes clear, there was no easy classification of region with party. Nor is it easy to classify the political histories of these states. Before the solidification of the second-party system, politics in the Old Northwest was highly personal, characterized by rivalries between leading figures such as Arthur St. Clair and Thomas Worthington in Ohio, Jonathan Jennings and William Henry Harrison in Indiana, or Ninian Edwards and Jesse B. Thomas in Illinois. In this early period, disputes arose over the distribution of offices and the placement of state capitals. The second-party system cohered those rivalries around a set of issues including banks, tariffs, internal improvements, and territorial expansion. Historians of the Midwest describe the antebellum period as one of "balance" between Whigs and Democrats, who alternated holding power. Margins of election were often narrow. In Indiana and Illinois, Democrats controlled the governor's office and won the vote for president for much of the 1840s and 1850s, while in Ohio Whigs often broke the Democratic hegemony. Whatever the local variations, and there were many, Midwesterners were able to define themselves by nationally recognizable labels. They were Clay men such as Abraham Lincoln in Illinois or Jackson men such as Congressman John G. Davis of Indiana. In those affiliations lay the basis for ignoring or downplaying where one or one's parents had been born.[25]

Whatever sectional unity existed between Midwestern Northerners and Southerners was shattered, however, by the national sectional conflict of the 1850s. After the Kansas-Nebraska Act passed, Congressman Davis was informed that, in his district, it was now "Eastern born men" versus "Kentucky & others from Slave States." For Northerners, the Hoosier story detailing the comic misadventures of residents of Indiana became a weapon: They could attack the Southern way of life by ridiculing its descendant in the Old Northwest. Commentators described the Midwestern states in the same language formerly used to condemn the backward South, or to condemn the Old Northwest during its colonial period. Once again the Old Northwest was seen as an extension of the slave states, with all the evils Republicans and Northerners saw in those states. An Illinois newspaper called the southern parts of Indiana and Illinois "proverbial for the intellectual, moral, and political darkness which covers the land." The *Illinois Daily Journal* greeted the founding of a newspaper in southern Illinois with a lengthy peroration on the long-overdue progress of southern Illinois. At last, "the people there are waking from their lethargy and are adopting measures for their own advancement." The *Journal* had long believed that southern Illinois's poor reputation for farm land and commerce lay not in the region's lack of natural advantages, but rather in the failure of its people to take advantage of them: "The early settlers of the country, to some extent, did not avail themselves of the advantages of their position, for enterprise and improvements. While in the more northern parts of the State, everything seems to be conducted on a go-ahead principle, in many portions of the South but little change has been seen within the last few years." An Illinois resident agreed in 1850 "that where New England emigrants do not venture, improvements, social, agricultural, mechanic, or scientific, rarely flourish."[26]

Some Southern settlers in the Midwest agreed in denigrating the economic and social condition of the South. In a debate in the Ohio constitutional convention of 1850, delegate Van Brown, born in Virginia but a resident of Ohio for 38 of his 48 years, vigorously denied that

Kentucky's use of biennial sessions provided a useful example for Ohio to follow. Infrequent legislative sessions, he argued, might not harm a state that had "no revenue, no commerce, no trade, no ehterprise, a sparse population, and no wealth but a parcel of niggers." But this policy could only be detrimental in a state such as Ohio, which was "alive with industry and enterprise." Brown professed to find Kentucky's system of biennial sessions, and its social system of slavery, equally inappropriate for Ohio.[27]

Another Midwesterner of Southern origin was inclined to see the South as disorderly, lawless, and passionate in comparison to the orderly, law-abiding, reasonable North with its "steady habits." Yet when challenged as to his credentials, Abraham Lincoln was certainly willing to affirm his ties to the Upland Southern voters of Illinois. "Did the Judge talk of trotting me down to Egypt to scare me to death?" he asked the listeners at the third of the Lincoln-Douglas debates in Jonesboro. "Why, I know this people better than he does. I was raised just a little east of here. I am a part of this people. But the Judge was raised further north, and perhaps he has some horrid idea of what this people might be induced to do."[28] Lincoln both asserted his Southernness and pointed out that it was Judge Douglas, the man from Vermont, who was the alien in "Egypt." Lincoln attempted to use his Southern background to political advantage, yet this very attempt highlighted the increasing salience of sectionalism in the Midwest. The party ties that helped to overcome sectionalism had been severed by the slavery controversy.

Southerners in the Midwest also were reminded of the worst of New England traits as the controversy over slavery grew more heated. A glance at the statistics reveals that the New England portion of the population was relatively small compared to the Southern population or even that of New Yorkers and Pennsylvanians. Nonetheless, the New Englanders were a formidable cultural presence, asserting themselves much more forcefully, out of proportion to their numbers, than any other regional group in the Midwest except for the Southerners. As leaders of reform political causes such as temperance and abolition, and viewed through the jaundiced eyes of their neighbors, New Englanders often appear in the Old Northwest in the stereotypical roles of zealous reformer and abstemi-ous Puritan. A Dayton, Ohio, man noted in 1854 that the chief character-istics of "Puritan blood are bigotry & propagandism." New Englanders brought these "peculiar ideas" to the Midwest and forced them on the rest of the region through legislation over education, temperance, and slavery. New Englanders were incapable of "sound & proper reflection upon the question of slavery," hence their continual agitation of the question. To discredit Lincoln's Southern credentials, the Democratic paper in Council Bluffs, Iowa, called Lincoln "a southern man with Northern principles, or in other words, with Abolition proclivities."[29] If Lincoln could be painted as a Northern sympathizer, the rest of the Northern cultural baggage could be attached to him, including abolition and disunion sentiments.

The English radical, Fanny Wright, believed that the new states forming in the West would prove "powerful cementers of the Union," bringing North and South closer together.[30] In fact, the new states were subject, internally, to the same sectional stresses that bore on the Union as a whole. Upland Southerners were remarkably willing, given their dislike for the newcomers, to incorporate them into the society of the Midwest. That incorporation was made possible largely by the shared party affiliations of the Jacksonian period, the shared political ideology of republicanism, and the shared sense of Westernness. This fragile sense of commonality which reflected the forces that held the young nation together fell victim in the 1850s to the renewed sectional hostilities that severed the Union. All Americans were republicans. Yet as early as the territorial period, Upland Southerners interpreted republicanism differently, creating the possibility for sectional misunderstanding.

TWO

❧

Statehood

FOR THE SOUTHERN-BORN SETTLERS of the Ohio Valley, attaining statehood was a second war for independence. In the battles of this war, they used all the ideological fervor they had learned during the revolutionary struggle to form a republican society. The settlers feared that the territorial executive would be able to establish himself, his relatives, and his cronies as a new aristocracy, which Southerners viewed as incompatible with republican liberty. During the statehood period, beginning in Ohio in the 1790s and culminating in Illinois's admission in 1818, Upland Southern Midwesterners became preoccupied with a fear that would dominate their thinking until the Civil War. They fervently believed that an oligarchy was conspiring to set itself above the people by means of its political power or its great wealth.

This fear arose out of a republican ideology that was common property in all regions of the new nation. But what should have provided a common tie between governors and governed often produced conflict instead. Governor of the Northwest Territory Arthur St. Clair, a Pennsylvanian and Revolutionary War officer, attempted to appeal to that common political culture by scoffing at accusations of his antirepublicanism. After all, what man in the country was not a republican, St. Clair asked, "both in principle and practice"?[1] But St. Clair's republicanism contained a strong emphasis on paternalism, which the Southerners who backed statehood rejected. Instead, their interpretation of republican ideology emphasized the ever-present threat of conspiracy, especially from aspiring aristocrats. Tyranny, not liberty, was the world's norm. This made liberty all the more valuable, yet all the more vulnerable. The longer Ohio continued under St. Clair's control, however benign its intent, the more powerful would the governor and his entourage become, until the people lived under a permanent despotism. In Ohio during the 1790s, the Southerners who led the statehood movement used this rhetoric of conspiracy and liberty to rally Upland Southern settlers to the statehood cause. But the elite Upland Southerners who came to political power in St. Clair's wake were capable of considerable paternalism themselves. The same tactics used against the Federalist St. Clair were turned by another generation of statehood agitators on an aristocratic Republican Virginian, William Henry Harrison, territorial governor of Indiana. Harrison, however, understood the rhetoric and replied in kind.

The early colonial governments of the Old Northwest were greatly concerned with the proper role of the national government in its territories. Congress's reservations about the loyalty of the frontiersmen and their ability to sustain republican governments led Congress to design a period of tutelage in which territories, under the guidance of their appointed officials, were given time to develop bonds to the new national government.[2] Officials of this government found the settlers of Ohio just as unruly. Acting Governor Winthrop Sargent struggled with the problems posed by settlers flocking onto lands below the Miami River, attracted, Sargent said, by the distance from the authorities of Knox County and the desire to be *"free as the Natives."* Sargent argued for delaying statehood "until the majority of the Inhabitants be of such Characters & property as may insure national Dependence & national Confidence." He repeated that he lacked "faith in the national Attachment of the people from the Indian Line quite up to the new England Settlements upon Ohio Company Lands." These settlers were too independent for Sargent's taste and were "not the *very best* of a neighbouring State of Doubtful politics," meaning that they were Virginia riff-raff.[3] Sargent was not the only territorial official to consider the Virginia immigrants of lesser quality and more doubtful loyalty than the New Englanders. Governor Arthur St. Clair echoed the fears of his subordinate:

A multitude of indigent and ignorant people are but ill qualified to form a constitution and government for themselves; but that is not the greatest evil to be feared from it. They are too far removed from the seat of government to be much impressed with the power of the United States. . . . Fixed political principles they have none, and though at present they seem attached to the General Government, it is in fact but a passing sentiment, easily changed or even removed, and certainly not strong enough to be counted upon as a principle of action; and there are a good many who hold sentiments in direct opposition to its principles, and who, though quiet at present, would then take the lead. Their government would most probably be democratic in its form and oligarchic in its execution.[4]

Mixed in with St. Clair's distaste for the Ohio settlers and his fear that they lacked loyalty to the national government was the Federalist fear of the kind of government Jeffersonians would create. Those taking the lead in the new states would be Southerners such as Thomas Worthington and Nathaniel Massie, who might establish a government democratic in form but oligarchic in practice, like Southern plantation state politics. St. Clair defined the "General Government" as the Federalist administration of President Washington, thus consigning the Upland Southerners with their Jeffersonian Republican sympathies to the nether regions of dubious loyalty.

What government officials saw as a distressing lack of governability seemed to settlers only a matter of local self-government versus the encroaching imperial tendencies of the national government. Early settlers at Losantiville (later Cincinnati) met under a tree to draw up their code of laws. When all had pledged to abide by these laws, they organized a court and elected a judge and a sheriff. Patrick Grimes had the honor of being the first man prosecuted under the new code. The jury sentenced him to twenty-nine lashes on his bare back for stealing cucumbers.[5] This incident reveals that settlers preferred to handle justice in an informal, and what others might call a lax, manner, but that they had established protocols for the enforcement of rules agreed upon by the community.

In view of such local justice, it is not surprising that courts became a matter of dispute between Sargent and the settlers. In fact, the Losantiville settlers had already come into conflict with representatives of the national government over the case of Patrick Grimes, convicted cucumber thief. Grimes was a soldier. The commander of the nearby garrison at Fort Washington objected to Grimes's sentence. The commander ordered Judge William McMillan, a Virginian of Scotch-Irish descent, to dissolve his court; McMillan refused. The commander sent four soldiers to arrest the judge and in the ensuing scuffle, the soldiers were driven off and McMillan was badly hurt. Some months later, St. Clair succeeded where the military had failed; he dissolved the court, despite the reluctance of the settlers to yield to the authority of the national government. The settlers of Indiana and Illinois were no less difficult to govern. The early Kentucky settlers in Illinois, noted one visitor, were reluctant to give up "their right of defence against every aggression, even to the laws which themselves have constituted." This attitude encouraged taking the law into their own hands. The Kentuckians did not hesitate to commit deeds of "ferocious violence" against someone public opinion judged guilty, regardless of the verdict of the courts.[6] No matter how unorthodox territorial officials may have found these methods, the settlers had constructed a system of justice and were operating under norms that satisfied the frontier community. The impositions of the territorial government seemed unwarranted intrusion and dictatorial meddling in local affairs.

St. Clair had his own problems with local justice. On Christmas Eve and Christmas night, 1801, in Chillicothe, men gathered to burn the governor in effigy. Writing in his chambers, St. Clair heard a commotion below. Investigating, he found the house full of people harassing the territorial legislature and even threatening one man with a dirk. St. Clair called the sheriff's deputy and magistrate to disperse the crowd. When its members were tried at the next quarter sessions, however, the magistrate, as he informed St. Clair, found them not guilty and dismissed them. Although the magistrate eventually resigned, the evidence of St. Clair's unpopularity and the power of the statehood group (statehood leader, Thomas Worthington, helped to calm an angry intruder) was manifest.[7]

While officials worried that the settlers were too independent, settlers fretted under the "degrading" "colonial yoke" and looked forward to breaking the "chains of aristocracy." Settlers saw themselves not under the benign tutelage of a benevolent national government but in danger of permanent rule by an aristocracy. Those who opposed statehood were satirized as wishing to create an order of nobility to restrain the swinish multitude. "Peter Squib, Knight," "Nibletongue Hornet, Marquis of Cincinnati," and "Bruin Etherside, Duke of Hamilton" wrote,

> we tremble with dismay at the present unhappy prospect of our being erected into a State, wherein the hardworking and illiterate populace will have a ruinous power of interfering in their own political concerns; and that we view this dangerous innovation with disgust, being conscious of our abilities to manage the public affairs of this country much more favorably, to our own private interests at least, than the people are likely to do, under the new arrangement.[8]

Instead of nurturing the territory until it was ready for full political rights, the territorial government seemed to oppose popular government and to favor the special interests of a privileged few. Furthermore, the settlers saw the territorial government as having nothing but contempt for a "hardworking" but "illiterate" population. Self-government would end the profitable self-aggrandizement of those now governing the territory.

St. Clair spoke with well-justified bitterness of the oligarchic tendencies of statehood leaders such as Thomas Worthington, a Virginia planter with distinctly anti-egalitarian views. However, no matter how self-interested Ohio statehood leaders were in their desire to defeat political rivals in the territorial government, they managed to tap into the Upland Southern sentiment. The statehood movement's rhetoric was exaggerated and overheated in its description of the threat posed by St. Clair's government. Certainly, it was not necessary for the people of Indiana and Illinois to resort to quite so vicious an attack upon their territorial executives in order to gain statehood. Yet their struggles for statehood came upon the heels of the defeat of aristocracy. Ohio had proved that the people would triumph over the aristocrats and that it was no longer necessary to wage the battle as fiercely as Worthington and the Ohioans had. In addition, Ohio's struggle for statehood took place in a period that was marked, at the national level, by a particular viciousness of language.[9] Little wonder that Republicans in Ohio should find it difficult to credit St. Clair with enlightened motives when republics were known to fall prey to ambitious and tyrannical men. The statehood leaders did not anticipate that republican hyperbole would eventually be used to condemn territorial officials, born in the South, who aspired to aristocratic status.

While the leading advocates of Ohio statehood had come to the area to achieve for themselves the gentry status familiar to them in Virginia, these men depended on other kinds of Southerners for political support. Upland Southerners came to Ohio to escape the very gentry that Massie and Worthington aspired to become. As Ohio statehood leaders strove to recreate elite plantation society, that very society was in the process of democratization. The aspiring Virginia gentry of the Ohio country had to appeal for support to a large population of yeoman Upland Southerners who had demanded and received an increasing amount of participation in the politics of the Upper South.[10]

Republicanism and the increasing democratization of the Upland Southern states caused settlers to feel deprived of their rights when they came under the tutelage of those enforcing the Ordinance of 1787. St. Clair argued that, although the Northwest Ordinance created a colonial government, it offered terms which everyone was free to accept or reject. Those who implicitly accepted the terms by moving into the Territory "ceased to be citizens of the United States and became their subjects, and the right of making law, particular law, for them at all is derived from that source only." The governor schemed to prolong Ohio's territorial period by dividing the Northwest Territory into three parts, none of which would have sufficient population for statehood. Ohio's delegate to Congress, William Henry Harrison, found St. Clair's plotting appalling. He professed disbelief that its supporters expected the people to submit to delaying their "emancipation" from the "arbitrary gov." they currently endured. The disagreement between St. Clair and Harrison was more than partisan; it revealed how the first territorial governors and the Southern settlers interpreted territorial status differently. St. Clair said the settlers were subjects of the U.S. government, having forfeited their rights upon entering the territories. The settlers maintained that they had not forfeited citizenship upon entering the territories and therefore their goal became the speedy restoration of their rights. A Fourth of July toast drunk at Mr. Frazer's tavern in southern Ohio, in 1800 proposed, "May the day soon arrive when the citizens of this territory shall be re-instated in their ancient and native rights."[11] They did not anticipate graduating from some territorial school of republicanism; rather, they looked forward to a restoration of rights unjustly taken away.

Once deprived of their rights, the settlers would be kept in a permanently dependent state. "A Friend to the People" of Ohio warned that many who had opposed statehood and promoted the "detestable" idea of dividing the territory now claimed to favor state government and attempted to gain election to the convention. "[T]heir designs are to lull us, as it were, to sleep, to put us off our guard while they are secretly making use of every means to get in creatures of their own principles, that they may have a majority in the convention, and by this means render abortive all our pretentions to a free government." "Placemen," William Goforth agreed, wanted to prevent statehood by conspiring to divide the territory.[12]

The very idea of a governor not chosen by the people aroused discontent in the populace. Not having resided in the territory, the governor could not have any attachment to it. Having different interests from the people, selfishness would induce him to look after his interests: the accumulation of property or personal fortune. As one historian has pointed out, the structure of the Northwest Ordinance made the governor the center of political faction because of his ability to grant jobs, to lay out counties, and appoint officeholders. The governor could hardly avoid being controversial. He possessed all the power of a "British Nabob," including power "to convene, prorogue and disolve our legislature at pleasure," and possessed unlimited power to create offices. This naturally led men desirous of political advancement to court the governor's good graces. Governor Ninian Edwards forwarded to Congress a petition from the territorial legislature of Illinois avowing no dislike for Edwards himself but a dislike for the extensive powers he held: "we consider the concentration of so many, and such important powers, in the hands of any one man . . . to be a badge of Colonial degradation, inconsistent with those principles of Republicanism which have been consecrated by the wisdom & virtue of every State in the union; subversive of the just & equal rights of freemen; & at the same time wholly unnecessary, as a means of protecting the interest of the United States within this Territory." Settlers made specific objections to the veto power. "[A]lthough we have the Expences of a Legislature," citizens of Jefferson County, Indiana Territory, told Congress, "we have but the name in operation and Effect; the ordinary powers with which Such bodies are clothed being in this Territory So entirely Surrounded and Circumscribed by the Unlimited power and authority which the ordinance gives to the Governor, inasmuch as his veto can prevent any Legislative act however wise & necessary from becoming the Law of the land, by the voice of the people." Ohio statehood advocates called Governor St. Clair "old *Veto*," indicating that in their eyes, this was the governor's prime sin: thwarting the will of the people by his control over their legislature.[13]

Most controversy swirled around the role and person of the territorial governor. In addition to the "difficulties" inherent in the territorial system of government, one of the chief proponents of Ohio statehood argued that settlers suffered because the government was "administered by a man who is disposed to seize every power given him and usurp others." While disavowing his personal interest in statehood, Thomas Worthington maintained that his object was to free the people "from the clutches of a tyrant and his accomplices." Using the style of the Declaration of Independence's indictment of George III, Worthington listed St. Clair's many crimes: usurping legislative authority; vetoing "laws useful and necessary for the Territory"; demanding arbitrary fees and vetoing laws abolishing those fees; attempting to "dismember" the territory in order to prevent its advancing to self-government; granting commissions during his pleasure but making an exception for his son to be appointed Attorney General for a term of good behavior; trying to influence the judiciary; appointing people residing outside of a county to duties within that county; obstructing the organization of a militia; and avowing "hostility to the form and substance of republican government." Worthington, on another occasion, called St. Clair "a tyrant by his acts & intrigue."[14]

Others had the same or similar complaints against St. Clair. Judge John Cleves Symmes found him to be "[b]y constitution a despot" who had become "unsufferably arbitrary." He placed his confidence in "weak" and "guileful" men "who misguide and disgrace him." He neglected his duties, sought only adulation, and sneered at republican government. He vetoed bills of a "salutary nature." People fled the territory to escape from him. Nathaniel Massie charged St. Clair with attempting to prevent the formation of a state government hostile to the Federalist administration by trying to divide the territory. St. Clair also demanded "oppressive fees" "unauthorized by law," usurped legislative powers by creating new counties and fixing their capitals, preferred monarchy to republican government, and attempted to influence the justice of the peace.

Thus from the earliest days of the territory, the national officials came into conflict with Southern settlers over the question of rule. The governor was inclined to entrench his power by establishing his friends and family in office and by liberal use of the veto. Upland Southern legislators resented this attempt at control. Worthington defined the issue as a question of whether the territory would become an "independent state" or remain "under the present arbitrary government, better suited for an English or Spanish colony than for citizens of the United States." Those who opposed Ohio's becoming an independent state were "all who hold offices (with few exceptions) under our executive, our Governor himself & all good federalists who fear that our state will give three republican votes at the next election for president." Much about Worthington's protests was disingenuous. He wished for power in order to advance his party and his friends, but he appealed to a fear of arbitrary rule which St. Clair simply failed to comprehend. St. Clair saw himself as providing more time for the territory to become ready for the responsibilities of full membership in the Union, and as delaying the entrance of a state that would be politically opposed to his principles. The Southerners, on the other hand, saw only the indefinite continuation of second-class membership in the government and of exploitation by an aristocracy.[15]

Similar, often identical, objections were made to Governor William Henry Harrison's administration, proving that what lay behind the discontent was a deep commitment to certain standards of popular rule. Southern settlers had no intention of being ruled by any aristocracy, even a Southern one. Once again, the veto power was a major source of discontent. Abel Westfall attributed the desire to divide Indiana Territory to Harrison's rule, particularly to his use of the veto to maintain his "assumd powers." While Westfall seemed to accept the special nature of a territorial government, he asserted that Harrison "degrades the citizen much below what an American, especially an old veteran like me of *seventy six* can tolerate even in a Territorial government under the Auspices of the United states."[16]

The complaints against Harrison cited his disregard for the will of the people, unjust taxation, and the creation of institutions which operated outside the democratic process. Inhabitants of the Illinois country also submitted a long list of complaints against Harrison. They argued that the governor's misconduct far outweighed their inconvenient distance from the territorial government. In addition to arbitrary vetoes, which came in last on their list of offenses, Harrison had forced the country too early into the second grade of government, before the settlers desired it, in order to "increase his influence and lessen his responsibility." In order to gain the extra funds needed to pay for the new form of government, he had approved a law requiring that transcripts of approved land claims be delivered to the territorial auditor. In addition, he had approved another law taxing not only landholders, but also those whose land claims had not even been confirmed. He had also supported an indenture law that would allow slaves to be brought into the territory in defiance of the Ordinance. He established a court of chancery, independent of and superior to the territory's national court. He authorized a census and then ignored its results in order to deprive certain counties of representation in the legislature. Harrison was actively destroying "those feelings which ought to connect a child with its parents . . . and we cannot but ask ourselves if the American Government has yet to learn how to hold its Colonies."[17] The implicit threat to the tenuous bonds of union was particularly poignant during this period of the Burr conspiracy.

Harrison was also specifically accused of two major sins: the use of his position to speculate in lands and interference in elections. Harrison, it was said, bribed people not to bid on lands at auction and took bribes in return for not bidding. In one case, Harrison was said to have promised a choice tract of land to one man and then to have given it to another in return for four hundred acres of land. Secretary of the Treasury Albert Gallatin found Harrison innocent of the charges of bribery, yet held Harrison's involvement in a land company, which did such things, to be improper. As with St. Clair, many of these complaints originated with Harrison's political enemies. Some groups, such as antislavery residents of Illinois and Indiana, objected to Harrison's proslavery views. Forces other than the slavery controversy were also at work. Political rivals, chief among them Jonathan Jennings, wished to undermine Harrison's influence. Jennings, leader of Indiana's statehood forces, prided himself on exposing the ill deeds of his "great enemy the Governor," submitting depositions on Harrison's character to the president and gloating at rumors that the secretary of war doubted Harrison's integrity. When Harrison left his position to join the army in the War of 1812, Jennings noted in a postscript, "Harrison will no longer govern us / Triumphed at last has virtuous / perseverance." Whatever the motivations and the sense of genuine injustice that lay behind the accusations, the language chosen reflected the settlers' own concerns and the charges they felt would most effectively damage the governor with the national authorities. Chief among those charges was profiting personally from office.[18]

The second accusation against Harrison arose from a fear that those in power would thwart rather than carry out the will of the people. Petitioners also asked Congress to prevent officers of the national government from interfering in elections. They watched with "concern and indignation the unexampled interference of our Territorial Executive in our late Congressional Election, by haranguing the Electors at the Polls, and by writeing and Sending into many, if not all the Counties in the

Territory, violent electioneering letters . . . hostile to the very principles of the American government and derogatory of our rights as free men." Worse than electioneering was the self-interested motivation for it. Harrison was campaigning for his friend, Thomas Randolph, and even after Randolph's defeat, Harrison was accused of attempting to thwart the avowed will of the people.[19]

In defending himself against charges of corruption, Harrison appealed on the ground that "interested men" wanted to ruin him. As he petitioned the secretary of the treasury for compensation for presiding over the sale of public lands, Harrison concluded with this defense:

> if there should exist in [the president's] breast the least doubt of the correctness of my conduct it would give me great pleasure to have [my conduct] investigated in any manner and by whom he should think proper. In this Territory however it would be impossible to find an impartial person; nineteen twentieths of the citizens are my firm friends; but there is a small faction headed by a [illegible] tory and a few others, that would certainly hang me without Judge or Jury—with the exception of this faction I would appear before any persons in this western country that the President should name, and hold myself bound to prove that my whole administration has been conducted upon republican principles and, with respect to pecuniary considerations, as disinterested as that of any other office of the Government. The President is I am persuaded too just to suffer me to be made the victim of a few designing & intriguing characters, many of whom are neither americans from birth or principles and who are if possible as much his enemies as mine.[20]

Harrison first welcomed an investigation, but then denied the credibility of those whose testimony would be most useful, the people of the territory. Harrison not only impugned the character of his opponents as antirepublican, but also accused them of the very types of "designs" and "intrigues" that they objected to in his administration. The Virginian Harrison turned the same accusations made by statehood advocates against designing and unrepublican governors against his opponents. Harrison did not attempt St. Clair's method of proclaiming that all were equally devoted to republicanism. Rather he adopted the Southern settlers' rhetoric, by asserting that his accusers lacked republican beliefs and American principles. Nor did he follow St. Clair by characterizing the people as inherently unfit to make political judgments; but he warned of those few who were self-interested, designing, and intriguing. He claimed to have used his admittedly extensive powers on behalf of the "liberties of the people," and boasted that there were no charges of injustice or oppression against him. In contrast to St. Clair, Harrison reported that the settlers of Indiana were orderly and believed them to be "as much attached to me as any people ever were to a Magistrate not chosen by themselves." In his solicitation for reappointment, he cited his ability to acquire the love of the people. When Harrison ran for president, he was extolled for his virtues as territorial governor: for never having appointed anyone who had not received the vote of the people, for throwing the shield of government protection around a frontier threatened by Indians, and for hastening Indiana's attainment of the second grade of government rather than aggrandizing himself and his friends.[21]

In Ohio and Indiana, controversy swirled around the person and powers of the territorial governor. Illinois largely avoided that controversy, for Governor Ninian Edwards was genuinely sympathetic to the needs and wishes of residents. If Illinois moved into the second grade of territorial government, some residents complained, only the two counties presently making up the territory would be counted for representation. The governor had no power to make new apportionments of representatives when new counties were admitted. This would be left to the legislature, made up of the original two counties. The petitioners disliked the idea of relying on these counties to "magnanimously" resign their power. In fact, efforts were already afoot to keep the non-freeholders disfranchised by hurrying into the second stage of territorial government before land sales were held increasing the number of voters. Governor Edwards agreed with the petitioners arguing that though the actual danger was minimal "still such are the jealous and independent dispositions of freemen that they never will be satisfied to depend for the security of their rights upon the mere courtesy of others." Furthermore, Edwards argued, since the public land sales had been postponed, it was not the fault of the petitioners that they were unqualified to vote. Edwards also wanted the people, and not the legislature, to have the right to select the delegate to Congress during the second grade of government. If only the legislature of seven men and council of five selected the delegate "scenes of intrigue or to use a Kentucky term loggrolling will constantly present themselves—which . . . while they may gratify the ambition of individuals will . . . greatly disturb the repose and tranquility of any territorial gov^t and hazard much of the best interest of the best citizens thereof."[22] Here the source of intrigue was not a tyrannically minded executive, because the governor was openly sympathetic to the needs of the territory. Still, the long struggle with paternalistic governors had left its mark on the politics of the region.

The best the Southerners could hope to achieve would be to create republican state governments which checked all tendencies toward privilege, intrigue, and aristocracy. Ohio's state constitution rejected the monarchy of a strong governor and reflected the growing distrust of executive power. Without the powers of veto or appointment, the governor became a "figurehead" unlikely to become the center of a political organization. The statehood struggle in Ohio helped define "republican" government and set important precedents for the establishment of states in other parts of the Old Northwest. All three states strove to create a political atmosphere in which a large majority of the adult male settlers would vote, in which legislators and governors would change office frequently, and in which the power of the governor would be circumscribed.[23]

During the statehood period, Southerners began to express the tenets of republicanism that would dominate their political culture throughout the antebellum period. They favored local control in the name of democracy and denounced the paternalism of national officials as evidence of aristocracy. St. Clair, the non-Southerner, was never able to counter this rhetoric because he never took it seriously. Virginia-born Harrison not only took it seriously and understood its appeal but used it when he himself came under attack. Another Virginian, Edwards, avoided such conflicts because he avoided offending the political norms of the settlement community. Despite the provisions of the state constitutions, settlers could never rest assured that potential aristocrats were not waiting for the right opportunity, when the people relaxed their vigilance, to acquire power. Despite their victories over the territorial governments, Upland Southern Midwesterners remained concerned about the creation of an officeholding elite.

THREE

❧

Manliness

POLITICAL IDEOLOGY PROVIDED one of the unifying forces in the
antebellum Midwest. Calls for civic virtue and public good, which
characterized republicanism, were also calls for Upland Southerners and
Northerners to put aside sectional differences and join together in the
struggle to preserve representative government. When Abraham Lincoln
spoke in 1838 to the Young Men's Lyceum of Springfield, Illinois, on
"The Perpetuation of Our Political Institutions," he spoke a common
national language which stressed the need for a virtuous citizenry and
feared the decay of virtue and the inevitable consequence of that decay in
the rise of ambitious and tyrannical rulers. Lincoln, about to discuss the
dangers of the mob, focused that concern internally. "If destruction be
our lot," he told his audience, "we must ourselves be its author and
finisher. As a nation of freemen, we must live through all time, or die by
suicide."[1] By examining the shared political ideology of republicanism,
one sees that Southerners maintained a distinct regional identity, even in
an aspect of political culture they shared with Northerners, by emphasizing values, such as manliness, that were particularly salient in Southern
culture.

Upland Southerners in the Midwest shared a fear that ambitious men
would destroy the republic. Citizens and editorialists throughout the first
half of the nineteenth century used similar language to describe the
process by which some men aspired to social distinctions and inequities of

power that threatened the liberty of others. "May the genuine spirit of republicanism totally annihilate the pernicous seeds of aristocracy," toasted the Cincinnati celebrators on the Fourth of July, 1800. Without defining the nature of republicanism, the toast revealed that Cincinnati's citizens viewed aristocracy as "seeds" likely to take root quietly and choke out the wholesome plants of republican self-government. A generation later, the rhetoric was the same when a committee of Richmond, Indiana, Whigs accused an unscrupulous candidate of attempting to mislead an ordinarily "enlightened community" by "endeavoring to excite the prejudices of the people." The common defense against demagoguery was to appeal to the people to elect men of good character. Not only would men of proper character be unlikely to have designs against the people's liberties, but they would also be able to resist "the seductions of designing men." Nevertheless, any man could call himself a republican and such a man, if elected without scrutiny, "will surely trample on your rights, and rob you of your privileges, if you give him an opportunity," according to a southern Ohio newspaper that urged voters in 1815 to scrutinize more carefully candidates' qualifications, particularly their commitment to republicanism.[2] Consequently, voters examined a candidate's demeanor for telltale signs of character flaws.

Southerners, however, possessed a unique way of discerning virtuous republican leaders from potential aristocrats. "Southern honor" with its heavy emphasis on manliness shaped the republicanism of Upland Southerners in the Midwest. Upland Southerners melded manliness with republicanism to form a unique blend that distinguished their republicanism from that of Northerners in the Midwest. While middle-class Northern professionals demonstrated manliness by their ability to provide for their families in an increasingly market-oriented economy, keeping their women and children in a state of economic non-productivity, yeoman Southerners strove to prove manliness in the more elemental fashion of brute courage and personal reputation.[3] The importance of manliness to the Upland Southerners, couched as it was in universal terms of republican virtue and independence, reveals the lingering importance of regional cultural values. A national political rhetoric of republicanism did not submerge the Southern identity of Upland Southerners in the Midwest, even after two or three generations. The importance of honor and manliness to their interpretations of republican virtue reveals the continuing importance of sectionalism in the antebellum period.

Honor, as defined by Julian Pitt-Rivers, manifests itself in a man's "feelings, his behavior, and the treatment that he receives." Upland Southerners considered honor essential to a man's personal and political life. Good character became an essential public attribute; reputation offered proof that one possessed and had always possessed such a character. At the heart of Southern honor, according to Bertram Wyatt-Brown, was the maintenance of one's reputation before the public. Since Southern immigrants assessed political candidates based on reputation, a politician's most difficult political task was to maintain that reputation. Tennessee-born John Tipton of Indiana advised his son in 1833 that the true path to happiness lay in *"unsullied Honour."* This father learned the importance of reputation from his own political career. A dozen years earlier, Tipton had found himself embroiled in a controversy over his conduct as sheriff and state representative. He felt his enemies were attempting to deprive him "of that honesty of intentions, which gives value to character, and renders man valuable to his country and himself." If the charges had merit, Tipton wondered why they had been withheld until the election in August, "my reputation being as near to me after as before the first Monday in August."[4] Reputation and good character, in turn, often depended on one's manliness. Upland Southerners accorded honor and political office to those candidates who exemplified masculine values.

The first element of manliness was sheer physical courage. In 1816, political opponents of a southern Ohio soldier objected that he could not be trusted because of his lack of religion. His supporters retorted that there had been no quibbling from "windmill patriots," hiding in their chimney corners, about the colonel's qualifications during the Indian wars when they eagerly engaged him to lead expeditions against the natives. As battling the Indians receded into the past, proficiency in the pastimes Southern settlers admired revealed courage. Stephen Douglas recalled during the 1858 debates that in years past, when both he and Lincoln were in the Illinois legislature, Lincoln

> was then just as good at telling an anecdote as now. He could beat any of the boys wrestling, or running a foot-race, in pitching quoits or tossing a copper; could ruin more liquor than all the boys of the town together, and the dignity and impartiality with which he presided at a horse-race or fist-fight, excited the admiration and won the praise of everybody that was present and participated.

Whether it meant proving one's manhood in battle, wrestling match, or fist fight, Upland Southern Midwesterners wanted men for candidates—not namby-pamby runts.[5]

When Peter Cartwright, an itinerant Methodist minister in Illinois, ran for office in 1838 he rode about Sangamon County on a get-acquainted circuit. Coming upon a group of men, he overheard one say that all Methodist ministers were rascals and horse thieves and that one Cartwright deserved a whipping for his impudence in running for office.

Cartwright, having no other path than straight through the group of men and not being one to back away from a fight in any case, rode up and challenged the man, telling him, "Cartwright is known to be much of a man, and it will take a man to whip him, mind you." When the hapless fellow protested he could "whip any Methodist preacher the Lord ever made," Cartwright identified himself and dared the man to fulfill his boast. The fellow hastily declined a fight, insisting Cartwright was lying about his identity, but on election day, satisfied with Cartwright's courage, he voted for the impudent Methodist.[6]

Violence at election time was common. Some historians have seen violence as a way Southern plain folk asserted their equality in an unequal and competitive world by resisting every verbal affront with physical force. Certainly, Southerners existed in a world where the importance of honor made it vital to sustain that honor by public combat. Since honor rested on public acceptance of one's worth, all slights had to be resisted. To accept public belittlement would proclaim to all that one was not worthy of being honored. The form that violence took depended on class: Upper-class Southerners dueled and lower-class Southerners brawled. But any engagement in violence was also an affirmation of equality. One may shrug aside an affront from one's social inferior with impunity to one's honor. To fight a man because of an insult implies that one accepts him as an equal. Among the Southern backcountrymen, violence took on a particularly barbaric flair with an emphasis on disfigurement, eye-gouging being the equivalent of a knock-out punch. One eyewitness to such a "rough and tumble" among the backwoodsmen of Ohio reported that they fought for "the most trifling provocations," but in the most deadly fashion, "tearing, kicking, scratching, biting, gouging each others eyes out by a dextrous use of a thumb and finger, and doing their utmost to kill each other." Often an isolated combat would expand into a general free-for-all in which all the spectators joined the battle.[7]

Political violence also occurred in the Ohio Valley and often the incidents were defenses of honor. In Belleville, Illinois, in the early 1830s, Virginia-born Ninian Edwards described an attack on himself by Judge Smith. Edwards was leaving the home of a sick friend, Mr. McKee, when McKee's enemy, Judge Smith, and Smith's henchman arrived to seek revenge on McKee. Smith accused Edwards of caucusing against him, and when Edwards denied knowledge of, or participation in, the alleged caucusing, Smith retorted that Edwards's "damned dogs" were involved in it. Smith called Edwards a "damned dog" and drew pistols on him. Edwards knocked Smith down and caned him until the two were separated. Smith, Edwards claimed, still threatened him and McKee with violence. Edwards protested that peaceable citizens were forced to arm themselves against "the ruffian violence, or murderous violence of a Judge of the Supreme

Court, whose oath of office binds him to keep the peace, and who is under every moral obligation to set a good example to society." It is significant that Edwards responded, or later said he did, to both a verbal insult ("damned dog") and a physical threat, the pistols. The confrontation was as much an attack on Edwards's honor as on his life. It is also interesting that Judge Smith's exalted position and responsibilities did not prevent him from engaging in a street brawl.[8] In a society of touchy honor, even the leaders fought, like common gougers, in the street.

In 1840, Abraham Lincoln reported that Stephen Douglas, "having chosen to consider himself insulted" by a newspaper report, tried to cane the editor, Simeon Francis. "Francis caught him by the hair and jammed him back against a market-cart," before they were separated. Lincoln considered the affair "ludicrous," but acknowledged that Douglas was not laughing. Lincoln even maintained a tongue-in-cheek attitude about his own affair of honor. James Shields, born in Ireland and a prominent southern Illinois politician, had demanded to know if Lincoln was the author of the "Lost Township" letter that had appeared in the *Sangamon Journal* and which Shields felt "degraded" him. Lincoln admitted authorship, but instructed his second to give Shields a note saying Lincoln had no intention "of injuring your personal or private character or standing as a man or a gentleman" and that he did not believe the article had done that. Friends prevented the duel, but that Lincoln took the affair seriously as a matter of honor is shown by his refusal to back away from a duel until Shields would retract an insulting letter he had written Lincoln. According to Lincoln, dueling fever became contagious thereafter with Shields challenging another man and Shields's second challenging Lincoln's former second. Lincoln anticipated a street fight. Once again, in relating the challenges, Lincoln used the phrase "chose to consider himself insulted by" to explain why the challenge was issued. Clearly these were matters where the durability of a man's honor, when he "chose" to consider it affronted, determined the challenge. Although Lincoln treated the matters facetiously, he and others made elaborate preparations as to time, place, and weapons.[9] Despite the Kentucky-born Lincoln's resistance to the use of violence, he clearly lived in a community where such violence was common and where physical courage was necessary to maintain one's honor and the respect of the public.

Another attribute of manliness was candor, the courage to speak one's opinions freely regardless of the possible loss of position or power. Republics needed "frank and manly political discussion." Recommendations to the public should be made in "respectful, tho' manly and independent language." "M.," writing in *The Belleville* (Illinois) *Advocate,* called a campaign circular "a plain, bold, and manly" statement of the candidate's opinions on the issues. The circular contained "good sense and sound principles, forcibly and fearlessly expressed." A letter to an Indiana politician congratulated him on the *"bold* and *manlike"* tone of his speech as well as its true Democratic principles. Another constituent favored his "manly and honorable course on the Kansas question." Of course, occasionally candor and the physical characteristics of manliness were combined in one man. An admiring Illinoisan wrote that when Colonel John A. McClernand, a Kentuckian raised in southern Illinois, spoke at Albion, Illinois,

> He leaped into the arena with chaticteristick [*sic*] boldness. Those who were opposed to him were struck with admiration at his manly and fearless manner. He announced his principles with the utmost candor and independence, & urged them with a power and eloquence that won 'golded opinions' from all sides.

Manliness was equated with candor and independence, not just with physical prowess. The manly candidate did not dissemble and fearlessly accepted the approbation or disapprobation of the public. Such a man would not be inclined to intrigue or to become the tool of intriguers. Upland Southerners insisted that the man who said one thing before the public and another thing in private was dangerous to representative government.[10]

Politicians insisted that their motivations lay entirely open to anyone's scrutiny. In the Ohio constitutional convention of 1850, delegate Samson Mason of Clark County accused his opponents of refusing to vote openly against his proposition to make state bonds tax exempt. Instead, he claimed, they were trying to kill it by saddling it with an obnoxious amendment. William Sawyer rose to Mason's challenge. Mason, Sawyer objected, was implying cowardice on the part of his opponents. "I will tell the gentleman from Clark," Sawyer affirmed, "that I am prepared to vote against his proposition—right in its face." Mason, in his seat, replied, "That is manly." At a speech in Kalamazoo, Michigan, Abraham Lincoln accused David R. Atchison of resigning the vice presidency for the chance to make Kansas into a slave state. A voice from the audience objected, "He didn't mean that!" "Then why didn't he speak what he did mean?" Lincoln asked. "Why did not he speak what he ought to have spoken? That was the very thing. He should have spoken manly, and we should then have known where to have found him." Mason, Sawyer, and Lincoln shared the assumptions of "A Citizen" of southern Ohio a half century earlier who pointed out,

> It is impossible to know, correctly, the *real* character or patriotism of men whom we place in office, until we are taught by experience. Their corrupt principles, concealed under the mask of hypocrisy, may escape the public

notice until they are elected. Then, if they are appointed to office without specification of time, they may throw off the mask, appear in their true character, and rule like arbitrary tyrants, while we shall be left to regret our folly in their election. . . .

"A Citizen" recommended term limits for all government officials, including judges, but Southern culture had provided Midwesterners with another safeguard, manly candor.[11]

The importance of candor did give candidates a defense against charges of wrongdoing. When candidates were attacked, they often pointed to the accuser's failure to reveal his identity as evidence of the suspicious nature of the charges. The central Indiana politician, Martin M. Ray, responded to charges by "A Voter" by demanding that his accuser "uncover himself & give his name to the public," give specific instances of "the commission of some political crime . . . and not in this sly way at the very eve of the . . . election act the part of a sycophant and dastard, by sneaking behind the curtain and stabbing in the dark!" A southern Illinois politician injured by election-eve slanders argued, "To attack a man, in this manner, behind his back, when fair and open opportunities have been afforded, is no better than to break into his neat house and rob it, when there is no one at home to defend it."[12] Those accusers who violated the code of manly candor were labeled sneaky, sycophantic, back stabbing, and unfair. Their refusal to identify their motives indicated cowardice and identified those motives as personally or politically base.

Finally, physical appearance also revealed manliness. Central Illinois supporters of presidential candidate William Henry Harrison pointed out not only that his manliness had been proven in battle "where cowards dared not show their heads," but his appearance as an "erect figure" standing on the "loftiest rampart," with his voice rising in "trumpet tones" over the roar of the battle, contrasted with opponent Martin Van Buren's "effeminate and luxury-loving" self. John A. Matson, the Whig candidate for governor of Indiana in 1849, had been billed by Democrats as a "wealthy nabob." Consequently, the voters of Princeton, Indiana, expected to see a "straight laced fop, with feminine looks and haughty appearance." Imagine their surprise when "a stalwart figure with brawny limbs, plain attire, and a countenance which at once indicated his honesty and firmness of purpose," mounted the speaking platform. The Whig supporter who penned that description reported that Matson was gaining support, no doubt due to his manly exterior.[13]

Assessments of appearance were inextricably linked to the language of class. In the case of Matson, the support the candidate lost because of his wealth was made up by his manly qualities of brawn, honesty, and steadfastness. Voters associated wealth with effeminacy, but they did expect a certain refinement of appearance and manners. In contrast to physical courage, forthrightness, and brawn, which were universally admired as qualities of manliness, a candidate could also be criticized for not being "gentlemanly enough." A Whig writer in southern Indiana contrasted the attempted dignity of a speaker at a Democratic rally with the slovenly reality: "the postoffice rose up in a very dignified manner, forgetting to spit before he opened his mouth, for in doing so the slobbers escaped down each side, unstarching his clean shirt collar and bosom, and causing an illmannerly snigger all round." The Democratic press compared the appearance of Abraham Lincoln, speaking at a Republican meeting in Indianapolis, to that of state senator J. D. Williams, and found Lincoln "lacking that gentleman's grace of manner and intelligent look." Lincoln himself was sorely aware of his lack of gentility. He claimed that he set out in his campaign against Douglas in 1858 to conduct it "strictly as a gentleman, in substance at least, if not in the outside polish. The latter I shall never be, but that which constitutes the inside of a gentleman I hope I understand, and am not less inclined to practice than others." In line with the virtues of gentlemanliness, Lincoln intended to conduct the campaign with principle and fairness.[14]

In an increasingly egalitarian society, gentlemanliness was tainted by its associations with a deferential political order. More and more, however, gentlemanliness came to mean decorum in behavior and appearance. Historians have shown that middle-class gentility encompassed an array of behavior about dress, table manners, and conduct. Upland Southern Midwesterners judged their candidates based on a standard of manners that they labeled gentlemanly. Dudley Woodbridge, running for sheriff in southern Ohio, possessed "that urbanity of manners . . . which, added to his integrity and human feelings, eminently qualify him to fill, with honor to the county, the most dignified station in it." While increasingly rejecting the idea that gentlemen in society formed a class with legitimate assumptions of both social and political preeminence, voters did reject behavior that was grossly unacceptable socially. An Illinois Democrat described the Whig candidate for Congress in 1841 as "one of your largest and coarsest kind of men—vulgar in his conversation and slovenly in his deportment." A Southern-born Quaker of central Indiana preferred Free-Soiler Thomas Stanton, who was "mild, straight-forward and gentlemanly," to Democrat William Freeman, who "raved, bawled and bellowed worse than the noise at a donkey's jubilee." A central Illinois voter felt speeches should be candid and unmarred with "slang, low jokes or unwholesome puns and scurilous attacks upon personal character." When David Davis recommended an old friend, John M. Scott, for a European consulate, he described him as "a gentleman of fine manners" and "a gentleman of fine acquirements."[15]

The virtues of gentlemanliness, however, included more than just the minimum standard of good manners. The true gentleman was "candid, sincere, frank, intelligent & ever faithful to himself & others." Manliness and gentlemanliness were thus complementary characteristics because they both typified different aspects of honor. Manliness meant a man was candid as well as brave. Gentlemanliness was a guarantee of integrity. Kentucky-born Richard Yates used "honorable" to mean honest in a letter of introduction for Alexander Briscoe: "he sustains the highest character as a citizen, a neighbor and a christian—He is honorable in all his dealings—a man of true integrity and of high moral principles." David Davis separated honor from good manners when he described an old neighbor from Maryland as "an honorable man, of good address." A correspondent of the *Alton Weekly Courier* described Jehu Baker as elevated and "elegant" in style and "manly and dignified" in expression. Abraham Lincoln characterized the Democratic register of the land office as a "gentleman in the true sense." "Still," Lincoln continued, "he submits to be the instrument of his party to injure us. His high character enables him to do this more effectually." Lincoln accused the man of making fierce and "coarse" speeches against Zachary Taylor, "not quite consistent with his habitually gentlemanly deportment."[16] Lincoln found the man's lack of political honesty and integrity at odds with his otherwise honorable behavior. Casual observers might identify the gentleman by dress or demeanor, but a true gentleman possessed those characteristics of manliness that implied candor, honesty in announcing one's intentions and steadiness of purpose in fulfilling them.

Where gentlemanliness complemented manly values, it was an asset for candidates. Where gentlemanliness projected contrasting values, it was a liability. Chiefly the gentleman was condemned for not doing physical labor either out of physical weakness or because he considered himself above such labor. Proving both one's willingness and ability to work could overcome the handicap of too much gentility. The Whig candidate for sheriff of Morgan County, Indiana, managed to overcome the biases of Jacksonian farm workers even though he bore the added stigma of being a Quaker. When the Whig, Jonathan Hunt, arrived at a farm where the hands were cradling oats, he tied up his horse, "jumped the fence, and took the boys by their sweaty hands and gave them a hearty shake." When Hunt talked farming,

> the boys began to guy him; remarking he looked more like a book farmer than the Simon-pure article. Nothing daunted, he threw off his coat and vest, picked up first one cradle, then the other. Swinging them through the air to make sure of the best, then taking the 'rifle,' whetted a keen edge on the old four-foot blade and struck in at a lively gait. One of the men started

after him but to no purpose; the candidate fairly distanced him, doing his work in a neat and farmlike manner.

Hunt was elected. His Jacksonian opponent, "stiff and quite dignified in manner" was no match for that display of camaraderie. Abraham Lincoln followed a similar strategy in New Salem in 1834, winning the votes of thirty farm hands by cradling more wheat than any of the rest of them.[17] The saga of a frontier election in Indiana presented the dangers of taking gentlemanliness too far. One candidate for election pitched in, rolling logs at log rollings, basting meat at barbecues, and cheerfully helping out at all public meetings. His opponent, "a dandified fellow," never contributed his labor but remonstrated against the "uncouth" candidate for "wearing borrowed shoes and for doing other things which he considered beneath the dignity of a seeker after public office." After much humiliation, the native wit of the first candidate came to his rescue. He decided to drop the "B" in his dandy opponent's name, Jack Bass. "Not only was Jack B'Ass laughed off the stump, but out of the country."[18]

This suspicion of gentility led voters to judge candidates based on their occupations. Upland Southerners universally championed the rights of the "honest farmer and mechanic" over the pretensions of the wealthy or professional classes. The former were associated with demanding physical labor, the latter with luxury and weakness. "Countryman" urged southeastern Indiana voters to elect "men who know what it is to eat their bread in the sweat of the face, and they will know how to represent your interest." If not, "the produce of our labor shall be filched from us to support an aristocracy, that in the end will overturn our liberties." As a southern Illinois candidate for office said, "Offices of honor and profit should be open to all classes alike; to the farmer and mechanic, as well as to the professional men." However, if anything, the prejudice was in favor of the laboring classes. The ideal combination of qualities for a legislator was expressed in this poem by a Hoosier:

> Blest Indiana! in her soil,
> Men seek the sure rewards of toil. . . .
> Men who can legislate or plough,
> Wage politics, or milk a cow,
> So plastic are their various parts,
> That in the circle of the arts,
> With equal tact, the 'Hoosier loons'
> Hunt offices, or hunt raccoons.

The farmer and mechanic were described in terms of their physical brawn and hard work, elements of manliness. Edward Archbold, born in

Washington, D.C., and a delegate to the Ohio constitutional convention in 1850, stressed his affinity with the sons of toil "whose hands are hardened by wielding the ponderous sledge and the axe."[19]

In contrast to the honest farmer and mechanic's manliness, the wealthy were depicted as idle, luxurious, and effeminate. A Harrison opponent in southern Illinois called the log cabin campaign a ruse on the part of "ruffle-shirt and silk-stocking gentry." A Whig, writing under the pen name "Cypher" denounced the "young sprigs of Locofocoism" who, without having done any honest labor themselves, condemned Whig "aristocracy." He had seen such a young man speaking on a street corner. Listening to the speaker one would think him "some sturdy republican, dressed in homespun clothes, a man with an intelligent countenance whose hard hands and sun browned face devoted to the toil by which his living was earned." But a good look at the speaker revealed, "a smoothed faced, soft handed coxcomb, arrayed in fine broadcloth, his pants nicely strapped down over a delicate little foot, covered with a pair of his aunts, or some other female relatives, prunella gaiter boots, his fingers ornamented with rings, his gaudy *ruffle shirt* set off with a costly bosom pin, a gold elegant walking stick in his neatly gloved hand." Obviously such an effeminate and dandyish man shared nothing in common with the laboring classes he claimed to represent. His anti-Harrison diatribe held no charm for the crowd. One man told the speaker he was a fool; another, wiping the sweat from his brow, observed that the speaker wasn't worth licking, "but I reckon if you should call old north bend a coward down on the Wabash you'd catch it!" The crowd went off singing Harrison campaign songs while a "weatherbeaten farmer" offered to treat all to hard cider.[20] The young speaker's gentility, taken to the extremes of luxurious dress and feminine demeanor, did not entitle him to the respect due a speaker who showed signs of the manly life of hard work and toil.

While Upland Southerners looked down on dandyism and effeminacy, and associated these traits with gentility, they did not disdain wealth or status, if it was earned. The Springfield, Illinois, Whig paper related the parable of a girl who "turned up her little nose" at her mechanic suitor only to wind up the wife of a drunkard. Her former suitor became wealthy and illustrated the principle that "In this country, no man or woman should be respected . . . who will not work bodily or mentally, and who curl their lips with scorn when introduced to a working man." Only one kind of aristocracy was grudgingly accepted, that "natural" aristocracy that arose when men of talents and industry achieved success. Such success was expected and even welcomed as long as it bore no taint of having been obtained by favoritism or intrigue. "The union of virtue and talents, may the preference that is justly given to them, form the only Aristocracy known in the United States," was a sentiment uttered by southern Ohioans at the turn of the nineteenth century that was still widely held, if expressed in other terms, a half century later. Southern settlers were not against men becoming wealthy, but they reserved the right to scrutinize how wealth was attained. Stephen Douglas, newly arrived in Illinois, reported that "no man acknowledges another his superior unless his talents, his principles and his good conduct entitle him to that distinction." For this reason, Upland Southerners distrusted the claims of the gentry to political office. Colonel Dement, state treasurer of Illinois, was attacked by Colonel Field for Dement's lack of the proper background. Dement had been a farmer to support his widowed mother and therefore

> was not able to acquire either a fortune or knowledge of any of the professions which col. Field would call honorable, such as Lawyer, Doctr, &c. &c., but the little rascal just kept farming ahead with his oxen, horses &c. until . . . he learned the way to Vandalia; where the little rascal never learned any better sense (being no professional man,) than to always be trying to find out in what way he could serve his constituents most.

This devotion to duty was more than Dement's enemies could bear. The "little rascal" was not only a plain farmer elevated to the position of state officer, but as treasurer, he refused to pay proper homage to the "Lawyer Stump Orators, &c." If Dement had wanted to win their favor he would have had to become "genteel"; he would "have pocketed a handsome portion of the peoples money, and to have made a gentleman of himself, at once, not kept ploughing and farming for his living, and remained as he is, a tolerable poor man."[21] Dement's saga revealed an intense hostility to the genteel pretensions of the professional classes. If they did not labor for a living, whence came their affluence? The answer must be that it was ill-gotten.

To defend themselves against charges that their wealth ill-fitted them for political office, candidates often asserted their rags-to-riches personal histories. A meeting at Belleville, Illinois, stressed that candidate William Kinney came to the west "poor and almost friendless," had endured the privations of life on the frontier, and after many years of farming "has risen to competency and influence." The man who had risen above his farmer origins was expected to maintain a sympathy for the interests of the people. One Whig candidate was touted as a log-cabin-dwelling farmer. An orphan, he had become a mechanic and then a lawyer. He was the "'FARMER OF LONG PRAIRIE'—one of the PEOPLE—whose interests are theirs—whose fortune is identical with every producer in the District." Martin M. Ray, Democratic candidate for Congress, had started out in life as a blacksmith and had, despite the obstacles in his path, become a lawyer and earned a reputation at the bar. Nevertheless, he remained a man of the people, and the Democrats put forth not "Martin, the lawyer" but "Martin, the blacksmith," as the champion of the Democratic cause.[22] The common man might vote for a man of higher economic or social class secure in the knowledge that he voted for a man who had known hard work and who would represent the interests of the "honest farmer and mechanic."

Campaigns and elections might be periods when the people chose their representatives, but they were also periods of lively suspicion: The people's representatives had to be prevented from becoming the people's masters. Upland Southern culture provided a standard of manliness by which to judge the fitness of candidates for leadership in republican society. Manliness embodied many of the virtues Midwesterners looked for in their candidates, while gentlemanliness provided a leavening of decorum to what might otherwise verge on a contest of brute strength. Yet gentility remained valuable only where it reinforced qualities of manliness—honesty and integrity. Aspects of gentlemanliness such as laziness, physical weakness, luxury, effeminacy, and pride that disdained working with one's hands injured a candidate's appeal. Upland Southerners did suspect that gentlemen of elevated rank and dignified manners, a category that increasingly included the growing ranks of professional men, lacked the requisite manly qualities possessed by those who did manual labor. Wealth and gentility, however, did not automatically disqualify one from office. The candidate who had once labored, even though now a professional, qualified for the support of the "honest farmer and mechanic." In this way, Upland Southerners injected Southern values of honor and manliness into a political culture they shared with Northerners that stressed republican values of virtue and the common good. The political culture of the antebellum Midwest thus provided a common political language for building a new region. At the same time, it did not destroy the real differences of emphasis and belief rooted in the cultures of the different sections.

FOUR

❦

Interest

PARTISANSHIP, AS WELL AS the common language of republicanism, disguised regional differences in meaning. Certain geographic areas were known for their party affiliations. Congressman John G. Davis, representing a heavily Southern-populated district of Indiana, assured another politician that Parke County, Indiana, would go Democratic: "it is not in the nature of things for her to be otherwise." But as a general rule, region of origin did not determine party loyalty in the Jacksonian period. Only in the far southern portion of Illinois—Egypt—were Upland Southerners consistently Democratic. In Ohio and Indiana, Southerners split their support between the two parties. Yankees in Ohio were more strongly Whig and Republican than other groups, but Southerners also belonged to these parties as well as to the Democratic Party. The South itself possessed a dynamic two-party system in the antebellum period and, after 1840, party loyalties remained strikingly stable until the Civil War.[1] That sectional issues finally destroyed the two-party system reveals perhaps more about the overpowering strength of the slavery issue than it does about the weakness of party attachments.

That region did not determine party does not mean that Upland Southerners viewed party or partisan issues identically with other Americans, even those with whom they shared party affiliations. It was common for nineteenth-century men and women to speak of interest, the advantage accruing to the individual from a particular course of public policy.

Nonetheless Upland Southerners viewed interest and its close relative, influence, with a deep suspicion that other Midwesterners did not share. This suspicion caused the Southerners to perceive the instrument of party differently and to justify their eventual intense partisanship on other grounds. One issue of the antebellum period, internal improvements, reveals the dynamics which occurred when local interests conflicted with other loyalties.

Northerners in the Midwestern states tended to admit openly that candidates and regions had interests and to accept the machinations of private interest as part of the normal workings of politics. When the people of northern Illinois wanted support for internal improvements projects, they reminded southern Illinois voters that Cook County would play a major role in selecting the new state capital, which Springfield aspired to be. One author suggested a straight quid pro quo: Springfield's support for internal improvements in return for Chicago's support for the state capital. It was to the mutual interest of both sites to cultivate feelings of good will. In another case, the *Chicago American* supported a Southerner, Colonel Richard I. Hamilton, for Recorder of the Deeds of Cook County. His defenders pointed out that a Southerner would be useful in persuading Southern legislators to support a canal bill. In reply to allegations that Hamilton did not support the bill, the writer protested that the colonel would not so sacrifice his own interest and that of his county. Hamilton himself made no mention of interest and merely denied the charges.[2] Northerners might openly admit to hiring help in gaining their interests; Southerners denied it or remained silent.

In contrast, Southerners publicly spoke only of constituents' interests, often assuming that a representative's own advantage would be at variance with the interests of those whom he represented. Vermilion County, Illinois, residents demanded "a man who is for the people's interests and wants, not a political truckler and intriguer. We know our rights, and will, and do demand them. The people should be the directors of their own affairs. The officers should be the mere executor of their will." At election time, one should vote based on one's "dearest rights and interests," wary of the politician's attempts to make his interests your own.[3] The majority's interests, expressed during the electoral process, were not to be feared; they were the desired results of a free and representative government. What had to be watched, however, were a politician's attempts to persuade voters that his special and personal needs reflected the public good.

Presumably the best interests of the common man were the common good of society, but the best interests of the few were claims to "exclusive privileges." Residents of Brown County, Illinois, resolved "That Legislation should be for the general welfare of the People, and not solely to promote the private interests of a few individuals, classes, or communities." Taken to an extreme, this meant that the individual politician mattered not at all as long as he served as a vehicle for conveying the public will. The correspondent of an Illinois man believed, "In selecting a candidate for the presidency, we should think principally, of the great interests of the country. It is a matter of small consequence who administers the government, but it is all important, that a correct policy should be pursued."[4]

Southern settlers tried to deny the force of particular interests in politics. They distinguished between the general, common, or "best" interest of all and the special interests of different groups or individuals. The latter were to be guarded against, and politicians were to subordinate their private good to the needs of the country. Northerners, however, saw those special interests as energy to be channeled into causes they supported. But the ideology of the common man also presented a way for Southerners to reconcile special interests with their own goals. If a man felt himself to be basically the same as other men, then what benefited him, benefited all. One southern Illinois politician insisted that as a working man his views were identical with those of his prospective constituents. "I have no interest myself which is not identified with the interests of those whose votes I solicit. Like the mass of them, I earn my bread by the sweat of my brow, and with the labor of my own hands. My condition identifies my interests with that of my fellow-citizens; and my feelings and sympathies are with them."[5] Being a common man, he had the common good at heart.

Politicians often admitted they were not common men, but insisted that they possessed the personal self-restraint to be disinterested. Jonathan Jennings, running for Congress, defended his tenure as governor of Indiana by denying that he had exploited position for personal gain. "I feel a conscious pride that I have never earned in the exercise of a public trust, in any manner which has resulted to my private advantage. In the exercise of a public trust, I have always made my personal interests yield to the paramount consideration of the public welfare, and in soliciting the suffrages of the people, I seek that only to which other citizens of the state are eligible." He did not avow that his interests were identical with the common man's, but he did insist that he had denied himself those opportunities to benefit from office. Patrician William Henry Harrison of Virginia also denied vigorously that he ever used his political authority to gratify "a despotic spirit or to promote any individual advantage." He insisted that if he had ever voted, spoken, or acted against his political principles or betrayed the confidence of the people "then I will acknowledge that I am unworthy of the further support or confidence of my countrymen." His seriousness reveals that, although an officeholding elite may have held actual political power, among Upland Southern Midwesterners that elite was controlled by the political principles it shared with the people.[6] No politician thought to deny that opportunities to profit from office existed. The political system relied on the forbearance of the politicians and the astuteness of the voters to prevent wholesale abuse of official privilege.

If officeholding led to the acquisition of power, wealth, and the ability to forward a personal interest at the expense of the public good, it also led to the acquisition of "influence." Influence was not necessarily an evil thing. A man could acquire influence based on his reputation for honesty, manliness, and wisdom. Others would then accept his advice and opinion as worth following. A Joliet man had signed a petition for a candidate for postmaster without knowing that another man also sought the post. He especially favored this second candidate and said he would not "knowingly, lend my name, without influence as it is, to prejudice" the second man. He associated his name or reputation with his influence. One Illinois man told politician Richard Yates that he had contributed his "'mite' of influence" to furthering Yates's election.[7] Significantly, as in these examples, men tended to disparage the influence they might possess and to link it with their honor and reputation.

Influence took on more sinister connotations when it meant powerful connections. Tennessee-born John Tipton was advised that the Delphi, Indiana, post office was being mismanaged by postmaster Henry Chase. Chase had announced that his job was safe because he had used his "influence" to help Tipton to the Senate and Tipton would protect him. Tipton's correspondent asked the senator not to obstruct efforts to restore the post office to proper working order. A generation later, Maryland-born David Davis marshaled his political connections in an endeavor to get the office of commissioner of the land office for "our friend Lincoln." Unfortunately Lincoln had made promises which tied his hands in politicking for the office so Davis wrote urging other friends to "Please, without the least delay, get such influence at work as you can" to see the papers favoring Lincoln reached the appropriate office.[8]

The line between proper and improper use of influence was a thin one. Isaac Trimble, of a Virginia family, wrote home to Ohio that he regretted having tried to aid a reformed drunk named Mallory. He had done it as a favor to Mallory's brother and to encourage Mallory in his new life of sobriety. To his dismay, Trimble had discovered that "Mallory has used my name to the full extent of its influence" for his own nefarious purposes. Trimble had not authorized Mallory to use his name or influence "in any way whatever, or to effect any purpose whatever, except to give my respects to my friends" in Ohio.[9] Influence might be a benign or even beneficial aspect of a man's character, yet it could also be used in insidious ways to thwart the proper workings of republican government.

Southerners in the Midwest had trouble locating the best ways to preserve the people's interest. Political debate revolved around the need to maintain the common good despite the conniving of special interests. Political parties, traditionally viewed as inimical to the best interest of the nation, became seen as tools for achieving the common good. Northerners, less preoccupied with the evils of pushing vigorously for one's own interest, were less hesitant to accept and use parties in this manner. Upland Southerners still tended to stigmatize parties as special interests because of their use of patronage and their control by an elite of party bosses. Southerners in the Midwest, however, increasingly justified their party allegiances by defining parties as the most powerful means of ascertaining and carrying out the will of the people.

By the advent of the Civil War, parties elicited intense loyalty from their followers. Party affiliation was lifelong, changed only for the most serious of reasons and at the risk of rupturing old friendships and connections. Thomas Marshall, Woodrow Wilson's Hoosier vice president, recalled that during the Civil War, his family's Methodist minister notified his father and grandfather that their names would be stricken from the church rolls if they continued to be Democrats. Marshall's grandfather "announced he was willing to take his chance on Hell but never on the Republican party." Although debate continues over how programmatic parties were and to what extent they began and remained instruments to gain election, increasingly in the 1830s and 1840s, candidates remained party men long after the campaign hoopla had died away.[10]

Throughout the antebellum era two images of party remained in the Upland Southern mind: an irresponsible faction and a promoter of the public good. Upland Southern Midwesterners did participate in party activity, but they did so with some reluctance and with deep misgivings about the nature of parties. This reluctance was related to the ever-present fear of interest. Upland Southerners saw parties as conglomerates of interested men pursuing a private goal, perhaps at the expense of the public good. Party loyalty meant submerging personal integrity to party will in the hopes of profiting from public office. In many ways, party was a sordid affair that Upland Southern Midwesterners deeply distrusted. Yet parties could also be presented as unions of principled men in pursuit of a common good. In that guise, parties achieved success among the Southerners. Gradually ambivalence gave way to such strong party loyalties that those who left the party and abandoned its principles were branded traitors in the most vivid terms.

Southern settlers in the Midwest were slow to accept the validity of party labels. Settlers during the territorial period found party sentiment distressing and toasted "Unanimity" rather than partyism on the Fourth of July. Virginia-born Noah Noble of Indiana could think of "no reason why members of either party should not support individuals of the other side." Another Indiana politician also felt that "correct men," regardless of party, should be in office. In 1834, the citizens of New Salem, Illinois, declared that a state's chief executive should be "free from and above party and sectarian influence."[11]

As late as 1860, politicians were still referring to personal electioneering as a matter of "delicacy." Richard Yates, running for governor of Illinois, wrote to Senator Thomas Marshall, who had also been suggested as a candidate for that office. Yates was both informing Marshall of his intention to run and sounding out Marshall as a prospective opponent for the party's nomination. Yates disavowed, however, any intention to electioneer, unless "a letter like this to an old friend asking his advice may have that appearance." Yates confided that both men were caught in a bind. They might be defeated at the convention because they had not "used the appliances of the politician" to gain the nomination. Obviously, however, Yates was loathe to use those appliances. He felt sure of the support of central Illinois and asked for Marshall's assessment of his chances in the south. On the proper attitude of the candidate for office, Yates was ambivalent. "I believe that proper ambition is a virtue, and confess that I have as much as I ought to have, yet I far prefer the quiet of retirement to an uncertain and doubtful struggle for the nomination—If aprised of support from your section, without effort to attain it, I might consider my chances for the nomination good enough to suffer my name still to be used." It might seem that Yates wanted to eat his cake and have it too, but he was caught in the bind of wanting office yet feeling it unseemly to show that desire.[12]

Submitting to the dictation of party seemed to many Upland Southern settlers to be at odds with the character of the republican citizen. In the Kaskaskia, Illinois, newspaper, "A Voter" related a conversation between a farmer and a mechanic, archetypes of the true republican citizenry. The Mechanic lamented, "I have seen men elected to represent this county, who, in reality, were no more the choice of the people than my cow; and yet they succeeded, because it was the wish of some of our big bugs here. This kind of slavery or vassalage . . . is a foul stigma upon our republican character." The Farmer agreed that "Candidates should not be known personally to the people; they should be known by *character* only—In this case, this odious and disgraceful system of *promising, hugging, courting, hobbying,* and all other electioneering *juggling* and deception would cease, and men would be voted for according to their merits." "You are no *party-man* then?" the Mechanic asked. "Thank God, I am not," avowed the Farmer, "There is nothing so sickening to me as these little nasty parties we have in this county. If the under-strappers and lick-spittles on either side offer me their tickets on the election day, there will be trouble in the camp; I will offer them my hickory, and that devilish soon." The Mechanic believed the parties to be about finished and that "The great body of the people will vote independent of party feelings. Party discipline is nearly done away with." The Farmer had the last word on the nature of parties: "Every man should be a party man when there is any question before the people, but not otherwise; but those who can follow in the wake of a few individuals, be the humble followers of those who are elevated above their fellows, not by superior intelligence but by hypocrisy, are unmindful of the high character of a republican citizen."[13] The Farmer's conclusion reveals that the source of the objections was not parties so much as party discipline. When parties stood for principles, they should be followed. But when they called for mindless loyalty, they called for slavery and subjection, and made the citizen the tool of an aristocracy, something republicans could never accept.

Objections to parties centered around the ever-present question of interest. Party interest differed from public interest and actually led to the abandonment of the people's interest. The "supple creatures of a faction, the veriest tools of a party" desired office "in order to effect some interested or ambitious views of those who have helped them to power." In the name of party interest, men stopped at no injustice against those who stood in their way. J. F. Polk, running for the Indiana General Assembly, pointed out that a party man could not possess that "unprejudiced and equal mind" a representative needed. Instead, a party man had to favor his party if he hoped for future advancement. Polk called party spirit "the greatest of public evils, and almost the assassin of liberty."[14]

John Tipton of Indiana had early in his political career proclaimed that he was "unbiassed by political men and aloof from parties." He intended to "serve the People, and not a party or party-men." Running for senator some years later, Tipton explained that since he did not owe his place in the Senate "exclusively" to party, "I am at liberty to pursue the best interest of the state & Nation." He regretted that he disagreed with the Democrats on the bank and internal improvements, but dissent within the party was not for him the crushing experience it would be for politicians a generation later. Tipton merely expressed his intention to act with the Jacksonians "where I can," and where he could not "they must go without me." Tipton strongly distrusted party and had opposed party conventions because "those men who are constantly clamoring about convention and party care nothing for the interest of the people. Some of them have obtained office, and others, following their footsteps, seek office by *party*, not merit." He maintained that he did not consider his election to office as a "party victory" and wrote that, considering his help in gaining office for members of the opposition, *"I am at a loss to know why any man could think I am a partisan."* One Hoosier congratulated Tipton on his election to the Senate, despite their difference in political views, because he believed in Tipton's "independence, & [did] not believe that [Tipton] can be prevailed on to sacrifice the interests of the State to further the views or wishes of any political party."[15] Tipton's career spanned the period when parties were becoming influential, and it reveals both their increasing place in political life and the ambivalence that even established politicians felt about their importance.

Even in an era when parties were accepted, the charge of special interest became a potent party weapon. The Whigs accused Democrats of nominating party men who "have attended to their own private concerns, *not ours."* The Whig convention, however, nominated "men of substance; men, who by honest industry have made themselves; men, who, in private life we all respect; men whose interest are subserved when the interests of the county are, and not the party." Whigs also accused Democrats of requiring subservience to the will of party leaders and of carrying out political intrigue "upon the people—in the name of the people—and against the interests of the people." Each party could summon examples of incompetents whose only recommendation for office was party affiliation. When the nation seemed to be coming apart in the 1850s, one Democrat blamed the crisis on Whigs who viewed the sacrifice of the Constitution and of the South's rights as "a legitimate party trick, if thereby they can secure for themselves *party* ascendancy."[16] Parties, it was believed, were a special interest in and of themselves. Party men cared more for the welfare of the party than for that of the people or the nation.

From the first, party service was related to the acquisition of places of pecuniary emolument. In the 1830s, citizens of southern Illinois suspected that bad legislation resulted from the actions of "men ready and anxious to step into the office of profit which they assisted to create . . . sharing out among themselves nearly every appointment within the control of the legislature without regard to the public interest" and from entrusting the public money to men with the proper party credentials although lacking in personal fitness. Parties, it was charged, facilitated profiting from public office. The combination of forces to carry forward common principles, however, became necessarily linked to the acquisition of place and profit, and it was that linkage that frightened Midwesterners. After all, why would a man push himself on the public notice and organize others to nominate him if not to get near enough to "grasp the treasures of the nation."[17] Parties merely institutionalized greed and ambition by trading votes for offices.

Principles legitimized parties. Frederick Grimke, the South Carolinian

who was the brother of the famous abolitionist sisters, Sarah and
Angelina Grimké, and who became an Ohio jurist, voiced the reasoning
by which parties would become respectable. In his treatise on American
institutions, Grimke called parties a positive good. Parties were, in
Grimke's opinion, not only the natural result of elective government, but
also necessary to the survival of that government. Grimke began with the
assumption that men were motivated by "narrow and selfish" private
interests, by preference for a certain leader and not by policy. Men
attached themselves to party because individually they were too weak to
carry out a given program for their own benefit. Recognizing, as did most
Upland Southern Midwesterners, the presence of selfish private interests,
Grimke believed that parties provided an arena for differing opinions to
be discussed by many who were potentially affected by them. Rather than
pretend interest did not exist, parties contributed to the welfare of a free
government by "furthering the interest and advancing the intelligence of
the most numerous class of society."[18] Grimke envisioned a society in
which self-interested men worked together for their own good and yet
contributed through their machinations to a free discussion of the issues
and to actions that benefited the majority. Grimke's elitism led him to
minimize the common man's ability to be motivated by policy, but in
other ways he articulated much of what other Southerners were thinking.
It was essential to guard against private interests. Parties could accom-
plish this by choosing and advocating certain principles, so long as the
decision-making process remained in popular hands.

By the 1830s and 1840s, when parties were well established, the
methods they used to operate became a matter of controversy. Conventions took care of the mechanics of selecting candidates and satisfied, for
many, the criteria that government should emanate from the people.
Caucuses had been a way for early Jeffersonian Republicans in Ohio to
organize against the Federalists, but, by the 1820s, these same organiza-
tions were seen as undemocratic forums in which the elite chose the so-
called representatives of the people. Although conventions were accepted
as particularly well suited to the democratic ideals of the age, Upland
Southern Midwesterners were reluctant to accept the New England
innovation. They feared that the device would lead to manipulation.
Convention promoters often appeared to be on the defensive as they tried
to overcome the reluctance of Southern settlers to adopt the new system.
An address to the people of the Seventh Congressional District of Illinois
revealed that the Upland Southerners' distaste was rooted in a belief that
conventions also were corrupt. The speaker believed the convention's
nomination was the "free and spontaneous choice of the people," but
could not deny that trickery had played no part in earlier meetings. He
tied the convention to superior party organization. Lack of organization

had led to defeat in the past; the convention added to the party's strength. Yet he noted that much of southern Illinois remained apathetic to the convention system.[19]

On the offensive, proponents pushed conventions as the best means to ascertain the will of the people. The Randolph County, Illinois, Democratic Convention participants believed parties to be a natural result of any political system and it only remained to find a "system of party organization . . . which is best calculated to give force and efficiency to [the people's] will." The convention system was such a system. In contrast to caucuses, "midnight and dangerous instruments" by which a few intriguers might "effect their control over the public mind," conventions were expressions of the popular will, when care was used to ensure that they emanated from the people. All this was designed to overcome the distaste of the southern part of Illinois for the convention system. After all, some southern Illinoisans were still referring to party action delicately as acting in "concert with gentlemen entertaining our views and sentiments on political subjects."[20]

In the 1830s, advocates presented conventions to southern Illinois as the best way for party members to express their opinions on matters "touching their common interest." But southern Illinois refused to support any candidate simply because he bore the party imprimatur. They would only select one they had chosen: a candidate "fairly chosen by a convention in which every member of the party had an opportunity of being heard." Democrats in southern Illinois referred to conventions without even referring to party. Conventions were ways to "unite and concentrate the action and the energies of a free people" and to "elevate to office men who will implicitly obey the will of the people." The emphasis on the candidate as the choice of the people made life difficult for politicians. One candidate for Congress from southern Illinois said that, although several southern counties had failed to send delegates to the convention to select a nominee for governor, he would support the convention's choice on the principle that they were all Democrats together.[21]

As well as reflecting the will of the people, conventions were supposed to reconcile the conflict between special interests and the public good. Gallatin County, Illinois, citizens supported a district convention as "the only representative expression of the popular will allowed to us in our primary capacity" which could "harmonize conflicting interests." Many continued to advocate conventions as the best way to overcome the "local and sectional feelings" that divided the Democratic Party and to "harmonize conflicting interests." In fact, submitting oneself to party interest could be a way of submerging those troublesome motives of personal self-aggrandizement that so bothered voters, who were considering a candidate's worth.[22]

As parties were vehicles for both principles and personal advancement it was very important to distinguish those who were "true" Whigs or Democrats from those who merely wished to profit from a party's success. An Indiana Democrat denounced a fellow Democrat who had defected to the Republicans because he believed them more likely to win the 1860 election:

> What poor reasoning this is; how effeminate is such a statement. The honest and earnest Democrat loves principles, and can not be led astray by any motives; success is not his duty, but to act in conformity with what he considers to be the true doctrine of his party. The consistent Democrat wishes rather a hundred times to be defeated, than to gain a hundred victories under a flag which is not his own.[23]

"A Farmer of Macoupin" warned against such deserters "from the camp of the enemy, after that enemy had been routed 'horse and foot,' and had no more favors to bestow."[24] Those who used the party for financial and personal advancement betrayed the true nature of the party as an organ for carrying out the principles held by its members. This combination of principles and patronage produced ambivalence about the distribution of office, rage against those who left the party, and constant examination of the motives of party members.

In 1825, Rollin C. Dewey of Bedford, Indiana, solicited the help of John K. Graham to get the position of enrolling secretary in the state senate. He referred Graham, since they were not personally acquainted, to gentlemen who could vouch for his ability to discharge its duties and made no mention of party services. This was a telling omission and reflected the period in which the request for office was made. Appeals for office, of which incumbents received vast numbers, overwhelmingly stressed party service during the era of the second-party system. One hopeful applicant wrote, "I have at least <u>tried</u> to do, if not the state the Democracy some services at great pecuniary sacrifices."[25] One letter to Congressman John G. Davis of Indiana, however, revealed a deep ambivalence about requests for office in its repeated assertions that there was nothing wrong in such a request and its comparisons to begging:

> I have laboured hard for the party commencing with Jackson's first campaign about Thirty Years, have spent mony and time because I thought it was my duty to do as an American Citizen, and have received nothing from the party, but have always been satisfied having believed it was my duty to do so, but now when I am getting old I have determined to ask an alms of the party. I don't want to set at the table and but only to be

permitted to pick up the crumbs that fall from the great democratic table. To the Victors belong the spoils, it is right, there is nothing rong in it, and I now ask you at a proper time to aid me in obtaining a situation.[26]

Another supplicant for office reiterated that circumstances of age and finance forced him to benefit from his party labors. "I have been a laborer in the Democratic Party for thirty years, and have not until of late asked for any alms from Government," wrote J. N. McNamar. "It is not that I charge for my labor that I do this, but it is from necessity."[27] Mixed in with unashamed requests for favors in return for service were lingering remnants of an older idea that party service should be based on principle alone and not expectations of personal gain.

Certainly by the 1840s, any remaining reservations about partisanship were quickly squelched. A Fourth of July toast revealed the prevailing spirit: "The Democrats and Whigs—Like man and wife, will fight like the devil among themselves, but death to the man or nation who troubles either." Even men of great conscience found it difficult to deny party ties. Thomas Corwin of Ohio felt deeply the scorn of abolition friends who derided his attachment to the Whig Party. He could not leave the Whigs, as his friends desired, "consistently with my notion of duty." He recognized the conflict in which this placed him as a Whig in 1848: "Believing the Mexican War as I do, to be a great national sin, I shall vote for the man that fought it. Holding slavery to be a great evil, I shall vote for him who owns . . . 200 Negroes." An Indiana Democrat, appealing for party unity during the election of 1860, believed it better to vote for an "erring Democrat," Douglas, "than the best Republican." He vowed to lash himself to the last plank of the storm-tossed ship Democracy until the "good old ship" could be reunited in calmer times.[28]

Indeed, when Stephen Douglas wrote about withdrawing his name from consideration at the Baltimore Democratic convention of 1860, the fate of the nation and of the Democratic Party were so inextricably bound together that it is impossible to discern which concerned Douglas more.

The safety of the cause is the paramount duty of every Democrat. The Unity of the Party and the maintenance of its principles inviolate are more important than the elevation or defeat of any individual. If my enemies are determined to divide and destroy the Democratic Party and perhaps the Country rather than see me elected, and if the Unity of the party can be preserved and its time-honored principles maintained and its ascendancy perpetuated by dropping my name and uniting with some other reliable, Non-Intervention, and Union loving Democrat, I beseech you in consultation with our friends to pursue that course which will save the Party and the Country, without regard to my individual interests.[29]

Another Democrat was not willing to contemplate the sacrifice of party even to save the Union. J. B. Otey of Terre Haute, Indiana, protested that President Buchanan "seems to think no sacrifice of principle too great for the North West to make so the South is satisfied I would go as far as any man living to do the south Justice . . . but when she seeks the Destruction of the Democratic Party to suit her notions . . . I never will submit to such an outrage."[30]

Upland Southerners originally condemned parties as tools of interest. By the 1830s and 1840s, however, they came to champion them as the means by which the people expressed and carried out their principles and rewarded those who fought for those ideals. As such parties became an important source of identity for antebellum Upland Southern Midwesterners. They also became the source of some mixed feelings. The link between individual interest and party interest was too strong for the comfort of many. Southern settlers had resisted the self-aggrandizement of special interests only to succumb, albeit with some misgivings, to the dominance of party interest. In so doing they did not lose their fear that special interests were at work. Rather, they now assumed that those evils were busy within the party, perverting the purposes of the convention and ensuring that men unworthy of reward received party favors. As long as party interest could be equated with the people's interest, then none of the party's operations or goals were suspect. Gradually party allegiance took a stronger hold until only the other party was suspect under the old ideals, and party interest became national interest.

Widely hailed in the West as the generators of economic prosperity for the region, Indiana, Illinois, and Ohio funded and built internal improvements during the antebellum period. Behind the general atmosphere of enthusiasm and boosterism, however, was the need to reconcile conflicting interests. Even those who wanted improvements argued about where to put them, about who would benefit and at whose expense. The subtleties of influence and interest were constantly at work: Sometimes Midwesterners saw another part of the country benefiting at the expense of their section; at other times, as in Illinois, the disputes were between different areas of the same state. And when the enthusiasm soured in the face of overwhelming debts and unfinished projects, people blamed the disaster on the insidious effects of interest.[31]

Midwesterners initially saw internal improvements as harmonizing the differing economic interests of the community. According to the report of the committee that studied a projected canal between Lake Erie and the Ohio River, such a project would bring prosperity to the farmer, commercial advantage to the merchant, and easier transportation in time of war to the government and would forge a "new bond of union and concord between the distant members of this rising empire." Instead of conflicting interests benefiting themselves at others' expense, the canal would benefit every class of society and bind the disparate sections of the country together as well.[32] Local and sectional interests arose, however, when money was dispersed. Yet a project's boosters stressed the unifying nature of improvements, tying one part of the country to the rest and one class of citizens to another.

Ohioans argued in the 1820s that the two great, and often antagonistic, economic spheres, agriculture and manufactures, would both benefit from canals because both would receive wider distribution of their products. Twenty years later, a booster in the Scioto Valley still backed improvements, this time railroads, and saw no inequity of benefits between the classes:

> To the farmer, it will be felt in the increased value of real estate; in the ready sale of all his productions; and in the facilitation of access to the most profitable market. To the town, the result will be the introduction of Manufactures; encouragement to the mechanic; the promotion of industry; and a repaid increase of our population, intelligence and resources.

By this time, however, the writer urged the legislature to approve the funds quickly before local jealousies arose over the exact route of the new road.[33] Edward Coles waxed lyrical about the prosperity that would result from a joint venture between Illinois and Indiana in building canals and improvements on the Wabash River:

> the waters of the Wabash and Erie will mingle and waft on their bosoms vessels ladened with the products of their valleys, and with the richest treasures of all quarters of the globe, inspiring renewing industry & enterprise, defusing wealth and happiness and increasing the affection of our citizens by enjoying the benefits of a great interior commercial intercourse, with the largest cities, and most remote districts and bringing closer and binding more strongly together every part of our great and happy republic.[34]

Economic prosperity would also promote social and political benefits. It would disperse wealth and it would increase citizens' love of the United States and the affection of the sections for each other by tying their interests one to another. Internal improvements thus promised not only to bind together divergent interests in the economic sphere, but also to draw distant geographic areas closer together.

The citizens of Indianapolis envisioned that an extension of the Baltimore Railroad through Indiana would bring prosperity to all segments of the economy and tighten the bonds of union. Baltimore would increase in "wealth, population, and commercial importance." The stockholders would see their holdings increase in value. Most of all, the railroad would

> vastly accommodate the agriculture, manufacturing and commercial inter-
> ests of that immense region of country, through which this stupendous
> avenue is intended to pass; securing to the western farmers a safe, cheap
> and certain facility for the transportation of their accumulating surplus to
> profitable markets; and securing to the city of Baltimore the trade of the
> western country; affording to the United States an additional guarantee of
> perpetual union; . . . and creating for millions of civilized inhabitants, real
> and permanent advantages.[35]

Not only would the railroad help those petitioning for its continuation, but it would also spread vast benefits over the entire western country, if not over the entire nation. It almost seemed not to occur to the petitioners that any advantage would accrue to Indianapolis itself.

The argument that internal improvements were so generally diffused as to make moot the question of who benefits did not prevail. Whenever internal improvements were discussed, Upland Southern Midwesterners generally supposed that someone gained at someone else's expense. The popular disclaimer was that "it matters not" how roads got constructed so long as the roads were constructed and the people and the state benefited. But this argument became ultimately unconvincing as more localities clamored for the improvements necessary to ensure their access to markets. Citizens of Knox County, Indiana, asserted that access to markets assured prosperity. They wanted a canal between the Wabash and Miami Rivers because,

> We firmly believe that much of the prosperity of our country depends upon
> the free navigation of the Wabash, and its connection by a canal with the
> Miami of Lake Erie; that unless our citizens are enabled to get into the Ohio
> river whenever it may be navigable, we can never derive much benefit from
> the Southern market, and cannot expect traders to settle among us, and
> take off our produce; that unless we have a canal communication with
> Lake Erie, we shall be excluded altogether from a northern market, through
> the Erie Canal of New York, to which we confidently look, as one of the
> most important sources of our future prosperity and wealth; and that the
> time has now arrived when it is incumbent upon us to make every exertion
> to promote these improvements.[36]

They no longer spoke in vaulting terms about binding the new nation together, but rather they voiced the practical concerns about access to both the great national markets. Furthermore, it is not clear whether "our country" meant the United States, the state of Indiana, or the particular local interests of southern Indiana. While many were arguing for internal improvements to help promote great national interests and an economic boom for all portions of the population, particular localities sought ways to serve their special needs.

Politicians struggled to reconcile these demands with the finite resources at hand. Jonathan Jennings had tried to ward off that sentiment when he addressed his constituents on the subject of national improvements. Although he strongly favored them, "yet some settled system should be adopted, calculated to do equal justice, or we may have to meet, conflicts and jealousies among the states, calculated to retard a regular progress of the work, and operate most injuriously to the harmony and unison of action which should be cherished, each towards each other, by the states of the Union." What Jennings implied was that, more often than not, internal improvements were the source of great discord rather than of union and goodwill. Edward Archbold, delegate to the Ohio constitutional convention of 1850, took this fear of "conflicts and jealousies" to its logical conclusion when he argued that for the state even to build internal improvements was morally wrong: "The principle is intrinsically and heinously wrong, because a line of public improvement, which is constructed by means of taxes levied upon the whole people, will embrace some towns and cities, and confer upon them great benefits, while it may positively injure all the other towns and cities in the State." As an example he cited the canal built through Dayton, which benefited the local stone quarries but destroyed the business of the Urbana quarries. "And yet, sir, the citizens of Urbana are taxed for the construction of that same canal! By your system of internal improvements, you compel these ruined localities to pay roundly *for a first rate calamity!*"[37] Like Archbold, many saw the dangers more clearly in retrospect.

Few went as far as Archbold in condemning all improvements, but the belief that internal improvements would cement the bonds of union turned out to be far too optimistic. Southerners in the Midwest saw their section of the country pitted against other sections in a struggle for resources. Rumblings of discontent emerged during the Jacksonian period over the president's ambiguous policy on internal improvements. A convention in Indianapolis bemoaned the duplicity of the Democrats in representing the president as against internal improvements when appealing to the South and for them when appealing to the West. What, the convention asked, was the interest of Indiana? Certainly not the policies advocated by the Southern states, which the convention concluded would leave products to rot on the wharves and reduce markets at home and abroad.[38] Governor James B. Ray of Indiana challenged Jackson on the question of internal improvements, telling him, in an open letter, that the people of Indiana voted for him in the belief that he would support internal improvements. Ray argued that the people had a right to a return on the money

> which is constantly passing out of the country for merchandize and public lands, by aiding the states to make roads and canals, that the farmer may carry off the accumulating productions of his soil and labour, without being subjected to the present enormous tax, levied by bad roads and obstructed river navigation, upon every thing they raise for market, they could live in republican simplicity, and by long lives of temperance, industry and economy, enjoy the rich and abundant fruits of an incomparable country.[39]

The interests of the West were being sacrificed to those of the South and, worse than that, the West would be left as an economic backwater. The result might even threaten the foundations of the republic by undermining that vigorous economic independence necessary for republican citizens.

Jackson's attempt to duck the issue by advocating national improvements and opposing purely local ones left him open to the charge of betraying the West. Connersville, Indiana, politician Ezra Rodgers had supported Jackson in the previous election believing the general supported internal improvements. To Rodgers, the Maysville Road Veto was either an abrupt change of mind or evidence that Jackson had misled the people. In either case, Jackson was "no longer worthy the support of the West," and Rodgers planned to vote for Henry Clay.[40]

Arguing that when citizens paid taxes they deserved services in return, some claimed that the Western states paid in more than they received. In 1839, Indiana's governor complained that Indiana's generosity in supporting the federal government with revenue from the public lands was not being adequately recompensed. In return, the state's interests had been foiled in the matters of the Cumberland Road, the Wabash appropriation, and the land bill, which would have provided three million dollars to the state. The Cumberland Road Convention, which met at Terre Haute, Indiana, with delegates from that state, as well as Illinois and Ohio, argued that

> Whilst the Western Delegation in Congress were generously aiding, by their votes, the progress of our fellow-citizens at the East, North, and South, by making large appropriations for the building of ships of war, the improvement of harbors, the erection of fortifications, light-houses, &c. we were sorry to find in some instances a total lack of every thing like reciprocal good feeling manifested by these favored Representatives, in regard to our cherished interest.[41]

The West had, in the spirit of the public good, submerged its own desires and supported benefits that directly accrued to other sections. Expecting the same courtesy in return, they were stunned to see the other sections callously pursuing only their self-interest, oblivious to the needs of other parts of the country. The oft-repeated complaint was that while the federal government spent millions to support the Atlantic trade, it provided nothing for the Western rivers on the grounds that those were local improvements. The Democratic State Convention tried to argue that certain improvements the West favored, such as the Cumberland Road, the Illinois and Michigan canal, and plans to connect the western rivers to the Great Lakes, were proper improvements with national benefits.[42] Controversy over public funding of internal improvements helped to solidify the notion of the West, as Southerners and Northerners united to promote the interests of the new region in opposition to the desires of other regions.

Westerners in Congress demonstrated their unity in the votes they cast on internal improvements proposals. On the Bonus Bill of 1817, the Cumberland Road Bill of 1822, and the General Survey Bill of 1823, congressmen voted solidly in favor of internal improvements and to overturn presidential vetoes of those bills. While senators and representatives from the South, New England, and the Mid-Atlantic states divided their votes on these bills, Northwesterners voted for them as a bloc.[43]

While internal improvements tended to make the West suspicious of the intentions of other parts of the country and of the general government, in Illinois, internal improvements battles split the state between the northern and southern halves. On the Fourth of July, 1834, a resident of Manchester, Illinois, proposed the hopeful toast, *"The State of Illinois.— In her population she combines the East and the South.—May she soon connect the two sections by her internal improvements."* By the 1830s, citizens in southern Illinois watched with dismay the rapid growth of the northern part of the state. Internal improvements seemed the way to restore the balance. In 1849, however, a dispute arose over a proposed railroad route from Terre Haute, Indiana, to St. Louis, Missouri. The people of southern Illinois favored the route, but the Northerners in the legislature stymied it, unleashing an uproar of disapproval and heated sectional antipathy. The citizens of Marine, Illinois, not far from St. Louis, argued that the railroad could be built at a comparatively small cost, would be an abundant source of revenue, "preserve a unanimity of interests," "remove local prejudices," and unite the people of a diverse country. While they disclaimed any desire for partial legislation or laws that harmed the interest of any individual, they asserted that the road would benefit the general public and urged the legislature to approve the project.[44] The legislature, however, failed to pass a bill with a liberal incorporation policy for railroads that would have made the Terre Haute–St. Louis railroad possible. Southerners then reacted with dismay and accusations that local, in this case Northern, interests had prevailed.

In Mount Vernon, Jefferson County, the citizens wailed that the legislature had sacrificed the public good to selfishness. A "miserable, dog-in-the-manger policy of local interests" had won, and they protested being forced to buy and sell in the markets of certain locales "or have all facilities refused us, in the improved means of transportation." In their eyes, the rest of the state was attempting to force the southern portion into an economic dependency. They resolved,

> That while we would cherish all the local interests of the state, commercial and others, that are consistent with the right and interest of the community, yet we in all commercial as well as political policy, do depreciate local and sectional territorial distinctions, but we look upon the commerce of the country as belonging to the whole Union, no matter where the place in which it may be carried on.[45]

A correspondent of the *Daily Register* reported that when the people of the southern section applied for the charter they met local jealousy and opposition that killed the bill in the Senate. Another correspondent reported that the bill's failure was purely a Northern refusal to help the South as that region had helped the North in the past.

> The north is growing rapidly under the very advantages that we seek by internal improvements; and if we lie still, we must be dictated to by our northern brethren, and take what they will give us, and abstain from that which they forbid. It is not to be disguised, that there was a large portion of the north opposed to the construction of our railroads. A member of the senate, in my hearing, declared his opposition to them on the ground that they would interfere with the trade of their canal, by drawing the produce to St. Louis in place of Chicago. . . . The state at large constructed their canal; and when we ask merely for the right of way for companies to construct roads in the south, which are to cost the state nothing, put four millions into circulation among the people, we are assured and told that it will result in injury to *our* canal.[46]

Public meetings in Vandalia, Benton, Effingham, Greenup, and Crawford County protested the legislature's lack of action. In Effingham, the citizens argued that the road, necessary though it was to southern Illinois, "would tend to the rapid development not only of the agricultural interests but of all other interests." The legislature had acted unjustly, ignored the will of the people, "and treated the citizens [of southern Illinois] with unmerited contempt."[47] Southern-born Midwesterners immediately assumed that Northern interests were out to oppress them and to force economic stagnation on them, while they themselves wanted not only what was their due, but also that which would benefit all of Illinois.

The other side argued that the southern portion of the state attempted to advance its own selfish interests, and, worse, those of the "foreign" powers of St. Louis. The *Illinois Daily Journal* objected to the legislature building railroads with termini "nominally" inside the state but in reality benefiting other states. Such a policy was not in Illinois's interests. "The great AGRICULTURAL interests of the state, can only be promoted, and advanced as they should be, by such legislation, as will *multiply the home markets,* by encouraging the growth of cities and towns WITHIN OUR OWN STATE." The Whig paper in Charleston, slightly north of the proposed route, argued that "It becomes all true Illinoisans to unite in a prompt and vigorous effort to protect the interests of Illinois against the plots of the hireling emissaries of foreign cities and foreign speculators. These men are straining every nerve to advance *foreign* interests at a sacrifice of the interests of this State." These same men, the paper claimed, had helped to defeat a general railroad bill which would have diffused the benefits of railroads through many sections of the state, including Coles County. Now these men protested when their particular, "St. Louis" interest was denied. A meeting in Charleston agreed that the railroad would have enriched a "foreign city" and another state. They argued that agitation for a special session of the legislature to carry out the failed program was merely the agitation of "local purposes" and "St. Louis interests." The well-being of all of Illinois was at stake, and Coles County felt it behooved them not to sacrifice the interests of the entire state in order to promote the desires of one portion of the state. They objected to "remaining tributary to a foreign city built up principally from the profits arising from the transhipment of Illinois products, and over which the sovereinty of our state cannot be extended for the purpose of taxing the wealth thus exacted from the labor and industry of the citizens of our state." Instead of St. Louis they proposed alternative termini of Quincy, Alton, Galena, Chester, or Cairo. A northern Illinois politician agreed. The North was not being unfair to the South, the South was unjust in claiming the right to "build themselves up and St. Louis, to the destruction of our own towns, and to the central and northern roads."[48] The *Illinois Daily Journal* argued that Cairo should be the city to benefit from Illinois's internal improvements:

> The interests of the southern part of this State are more concerned in this matter than those of the middle, or northern Illinois.—It is a vital interest to the South—to Cairo—to all the country south of the proposed Cincin-

nati road. We can stand it in the north,—if we can stand any thing like a
sacrifice of State character and State interests to advance foreign interests.[49]

A Macoupin County meeting agreed that the proposed road would hurt
Illinois's best interests and would benefit Missouri at Illinois's expense. A
railroad meeting at Taylorville, in central Illinois, resolved "that it is the
duty of all citizens to promote the best interests of the state—that in the
construction of public works, the general wants, the general interest and
welfare of the whole people should be the paramount object of action
rather than the local interest of any one community." They believed that
"the individual and general interests of the people of Illinois at this time"
required the construction of railroads that would tend to build up the
cities and towns within the state.[50]

Calls began to go out for two different railroad conventions. The
Salem convention in Marion County supported the Terre Haute–St. Louis
road and requested the governor to convene the legislature to carry out
the constitutional provision allowing the legislature to pass liberal general laws to encourage internal improvements. The convention's opponents jeeringly described the delegates as openly admitting their subservience to St. Louis interests, but the governor did call the legislature
into special session. Another convention, to be held at Hillsboro, Illinois,
supported a terminus inside the state thus encouraging the prosperity of
Illinois's cities and saving the farmers from paying a "tributary tax of
ferriage incurred in transporting our productions to another State for
shipment to a foreign market." The Hillsboro convention objected that
the special legislative session had been called before the convention could
meet and argued that there was no justification for it. They approved of
the actions of the last legislature. If the Salem conventioneers objected to
northern Illinois running roughshod over the southern part of the state, at
Hillsboro the theme was the enslavement of the entire state to St. Louis
capitalists.[51]

One correspondent of the *Illinois Daily Journal* saw oppression and
tyranny in the furor. Farmers cared only about getting their produce to
market, the nearest and best market, he wrote. But others thought that
they should establish another market as the terminus of the transportation system. They told the farmer, "you don't know your own true and
best interest and unless you take what I am willing to give you, you shall
have nothing, but must remain content to be 'hewers of wood and
drawers of water,' to such of us as are determined to control you in this
matter."[52] In order to ensure equality, the government ought to ensure
that all citizens had access to markets. Residents of southern Illinois were
to be reduced to economic serfdom while others flourished because the
government backed certain programs and not others equally as worthy. It

was not suggested that government withdraw from the business of funding improvements, rather that government ought to fund all worthy projects in the interest of providing equality of opportunity for all.

Five years later, the dust still had not settled on the issue. The citizens of Bond County, along the line of the proposed road, were still petitioning for a special session of the legislature to remedy the situation. A convention in Salem reported that of two thousand miles of railroad track in Illinois, less than three hundred were in the southern part of the state. Still, the paper maintained that what was at stake was not the particular interest of that part of the state: "yet it is not these especial objects, nor southern Illinois alone, but the whole state, and its most important interests, that demand immediate legislation, on the one important subject of railroads." David Davis reported, "The railroad mania is still very active in our state." The legislature was currently debating whether to charter a railroad along the old Terre Haute–St. Louis route. The issue was fought along the same lines as it had been half a decade earlier: "A strong & hitherto successful party in this State, advocate the building up of our own towns—which they term State policy—The other side, say, the true policy is to grant charters wherever rail roads will be built—The fight waxes warm at Springfield."[53]

The controversy over the Terre Haute–St. Louis road posed problems for Southern-born Midwesterners. On the one hand, they accepted a culture that rejected the claims of particular interests and had to justify internal improvements in terms of benefits for a larger, general interest. On the other hand, they claimed that, having supported northern Illinois in its needs, they felt it was only fair now that their desires be met. When denied, they cried out against economic oppression. Illinois replayed on a smaller scale the Jacksonian era dispute between the West and other regions over internal improvements.

Ironically, instead of contributing to "individual and national independence," as Midwesterners had hoped, internal improvements often led to staggering financial difficulties. Indiana's ambitious internal improvements program, begun in 1836, left the state bankrupt by 1839. In the 1830s, politicians dismissed the fear that attempts to build extensive systems of canals would involve Indiana in debt far beyond its ability to recover.[54] By the end of the decade, the fear was beginning to be realized. When the canal boom busted, the fragile universality of interest, which had justified such expenditures, disintegrated.

Upland Southerners clearly wanted better access to markets and the prosperity that access would bring. As a result, they convinced themselves, briefly, that they could have that access without benefiting the interests of some more than those of others. In their initial enthusiasm, they touted projects as aiding all segments and regions of society and as binding the new nation together, cementing the loyalty of each section to the greater whole. Increasingly they found that internal improvements created sectional and class hostility rather than unity. Internal improvements issues did help to give all Midwesterners a heightened sense of their common interest as Westerners. At the same time, however, these projects exacerbated tensions with other regions, East and South, which seemed to receive more than their fair share of federal largesse. Internal improvements sharpened sectional divisiveness within these three Midwestern states by encouraging feelings of deprivation as it became apparent that government's scarce resources could not accommodate all interests. The internal improvements era left the Midwestern states an enhanced sense of Westernness and yet greater internal tensions.

FIVE

❦

Opportunity

THE UPLAND SOUTHERNERS who settled the region north of the Ohio River were familiar with a plantation society that reserved wealth, privilege, social status, and political power for an elite. Because equality of opportunity in the South itself was so closely linked to the social and economic status of slaveholders, Upland Southerners were less sanguine about the openness of opportunity than other settlement groups in the Midwest. The earliest debate involving equality of opportunity concerned that peculiarly Southern institution, slavery, and its importation into the Midwest. Midwesterners went on to debate whether government could secure equality of opportunity by establishing banks, protective tariffs, and public schools.

To the yeomen of the Upper South, freedom meant independence from others. Such independence required economic self-sufficiency. In the Midwest, many achieved those goals. Visitors noticed the "ease and self-possession" of the inhabitants and the lack of class distinctions based on wealth or rank far different from the deference of plantation society. "I have seen a veritable major invited to a corn-shucking; and the major went," a sojourner in Illinois reported. In a frontier community, struggling for survival, there was little time for "differences of education and station." The dependence on each other for survival led to "almost absolute social equality."[1] Conditions on the frontier did not eliminate social class distinctions—a major was still known to be a major—but such distinctions were less rigid, and while opportunity remained unfettered all could aspire to a higher status.

Republicanism confirmed and strengthened those tendencies. Indiana lawyer Calvin Fletcher's Fourth of July oration asserted that the Founding Fathers left a land "of equal rights and privileges—under a government that knows no distinction from birth or titles." Classical republicanism emphasized an independence based on property holding. These themes continued during the Jacksonian period. Jacksonian Democrats feared that governmental intervention in society and the economy invariably aided some at the expense of others. Jacksonians believed that if opportunity were left unfettered, a balance of power and wealth would be achieved. Government intervention only worked to upset the balance, not to create it. Thus the Democrats maintained that their true principles were "equal rights and privileges."[2] The argument against aristocracy drew on the Upland Southern fears of recreating the inequality they had known in the South.

Upland Southern Midwesterners self-consciously maintained that poverty should not be considered shameful. Self-sufficiency was essential to citizenship in republican ideology. Therefore, Upland Southerners asserted that poverty did not necessarily mean the dependence implied by republicanism nor the reliance on wealthy neighbors so often true of the South. A correspondent of the *Scioto Gazette* wrote, "We hardly know our next neighbor, if he is poor, but if rich, tho' he live miles away, we can speak of him with *admirable* self-complacency as 'our friend, Mr. such-a-one.' . . . Would to heaven the day was come . . . when we need not add to a poor man's obituary, 'tho' *poor, respectable*'—as if such a thing were an anomaly in society."[3] Abner Flack, candidate for the state senate of Illinois, pointed out that objections to his candidacy had been made on the grounds that he was a poor man.

> This is my misfortune, not my fault, for I have honestly struggled for my livelihood. I hope my poverty is not a *crime,* and I am sure no man is able to *buy* me, poor as I am. I was poor when I fought with others against the Indians twenty years ago, and I was poor when the Democracy of the whole State elected me to the honorable office of a Jackson elector; and, fellow citizens, whenever a *property qualification* is necessary to entitle a man to represent the People, I shall promptly decline being a candidate for any office.[4]

Flack insisted that poverty did not have to mean dependence. He pointed to his previous political services as well as his courage against the Indians and implied that if wealth were a qualification for office he would abdicate office on principle not because of his poverty.

More than simple access to office was at stake, however. Government must refrain from favoring the wealthy. One Indiana politician wrote that he would not give to an individual or group of men privileges not provided to all, because "the inmates of the palace are no more entitled to the fostering care of government then the tenants of the most humble cottage of the land." Even trivial matters of public business could be interpreted as solicitations for special government favors. "A Citizen" of Cincinnati reported that outbreaks of yellow fever had prompted some to advocate turning hogs loose into the streets. This had been done in Philadelphia and New York City and had supposedly reduced occurrences of the disease. "A Citizen" objected that in those cities gardens were walled; in Cincinnati, they were not, and the hogs would feast on the produce. But there was more to "A Citizen's" objections than the dislike of seeing his garden become a pigsty. He claimed that the hog owners wanted to fatten their livestock at others' expense and dismissed them as "whining applicants for exclusive privileges." New Englander Ephraim Cutler found this attitude quite frustrating. A bill providing relief for veterans of the Revolution met opposition because, although it might help hundreds of needy veterans, it might also "give a needless privilege to one in different circumstances." Scornfully Cutler asked, "Do gentlemen, indeed, wish that we should follow our retreating soldiers through New Jersey, in that darkest and most forlorn winter of the war, and scientifically gauge the puddles of blood shed from their shoeless feet; and then, by the butcher's rules, reckon up the compensation due?"[5]

Economic and class envy were doubtless behind some of these scruples. The scruples were, nonetheless, quite real and related to the perceived need of republican societies to preserve public virtue in the face of luxurious aristocracy. The *Indiana State Sentinel* pointed out that "it is as difficult for a nation to make haste to grow rich, and remain virtuously free, as for an endowed and beneficed clergy to retain the apostolic graces of primitive simplicity." An Illinois paper distinguished between the increase of national wealth and the accumulation of wealth by a few. The first was no danger to a republic and might actually be beneficial to liberty by improving the people intellectually, morally, and socially. The second, however, "must sooner or later debase and degrade the mass of the people both physically and mentally, converting them into mere beasts of burthen, and extinguishing in their bosoms the proud consciousness of republican equality and the generous love of liberty."[6] An uneven distribution of wealth led to the exploitation of those who were not rich and the conversion of the government into a despotism.

Declining possibilities for upward mobility was the chief fear underlying the concern with wealth and aristocracy. New Englanders assumed equality of opportunity existed and that government would foster it.

Southerners did not. Simeon Nash, originally from Massachusetts, and in 1850 and 1851 a delegate to Ohio's constitutional convention from Gallia County, accused radical Democrats of insulting Ohioans by calling them poor.

> And who is this rich man? The poor man, of thirty years ago; and who, by his enterprise, and industry, and self-denial, has made himself what he is. When railing at the rich man, you are railing at the arrangements of God, who has ordained that wealth shall attend upon such a life of self-denial and toil. . . . If to be rich, is to become an object of public hatred—is to be assailed and persecuted, what inducement has the young man to follow such a life of toil and self-denial, as has built up the mammoth fortunes in America? The sons of the rich, if unworthy, become the poor of the next generation, and the sons of the poor, become its rich men. Thus society changes—the industrious, and virtuous, and saving, inheriting the earth, as they deserve to do.[7]

Wealth is God's reward for hard work and is as easily lost as it is difficult to gain. Nash associated wealth with labor and argued that men moved both up and down the economic scale based on merit. This free-labor ideology, as Eric Foner has called it, stressed keeping opportunities for advancement open. An individual's economic progress was an accurate measure of his moral worth, for social and economic mobility were open to every one.[8]

Southerners held free-labor views as well as Northerners. Wealth itself was not in dispute between Northerners and Southerners in the Midwest. They did, however, dispute the means used to acquire it. New Englanders tended to look on the rich man as one blessed for his virtuous and industrious life; Southerners tended to see the same man as one who had squeezed a great deal out of those who were leading genuinely virtuous and industrious lives. Yet certain Upland Southern Midwesterners, Whigs and Republicans, held views closer to the New England one. Abraham Lincoln not only avowed that his own life was an example of upward economic mobility but also scolded his stepbrother, a more stereotypical Upland Southern Midwesterner, for too slovenly an approach to life.[9]

Property had always been a prerequisite for republican virtue because economic independence was necessary to the republican ideal. Increasingly in the antebellum period, Midwesterners from North and South believed that everyone could acquire a certain amount of wealth. Those who did would also possess the republican virtue society needed; those who did not lacked this virtue. Middle-class self-sufficiency, even wealth, did not frighten Southerners in the Midwest. What frightened them, more than it did Northerners, were conglomerations of the very rich and the very powerful who threatened to reduce them to positions of subservience. They had seen such combinations develop in the planter class they left behind, in banks, and in policies on manufacturing and education.

Southern settlers in the Midwest had strong feelings about one visible sign of wealth: slaves. Some fought the extension of slavery into the Northwest on abstract grounds of natural rights, but most were concerned with the economic results of slavery. They opposed slavery because it created an uneven distribution of wealth and power familiar to them in the South. A slave society closed opportunities for the poor to advance economically and socially. Poor men would be unable to accumulate the capital to invest in land and slaves necessary for economic betterment. A slaveholding elite would look down on the common white laborer, considering him a social inferior. Those who promoted slavery described a very different slave system from the elitist and closed society envisioned by those who opposed slavery's introduction into the Northwest. Proslavery proponents described a slave society in which many whites would hold a few slaves each, bringing general prosperity and avoiding dominance by a few wealthy planters. The argument over slavery reinforced sectional prejudices by causing Upland Southern Midwesterners to reexamine their ties to the South.

The South's expanding plantation system forced many yeoman farmers to migrate to the Northwest. Some objected to slavery as a matter of principle; others simply could not hope to compete with slave labor. While one observer noted that many Southerners migrated to Illinois to escape slavery, and called them "abolitionist" in their sympathies, he was forced to admit that another reason for leaving was "their want of means to become slaveholders, a man's respectability being, in a great measure, proportioned to the number of slaves in his possession." Yet racism kept most white Southerners sympathetic to white masters. This ambivalence about the slave system and the South continued throughout the antebellum period.[10]

Although Article VI of the Northwest Ordinance prohibited slavery in the Northwest Territory, it had limited effect on the slaves held north of the Ohio River. Local officials often did not enforce the ordinance's provisions. It was impossible, moreover, for authorities to prevent Southerners from traveling with their slaves and forcing blacks to accept "voluntary" indentures that met the letter of the ordinance but amounted to de facto slavery. The numbers of slaves in these three states were always minimal, but the result was that slavery was not expunged quickly from the Northwest Territory but rather died a lingering death.[11]

Not only did slavery linger on, but some Southerners made a concentrated effort to import it to the Northwest. The ensuing debate, largely among Southerners, forced an examination of slavery on three grounds: whether it could bring growth and prosperity to the region, whether it was a republican institution, and whether it would create an unwelcome aristocracy. In all three states, proslavery people argued that slavery would promote the growth of the state. Some prominent Jeffersonian Republicans were said to favor the introduction of slavery so that "men of wealth and independence" would come to Ohio. Petitioners from St. Clair and Randolph counties, Illinois, asked in 1796 and again in 1800 for exemption from Article VI which, they claimed, had deprived them of valuable property and left them in "Poverty and distress." The Vincennes Convention asked for a suspension of Article VI for ten years on the grounds that it had "prevent[ed] the country from populating."[12] They claimed to be arguing not only for their rights and the general good, but also for the best interests of the blacks.

Many more Upland Southerners objected to slavery, not only on the grounds that many of them had left the South specifically to get away from it, but also because of the degrading effects slavery would have on white labor and hence on the prosperity of most whites. To "A Hamilton Farmer" in Ohio, slaves were a symbol of aristocracy. Statehood would bring a stratified society with

> gentlemen enough, and their negroes too, and that's what they want to be at—if they could only get their negroes brought here, if one of us were starving we would not get a days work, nor a civil word from one of them, while they would be riding over us with their coaches, and we should be obliged to go out along with their negroes to make roads for them.[13]

In Illinois, "Martus" opposed efforts to call a convention whose widely regarded purpose was to introduce slavery. His opposition to slavery centered around its unegalitarian economic ramifications. Only rich men had the capital to buy slaves and "many an one would have to make a *slave of himself* a while, before he would be able to purchase a slave to serve him." Slaveowners would buy large tracts of land, driving up prices. Blacks were not profitable because they did not work as hard as white men do for themselves. The South would not sell Illinois its best slaves and the wealthiest men of the South would stay at home, leaving only slaveowners with little money to emigrate. Martus compared the prosperity of New York and Virginia and of Kentucky and Ohio to the detriment of the slave states. While some of Martus's arguments seem contradictory, the overall picture he presented was one in which the Southern planter class oppressed the yeomanry of Illinois either by introducing economic conditions that would make it harder for non-slaveholding Illinoisans to prosper or by exporting their least desirable planters and slaves to Illinois.[14] For nonslaveholding whites, slavery meant poverty and a form of serfdom through which they were degraded to the level of slaves.

In addition, Upland Southern opponents of introducing slavery doubted that black slavery was reconcilable with republican government. The Legislative Council and House of Representatives of Indiana Territory called slavery "repugnant" to the "principles of a republican form of Government" and blamed English rule for its origins in the United States. Other critics called slavery "repugnant to the inestimable principles of a republican Government." William Henry Harrison's republicanism came under attack when he supported bringing slaves into the territory. One Illinois man, writing under the pen name "Democracy," argued that while republics needed virtue, slavery destroyed virtue. The habit of commanding and threatening slaves, necessary to induce them to work, produced an "overbearing and tyrannical spirit, entirely opposite to republican simplicity and meekness." Slaveowning also produced debauchery and defiance of the law.[15]

Upland Southerners found the social class stratification resulting from the institution of slavery antirepublican. Slavery violated political principles by denying the truth that all men are created equal and undermined the republican system, for

> Who is accustomed to the servile obedience of humble negroes, cannot bear the erect attitude of men proud of their independence, and who can command a multitude of blacks, for no other consideration, than the obligation which his interest imposes, of keeping them alive, will not readily pay the price which a free man sets upon the exertions of his industry.[16]

Virginia-born Ohioan John Rankin believed "slavery tends to tyranny." The relationship of master to slave was that of absolute monarch to subject, and the customs of slave society showed that slave states were devoted to an inequality among men that was contrary to the Declaration of Independence.[17] These arguments about slavery in the Midwest revolved around whether economic and political opportunity would still be open to all white men in a slave society. Many feared they would end as slaves themselves to an aristocracy.

The early debate over slavery served, as did the later one which reprised many of its arguments, to strengthen sectional differences. The proslavery "Slim Simon" in Indiana derided the notion that slaveholding Kentuckians were less virtuous than nonslaveholders in Ohio. For the charge that proslavery men were aristocrats, he had only contempt. "Are the people of Kentucky, or the old volunteers, federalists and aristocrats?

Do the people of the State of Ohio occupy a higher grade of moral, political and religious virtue and excellence than those of Kentucky? . . . The idea would be preposterous." An Illinoisan scoffed at the notion that slavery would weaken Illinois. He asked where the "hardy freemen" of New England had been when the people of Kentucky and Tennessee had fought the War of 1812?[18]

Slavery provoked feelings of great ambivalence among Upland Southern Midwesterners. At the time of the Missouri Compromise, the publisher of the *Scioto Gazette* found himself in the midst of a controversy about advertisements for the recovery of fugitive slaves. J. Bailhache maintained that he was personally opposed to slavery but believed that to run such ads was his constitutional duty as well as necessary for the preservation of the Union. He would not risk disunion "for the sole purpose of teaching morality to the citizen of the southern states." Bailhache complained that denouncing the South as immoral was the current fashion, indulged in by those who forgot the South's contribution to the War of 1812, a contribution greater than that of the states who now saw themselves as the backbone of the Union. Bailhache also claimed to be doing Ohio a favor by helping to return runaways. Fugitive blacks who resided in Ohio decreased that state's physical strength, commerce, industry, morality, and religious feeling, according to the publisher. The man who had objected to the ads found himself ostracized in Ohio and accused of being prejudiced against the South, even though he was himself a Southerner, born and raised among slaves.[19] Bailhache's spirited defense indicated how touchy Upland Southern Midwesterners were with respect to this issue. On the one hand, many professed to have no sympathy for slavery, yet they resented fiercely any aspersions against the South and responded with vigorous sectional criticism of their own, misdirected though it was in this specific instance.

Upland Southerners' divided attitudes about the merits of bringing slavery with them to free territory were evident in the Illinois vote on whether to call a constitutional convention in 1824. A vote for the constitutional convention was widely held to be a vote for legalizing slavery in the state. While the majority of Egypt's counties favored the convention, significant portions of Egypt and southern Illinois opposed it.[20]

Although Southerners may have developed a rationale that reconciled slavery with republicanism,[21] those who came to the Midwest were deeply suspicious of planter society. They feared its aristocratic, unrepublican aspects, its tendency toward luxury, its devaluation of white free labor. They also feared that whites would be debased and enslaved politically just as blacks were physically. Proslavery proponents described a slavery with widely dispersed ownership of a few slaves, quite different from the feared planter dominance, but many Upland Southern Midwesterners, while susceptible to rallying cries on behalf of the South, disliked the aristocracy and denial of opportunity they associated with slavery.

Wealth creates power; power creates the ability to oppress. Nowhere was the equation more visible than in those "moneyed aristocracies," the banks. Midwesterners divided on the issue of banks because they could not agree on the effects of the credit system.[22] Did it, as many Northerners and a few Southerners argued, open avenues of opportunity? Or did it, as many Upland Southerners were inclined to believe, close those opportunities by providing another forum in which connections counted more than talent or hard work. At heart was a concern with opportunity, the same equality of opportunity that concerned Midwesterners when they considered the many economic avenues that led some to prosperity and others to poverty. Those who controlled wealth might deny it to others.

To some, banks could do a host of good things. "Civis" urged a liberal policy of incorporation, for as banking capital increased so could the expansion of population and the prosperity of the economy. "Well-dispersed capital," in the eyes of the citizens of Marion County, Indiana, had brought stability to the manufacturing, agriculture, and commerce of the Mississippi Valley. A Bedford, Indiana, man wrote that the West owed its prosperity to the fact that the Second United States Bank had disseminated its capital in the wilderness. Although favoring banks, these writers were also asking for a wider dispersal of money, not the concentration of wealth that was so feared by the community. They also asked for "sound" and "well ordered" institutions based on the experience, often unhappy, of their own and other communities or states.[23]

Others, however, had deep reservations about the workings of the credit system. A Chillicothe, Ohio, man lamented the existence of such small notes, because they provided a great opportunity for "frauds & impositions." The more radical Democrats could connect banking with pure evil. James Loudon, delegate to the Ohio constitutional convention from Brown County, and a Kentuckian by birth, countered the argument that the delegates little understood the banking business they discussed by agreeing, "Nobody, I believe, but his Satanic majesty himself, is capable of understanding the deep dark iniquity of those institutions."[24]

One group of men was well versed in manipulating banking to its own advantage. When some prospered although the economy failed, speculators were the universal scapegoats. The Democrats meeting in Petersburg, Illinois, in 1843 proclaimed banks to be evil, in part, because "They produce fluctuations in the prices of all kinds of property, whereby crafty speculators, stock jobbers, brokers and shavers are enriched by the distresses of the people." The Democratic state convention a few years earlier had blamed the bank managers for unsuccessful speculations and accused them of creating an unnatural privation in the midst of a prosperous country. If the evils of banks were not controlled, one Ohio man wrote, "our state will shortly be governed by a set of speculators and swindlers, who appear to thrive and fatten on the distresses of the country."[25] Whether they went by the name speculator or capitalist, public sentiment discerned a group of men ready to swindle honest people.

Why was there so much fear about the workings of banks? The obvious answer lies in the fluctuations of the economy in the first half of the nineteenth century and the inconvenience and frauds of the banks themselves. How could a man get ahead when circumstances were so unstable? Yet some seemed to prosper even when times were hard. How could this be? Southern settlers feared that equality of opportunity would be shut off, creating a society in which the rich got richer and the poor poorer because there was nothing else for the poor to do; and those fears seemed about to be fulfilled. Banks were institutions founded by rich men, for rich men, and made it more difficult for the poor to compete.

Banks, as corporations, violated the ideal of equality of rights and privileges. A bank charter, by nature, "confines the power and privilege to a few to whom it is granted." Such a charter was "establishing an aristocracy by law," and a "monied aristocracy" to boot. A charter granted powers denied to the many to a few, and that few always used those powers to injure the many. Such concentrations of privilege were monopolistic. Monopoly was the favored status of banks, enabling them to best exploit their advantages of capital and credit. Some might admit that banks brought economic advantages to a community, but this did not outweigh their ill effects on equality. Who used banks? Not the farmers, but only the rich men.[26] "A Farmer of Bond County," Illinois, wondered,

> As all the Banks make money, and RICH men alone have stock in them, it is a question to be asked, of whom do they make the great gains, and out of whose labor do their Presidents, Cashiers, Directors and Stockholders become able to live in fine houses without labor, and drive splendid carriages, and give sumptuous entertainments every day. The question is as easily answered as asked; it is by the labor of the Farmers and the Mechanics, and the day laborer; on their sweat and toil these rag barons revel, and dress in purple and fine linen, and deride those by whose labor they fatten.[27]

Bankers did not seem to be working at all. Their money appeared out of thin air, but the money had to come from somewhere—probably from those elements of the community that did work, the honest farmers and laborers.

Financial power enabled banks to exert influence in their own favor. They had the power to affect the nature of banking legislation. They could loan at usurious rates, use money to influence elections, and lobby those they had helped elect. They could also pick and choose to whom they would loan. The use of bank power to affect legislation threatened the political liberties of the people; the uses of bank power to control economic opportunity threatened the mobility of the people. Both were heinous crimes, and sometimes they were intertwined. "Justice" complained that a branch of the state bank of Illinois engaged in favoritism, renewing some notes without demanding payment of interest or discounting a draft without requiring security, and providing favors for the branch's president and his son-in-law. The *Indiana State Sentinel* reported that Dr. George W. Stipp, "a notorious and insolvent man" but with wealthy Whig friends, discounted $1,300 at the bank in Indianapolis. On the same day, the note of a worthy hog buyer was turned away.[28] Banks thus held back economic mobility by favoring those already wealthy or with wealthy patrons, while those who strove to better their condition were rejected. They also encouraged aristocratic notions by finding the hog buyer less acceptable than the professional man.

The result of these privileges was to transfer the property of the many to the hands of the few, pauperism for the former and opulence for the latter. Banks "furnish a means which is not neglected for the rich to make themselves richer, and the poor poorer." Banks prevented "free and honorable competition among all classes" and helped to "divide society into classes and castes; grading each by the amount of wealth it possesses." Instead of an ideal society of competition where men rose to wealth by industry and innate virtue, banks created a fixed society of caste in which the poor man remained unable to do better, was exploited, and yet was stigmatized for failing to rise. When banks possessed a monopoly, wrote Allen G. Thurman, their directors would engage in favoritism, helping the rich instead of the poor if only out of the purest of business motives. Thurman conceded that this policy tended to make "the rich richer & the poor poorer" and yet the only solution he saw was to impose competition on the banks themselves.[29]

Thurman's sentiments were those of Southerners, many Whigs and some Democrats, who believed in the credit system, but only if it could be kept open to all and so help the common man's economic and social advancement. Governor Joseph Vance of Ohio defended credit for having given Ohio "an equality of fortune" not to be found anywhere else. Banks could be part of progress, providing a way for men to move from laborer to middle-class independence. John J. Janney, a Virginia Quaker who settled in Ohio, defended the credit system and its agents, the banks, for their willingness to take chances on young men who could not pay right away. "By this means thousands of young men are enabled to commence and successfully prosecute a business, and assume at once that station of usefulness in society which they would be years in attaining without the aid of credit and perhaps not one in a thousand would obtain it." To this Southern Whig, banks facilitated upward mobility, a desirable social event.[30]

The bill to recharter the Second Bank of the United States, presented by Whig politicians in 1832, provoked President Andrew Jackson's famous veto message and "war" on the Bank. An analysis of the vote taken on that measure shows the ambivalence with which Midwesterners viewed banks. In the House of Representatives, ten congressmen from Ohio, Indiana, and Illinois, three of them born in the South, voted for the recharter. Of the five congressmen from these Old Northwest states who voted against the recharter, one came from the South. While the South as a whole split its vote on the recharter, and a majority within the Midwest tended to oppose it, congressmen with Upland Southern roots tended to favor the Bank against the president's wishes. Party affiliation gives an indication of why the votes divided as they did. Among the congressmen from the Old Northwest, four Democrats but only one Whig supported the president's position. Four Democrats, four Whigs, a National Republican (a precursor of the Whig Party), and one member without a party affiliation opposed the president. While this might seem to be an even split on the issue, two of the Democrats later became Whigs, suggesting they felt a closer affiliation to Whig policy than was normally true in their party.[31]

Southern settlers in the Midwest did not object to getting rich, only to doing so at another's expense. While they were extremely suspicious of rich people getting richer, they had no objection to a poor man rising in society. They supported banks that facilitated the rise of the poor, but often banks seemed to be tools of the rich, tools used to garner wealth from those who labored. Instability and fraudulent practice led to widespread distrust of banks and the men who ran them—evil speculators or wealthy nabobs. Banks committed a variety of crimes: They exploited the laboring population; they wielded too much influence and grasped for despotic political power; and they closed off the honest poor's chances of economic and social mobility. As with slavery, banking seemed to be yet another method to deny the poor economic opportunity. Slaveowners monopolized land, and banks controlled wealth. But because the banking issue lacked sectional connotations, it remained a partisan issue, rather than a sectional one. Upland Southern Whigs joined forces with Whigs from other regions to fight "King Andrew's" attack on the Second United States Bank, while Upland Southern Democrats united with other Democrats to attack the "monster."

Another antebellum partisan issue, the protective tariff, did take on sectional overtones. While at the turn of the nineteenth century, home manufactures and national independence were goals that transcended other partisan differences, by the Jacksonian period, protection of manufactures was an issue that divided the parties. Democratic policy sought to retard commercial and industrial development in the name of the egalitarian, essentially agrarian, society the party envisioned. Whigs favored a commercial society and advocated protective tariffs for manufacturing in order to encourage its growth. As a symbol of their commitment, prominent Whigs made it a point of honor to wear no clothing of foreign manufacture.[32] As with other economic issues, Southerners in the Midwest were not universally for or against manufacturing. Ohio's nine leading manufacturing counties, five in the Upland Southern–dominated portions of Ohio and four in the New England–dominated northeastern quarter of the state, split their vote fairly evenly between the two parties throughout the 1830s.[33] The southern halves of Indiana and Illinois had less manufacturing than the northern. This situation produced much rhetoric from the North about the backwardness of those areas and much defensiveness in the South. Within states, manufacturing and protection gave rise to local sectionalism, but on the national level, Midwesterners did not align themselves with the South or the North—they backed Western interests or party positions.

From the earliest period, the issue of manufacturing was bound to the need for national independence. In the 1810s and 1820s, manufacturing and agriculture were the subject of many toasts, the themes of which were independence and the harmony of the different economic sectors. "A free people, to be really independent, should manufacture their own clothing, as well as their own laws." Agriculture was "the foundation of national strength" and manufacturing "a grand source of national independence." Many times manufactures were feted as "the sure pledge of National independence," and many times they were coupled with agriculture in that regard.[34] The two sections of the economy, agriculture and manufactures, would exist in harmony.

The fear that the United States might, once again, come under foreign control spurred the quest for national independence. Just as the republican citizen needed to be independent of others, so the republican nation's first consideration was to secure its freedom from other nations. The threat of economic slavery to foreign goods necessitated a home-grown industry. "A Friend to Domestic Manufacture" argued that the idea of antagonism between agriculture and manufacturing, particularly the assertion that what promoted manufacturing hurt agriculture, was an idea spread by the English to ensure their command of American markets. Some Jeffersonian Republicans from Chillicothe, Ohio, advocated aiding manufactures with a protective tariff even if it meant a "sacrifice" for the majority of society. They reasoned that a dependent republic would lack the conviction to stand up to foes it was tied to by debts and commercial connections. They encouraged others to celebrate the upcoming Fourth of July by wearing clothes entirely of domestic manufacture, because "any Nation cannot be really Independent so long as they are obliged to procure from a foreign Nation any article whatever, that is necessary or convenient in life. . . . It is of the utmost Importance to the United States to be capable of existing entirely Independent of the aid or support of foreign produce or manufactures."[35] In this early period, people feared economic slavery to another government as much as they did political domination. Because encouraging manufacturing was in the national interest, it was supposed that no disharmony existed between it and other sectors within the U.S. economy. The goal was independence from Europe and there was as yet no hint in the Midwest that one region of the United States would become the dependent of another.

Whigs repeated these same arguments about the necessity of national independence during the 1830s and 1840s. For one Yankee Whig in Illinois, protection of manufactures was the defining issue that set him apart from his Democratic neighbors and family. For one Southern-born Whig in Ohio, economic independence of other countries was both necessary and practical, because no "good end can be attained by transporting wool and cotton 3000 miles to be manufactured into the clothing we wear and then bringing it back again to be paid for by the food consumed in its manufacture taxed with the same transportation." But where once the harmony of agriculture and manufactures had been accepted and toasted, now the benefits manufacturing brought to other parts of the economy, particularly the laborer and the farmer, had to be explicitly described. Manufacturing establishments provided more employment for laborers, demanded foodstuffs in such quantities as to raise their price and bring a greater prosperity to the farmer, brought more customers to the merchants and more taxpayers to the town, and increased the value of everyone's property.[36]

Congressional votes on antebellum tariff bills reveal a pattern of sectional and party alignment on the issue of manufacturing and protection. In 1828 and 1860, Southern congressmen in the House of Representatives overwhelmingly rejected proposed tariffs, unless those tariffs involved reduction of the existing rates. By varying margins, the Mid-Atlantic states supported most tariff bills while rejecting a lowered tariff in 1857. New England objected to the tariff of 1828 by a slight margin, divided almost evenly on the tariff of 1832, supported the tariff of 1857 by a five to one margin, and supported the tariff of 1860 unanimously. In contrast, congressmen from Ohio, Indiana, and Illinois unanimously supported the tariffs of 1828 and 1832 regardless of place of birth or party affiliation. However in 1857, they rejected the lowered tariff by more than a two-to-one margin with all the Democrats voting for the measure and the majority of Whigs and Republicans voting against it. In 1860, congressmen from the Midwestern states split their votes almost evenly on the Republican-proposed Morrill Tariff. Democrats from the region voted almost unanimously against it, while Republicans and Whigs voted almost unanimously for it. Clearly in the early Jacksonian period, Midwesterners saw protection as benefiting their section. By the late antebellum era, it had become a partisan issue.[37]

By the late antebellum period, the tariff was becoming a sectional issue in the sense that regions within states became polarized over the manufacturing issue. The *Daily Journal,* quite superior in its attitude toward the southern portion of Illinois, attributed part of southern Illinois's lack of progress to its lack of manufacturing:

> Mark the contrast in the growth of towns in Northern and southern Illinois. In the former every encouragement is given to manufacturers, and their growth is rapid, and they extend their influence to all the country around. In the latter, that our manufacturing should be done in England—not even in the Eastern States;—that there should be no banks to encourage the emigration of manufacturers, capitalists, and enterprising business men, as a general thing—is held as cardinal principles of democracy and the result is seen in the comparatively tardy improvements in that section of the State. In the north both the whigs and the democrats are in favor of progress; they adopt means which they know, by the results in other States, secures progress—and they are richly repaid for their discernment and their enterprise. There is no reason to be found in the natural advantages of northern over Southern Illinois, to account for the more rapid advance in wealth and prosperity.—Indeed, we have contended that the south had the advantages of climate; of natural access to markets, of timber, sufficient to over-balance any advantages of soil which the north might be supposed to possess.[38]

Not only were the interests of manufacturing and agriculture compatible, but manufacturing would lead the way in advancing economic prosperity. The *Daily Journal* argued that manufactures located in the center of an agricultural region provided a home market. The "best interests" of both farmer and mechanic were served by this arrangement, and so the paper was "most anxious to make our town a manufacturing town."[39] Manufacturing meant progress, and southern Illinois stood condemned as backward for its lack of it. Their hostility to manufacturing, and to measures to benefit U.S. manufacturing concentrated in the East, condemned the United States to perpetual vassalage to Europe. The *Daily Journal* still appealed to the idea that what benefited one section of the U.S. economy benefited others, that what benefited one region of the United States benefited all.

Some objected that at the national level the interests of East, West, South, and North were not the same. The West and the South were primarily agricultural, argued S. H. Anderson, candidate for Congress, and relied on foreign manufactured goods. A tariff increase would not only cost the consumer, but it would also depress the Southern market, which was crucial to Illinois's economy. Others shared the concern for the tariff's impact on western markets. Governor Wilson Shannon of Ohio agreed that the tariff was a tax on the farmers to help the manufacturer and would result in closing Southern and foreign markets to Western grain.[40]

Despite the repeated avowals that all sections of the country, manufacturing or agricultural, benefited from the tariff, many felt they were being asked to replace the tyranny of Europe with the tyranny of New England. A Putnam County, Indiana, Union meeting condemned the Republican Party's adoption of an "iniquitous sectional tariff, intended to enrich the New England States at the expense of the agricultural States of North and South." The Morrill Tariff, they claimed, would enact "a direct tax upon the industry of the West, the South, and the Middle States, for the benefit of Yankee mills, Eastern capital, and the purse-proud manufacturers of New England."[41] The men of Putnam County not only believed a class of rich manufacturers intended to exploit them, they located that class in a specific geographic area, New England, and denied any commonality of interest between agriculture and manufacturing or between New England and the rest of the country.

Resistance to the increasing importance of industry in the U.S. economy reflected more than just an agrarian mindset determined to preserve an older way of life. On the contrary, at the turn of the nineteenth century, a strong agreement existed that the interests of agriculture and of manufacturing were reconcilable. Only with a strong domestic industry could national independence and the republican experiment be preserved from foreign economic and, eventually, political domination. But manufacturing also possessed a strong class and regional overtone—rich manufacturers came to be seen as at odds with common farmers and laborers. Manufacturing and nonmanufacturing regions in the state or country began to believe that they had different interests. Those who were suspicious of manufacturing saw another attempt, akin to that made by slaveowners or bankers, to reduce them to poverty. Increasingly the arguments of the latter became sectional in tone as the belief in common interests between the sections faded.

Sectional divisions appeared clearly over public education. In general, New Englanders strongly favored state-supported schooling, while Southerners were, at best, apathetic and, at worst, overtly hostile to violating the rule of "let every man school his own children." Upland Southern Midwesterners felt that public education violated a man's rights by taking his money to pay for the education of another man's children. In the 1850s, an Illinois man noted that an educator had published a plan for an industrial university. While the proposal was well received in northern Illinois, citizens in the southern part of the state disliked it and even made personal attacks on the good professor. Not surprisingly, the movement for public education began in Ohio, where the New England influence was strongest. Three Ohioans of Massachusetts birth masterminded the passage of the public school system. Indiana and Illinois were more half-hearted in their actions to develop public schools. Officials there were lax in collecting taxes for the schools and squabbled over school organization. An 1825 Illinois common school law resulted from discontent in southern Illinois with a previous law. The new measure ensured that none would be taxed against his will to support public schools. Only in 1855, when legislators of Yankee background took control of the Illinois legislature, did the formation of public schools begin in earnest and then only after a compromise was reached with the southern half of the state. In return for paying taxes to support common schools, the southern counties received a double share of the state revenues. Some have noted that Southern settlers objected to Yankee meddling and to Yankee educational schemes designed to wipe out Southern cultural values. One historian has noted that suspicion of the "Yankee device" of public schools was offset by appeals that education was essential to both upward mobility and democratic society.[42]

In the antebellum South, Whigs, largely self-made men, led school reform. Indeed, some Upland Southern Midwesterners found the thought of children going completely without an education to be "revolting to the mind." Governor Thomas Carlin of Illinois, born in Kentucky, spoke of the abstract benefits arising from education: "happiness, virtue, and usefulness." Others objected to hiring the cheapest teacher, regardless of his qualifications or, more often, his lack of them. Men of "literary acquirements" rejected teaching as a profession because of the low pay, so that most teachers were "illiterate, indolent and much given to intemperance." But the fact that teachers were held in such low regard indicates how little most Southern settlers emphasized education.[43]

Also in keeping with the Southern perspective, however, were the suspicious grumblings in the *Illinois State Register* against fanatics in the legislature who believed "that the habits, customs and actual conditions of society can be changed by one sweeping act of legislation." The correspondent objected to the law's "coercive features," particularly the power to tax:

We cannot legislate men *learned,* no more than we can wise, moral and religious. Yet this law goes upon the principle that education will be in proportion to the tax collected, and hence every little petty school officer is vested with full power to levy taxes in his own discretion thereby intending to compel the attendance of children at school for at least six months in the year. Many of these school officers have neither property, honesty nor discretion: but mistaking power for discretion proceed with a more tyrannical and oppressive hand to levy these burthens than even did the Czar of Russia while carrying on the war against England and France in the Crimea.[44]

Enforced schooling was not popular, in fact it bordered on the tyrannical, but there were certain grounds on which education was promoted as beneficial. First, education secured the survival of a republican government. Secondly, the education of all children, rich or poor, was a way of ensuring equality of opportunity in the future.

Upland Southerners acknowledged education to be "the strong adversary of tyrants," "the safeguard of republics," and of the people's liberty. The Indiana Legislative Assembly had told Congress when it petitioned for admission to the Union that "the promotion of useful knowledge is the best guarantee to our civil institutions." Education enlightened the people and an enlightened citizenry was necessary to self-government. "A people thoroughly enlightened," intoned the Assembly, "can never be enslaved." The 1816 Indiana constitution called for a system of common schools on the grounds that "Knowledge and learning, generally diffused throughout a community [were] essential to the preservation of a free government."[45]

From the educated would come the leaders of this free people. "F. P. C." complained that too few children attended school and asked parents where they expected to find future congressmen and presidents. "Will they be Geniuses, on whom Providence has performed more than her ordinary duty? No!—They will be those who make close application of their time, in the execution of their studies in the schoolroom."[46] In an egalitarian society, the leaders are not exceptional men either by birth or rank, but are merely the common people trained up in the paths of liberty.

Education defended liberty and free government from "the polluting and enervating touch of aristocracy and despotism." In a land where the people ruled, decisions could not be left to an "ignorant, blind, unprincipled rabble." A free people had to be able to assess their own interests properly; they would not long remain free if they were the kind of men "any demagogue might deceive, and any traitor might stir up to rebellion." A young Richard Yates argued in an address delivered at Illinois College that education should be available to all classes in society, "for knowledge is power, and he who possesses it, must, to a certain extent, govern those who grope in ignorance." Only when all citizens had access to education would the constitutional promise of equality of rights and privileges be fulfilled, "for it is as much a privilege to be educated as it is to be protected; and we had better withdraw the protection of law, then take away the privileges of education." Yates still saw education as a privilege, yet one that all should enjoy in order to offset the growth of an oppressive aristocracy. James B. Finley encouraged parents to "embrace" public education or else curse their children to being "the dupes and servants of their better-educated fellow-citizens": "An ignorant man must always remain a Lilliput in intellect, and a Tom-Thumb-being in society." General education led to "that equality among the people" most congenial to republican government.[47] Universal education was more than just a general inculcation of morality and social virtue. Education had a definite bearing on the preservation of a republican society.

An older Yates, as governor of Illinois, avowed that should the U.S. government fall it would not be because of attacks from a foreign enemy "but from the seeds sown broadcast of national corruption and ignorance. . . . Despotism may point to her standing armies as the prop of the government, but I point to American school houses and meeting houses as the citadels of freedom—the rock-bound foundations of American liberty." He hoped that Illinois would never be populated by a "people rude and ignorant" because the state had neglected to provide them with an education. Yates, speaking at the opening of Normal University in Bloomington, took the opportunity to combine the themes of the survival of republicanism and of upward mobility. Education had a beneficial impact on morality as well as on material development. Education not only provided an enlightened citizenry but enabled any man to aspire to the heights of political power. Yates concluded that,

> Our Government, by giving to every man the equal right to vote, and opening the avenues to office to the humblest as well as the highest, holds out the greatest stimulus to education. A man, to give an intelligent vote must think, must reason, must discriminate, must be informed, and hence must be educated. If he aspires to office, he must be prepared to show qualifications for the discharge of its duties. . . . The boy at school imbibes the genius of our free institutions, and however poor says: "I stand as much chance to be President as any other."[48]

Education could provide equality of opportunity in a political sense. It provided enlightened citizens who were careful in selecting their leaders and who prepared to be leaders. Enlightened citizens became neither the dupes of tyrants nor tyrants themselves.

Education served another function that appealed to the Southern born; it was the gateway to equality for all classes. Education presented an opportunity for poor children to make better lives for themselves. Virginia-born Governor Thomas Worthington of Ohio made the usual references to education as necessary to "a perpetuation of that freedom, we now possess" in his 1818 message to the state legislature. Yet he also warned that if nothing was done to establish public schools, republican society would decay: "the poorer class . . . will be brought up in a state of comparative ignorance, unable to manage, with prosperity, their private concerns, much less to take any part in the management of public affairs: and what is still more to be lamented, unacquainted with those religious and moral precepts and principles, without which they cannot be good citizens." Northerners most forcibly expressed the idea that education was a "birthright" rather than a gift. Upland Southerners, however, did respond favorably to the notion that education could be a leveling device. Governor Joel A. Matteson of Illinois rejected the idea that schoolchildren should feel they were accepting charity. Educating all children did not attempt to achieve "equality of intellect," an impossible goal, but did aim for "equality of rights." The Southern born had argued for many years that state-supported education should be open to all children, rich and poor. It was suggested that by doing so the poor could end their poverty, thus removing them from the public's charity. But behind the discussion of state-supported schools lurked the idea that if government spent money on education, everyone should benefit.[49]

Education would allow those of virtue and talent to raise themselves from poverty and assume deserved positions in society. If charity required supporting the poor with public money, then so much more should the public be taxed to support public schools, "the most efficient means of removing poverty from among us." "Most of our great men have come from the middle classes," the Charleston (Illinois) Courier pointed out, "and many of them have struggled up from the lowest poverty. Let us extend the helping hand to those dear little ones, for our free country needs them all."[50] Once again, material success was associated with hard work and self-denial and was available, or should have been, to all who sought it. Education's mission was not to choose the virtuous and reward them, but rather to provide the virtuous poor with a level playing field on which to compete with their more fortunate peers.

While many Southerners contributed to the rhetoric in favor of schools, Southerners were more deeply divided over the issue than were Northerners. An Ohio man recalled that while New England immigrants immediately established public schools, Southerners were concerned only with institutions of higher learning. A Jacksonville, Illinois, man remembered that the poor people of southern Illinois objected to the 1825 school law. They did not welcome its offer of upward mobility; rather they feared it would render their children unsuited to and unhappy with life on the farm. "Observer" lamented the shortsightedness of parents who kept children out of school in order to save money. They not only robbed the children of the "privilege of cultivating" their God-given talents but endangered the "prosperity, permenance, and perpituity" of the republic. Caleb Mills showed that while counties north of Indianapolis overwhelmingly supported the 1848 and 1849 school laws, those to the south were about evenly divided for and against them. Mills provided a list which showed that all four of Indiana's counties with an almost fifty percent illiteracy rate were in the southern portion of the state.[51] Some Southerners were sympathetic to the arguments that education would provide equality of opportunity and safety for republicanism; others did not see the benefits as clearly.

Although complaints about the "apathy and indifference" of the Upland Southern Midwesterners continued throughout the antebellum period and retarded the establishment of public schooling,[52] the arguments used to break this indifference are revealing. General appeals to the "right" to an education or the ennobling effects of education on personal morality and character had more dispersion among the northern parts of the Ohio Valley than in the southern portions. In the southern sections, what mattered was whether education would contribute to the success of the republic by providing a citizenry capable of knowing its own interests and identifying the aristocrats and other subverters of liberty. What also mattered was how education would provide equality of opportunity, allowing the industrious poor to move up in society and preventing the solidification of a rigid class structure in society.

Entwined with the party divisions common to the antebellum era were sectional concerns. In some cases, party divisions did not enhance sectional divisions. Upland Southerners debated banking along party lines. In the cases of slavery and the tariff, however, sectional prejudices were resurrected. Upland Southerners, appalled at the idea of reinstating slavery, were cajoled unsuccessfully with patriotic references to the glory of the slaveholding states. The tariff created a Western section with distinct interests until it became a party issue in the late antebellum period. While Southern leaders spoke of the advantages of education, most of their constituents were reluctant to part with the tax money necessary to support it. In each case, however, Southerners defended their actions as promoting both republicanism and equality of opportunity.

SIX

❧✿❧

Rights

ABRAHAM LINCOLN, as a young candidate for office, stated his political views as "I go for all sharing the privileges of the government, who assist in bearing its burthens. Consequently I go for admitting all whites to the right of suffrage, who pay taxes or bear arms."[1] As Lincoln's statement reveals, the Southern born limited political rights to those able to exercise the responsibilities of citizenship, limits that excluded blacks and often the foreign born. But if these groups shouldered the burdens of society, how could Upland Southerners justify their exclusion from its privileges?

Upland Southerners expanded the definition of political rights when discussing temperance and land, but narrowly applied it to blacks and foreigners. Each issue in turn had its own impact on the sectional dynamics of the Midwest. Foreign immigration remained a partisan dispute, while black immigration pitted Northerners against Southerners and Upland Southern yeomen against planters. Western settlers united against Eastern influences, whether the national government or the speculator, over the land issue. North opposed South as Upland Southerners defended their liberty to drink from Yankee imperialism.

As a rule, Southern settlers resisted temperance movements more fiercely than did their Northern neighbors. While the Northerners condemned alcohol as a significant social and political evil, the Southern born feared the despotism and oppression inherent in the power to curb drinking. A significant number of Southerners, however, favored temperance. Some were Quakers and acted from religious principle. Others belonged to that group of middle-class Whigs and Republicans who looked on drinking as another of the backward, lower-class characteristics they wished to shed.

Those who resisted temperance did so on the grounds that it was no one's business whether a man imbibed or not. The Reverend James B. Finley encountered great resistance when he tried to enforce the Methodist Church's provisions against liquor on the Midwestern frontier. Finley remonstrated with the owner of the house where the minister was staying about a ten-gallon keg of whiskey the man intended for a barn raising. The man told Finley, "There is no law against using whiskey, and I'll do as I please." Finley refused to spend the night in that intemperate household. The next day at church, an old man told Finley to go home as he was doing more harm in the neighborhood than good. "And if you can't preach the Gospel and let people's private business alone," the old man concluded, "they do not want you at all." On an earlier occasion, Finley had tried to inculcate temperance values in the workers at John Dillon's ironworks near Zanesville, Ohio. Finley entered the lion's den, preaching at Mr. Dick's tavern while the workers drank and swore around him. Finally, he reproved them for their conduct and was told, "You go on with your business of preaching and we will mind ours."[2]

All religious men did not condemn drinking. Ministers often drank and even preached in the barrooms of taverns. Finley reported that "the ministers as well as the members of some denominations imbibed pretty freely." Yet Finley's reminiscences, and those of other itinerants on the frontier, included numerous anecdotes about the settlers' resistance to obeying what temperance principles their ministers preached. Southerners drank routinely at public events such as elections, militia musters, and court sessions. Southern temperance men attacked just those public events for becoming occasions to drink with friends.[3]

From the first, temperance was associated with sectional origin. By the temperance forces' own census, a third of temperance pledges came from New England, which had a sixth of the nation's population. The South, with 44 percent of the U.S. population, provided only 8.5 percent of pledges. As early as 1835, Stephen Douglas was writing home from Jacksonville, Illinois, that "Distilling & retailing Liquors is very proffitable but in these days of Temperance not very honorable, particularly among you Eastern People or 'Yankees' as the Suckers call you."[4]

Industrialization encouraged temperance. Two southern Illinois men, Mr. T. and Mr. S., owned a shop for which they hired only nondrinking laborers. So desperate did they become for a man with the proper skills for a particular job that they hired "L.," a notorious drunkard. They warned L. that he would be fired if he drank, and so L. learned to live without liquor. From a man who created a ruckus every election day, "bellowing and tearing up the dirt in the streets like a mad bull," L. became a temperance society member and churchgoer. Temperance was thus in part a class issue pitting laborers, the lower class, and all who clung to preindustrial work habits against the new manufacturing and industrial class.[5]

While New England industrialized, the Upland Southern portions of the Midwest remained largely agricultural. An abundance of corn and limited access to Eastern markets made distilling a profitable enterprise. In 1850, Ohio led the nation in the production of distilled spirits. Indiana ranked fourth and Illinois, fifth. A traveler in southern Illinois in the 1850s stopped and asked for a drink of water. The woman replied that whiskey was preferred to water and, at ten cents per quart, was cheaper than digging a well. Not until transportation networks linked the Ohio Valley to a national market, did Midwesterners strive for that efficiency and industry which many historians believe first led New Englanders to appreciate the joys of temperance.[6]

Where an agricultural economy remained, as in the Upland South, preindustrial work habits, including heavy drinking, prevailed. One recollection of life in Harrison County, Ohio, in the Jacksonian period, noted that, "At raisings, huskings, log-rollings, and all manner of social gatherings, it [whiskey] was used as an invigorator and a sign of hospitality; and the manner of taking it was from the neck of the jug, each man swallowing as much as he wanted." Farm hands expected alcohol for a normal day's work, not just on social occasions such as barn or house raisings. When, under the influence of temperance reformers, farmers stopped providing the expected refreshment, they replaced it with extra wages. Many hands simply refused to work if not given liquor. A temperance preacher advised farmers to give the men chocolates and coffee instead of whiskey as stimulants to hard work. He also advised women to stop driving their husbands to drink.[7] His proscriptions made up in zeal what they lacked in practicality.

Southerners pledged but without the fervor of New Englanders. A Carlinville, Illinois, Whig, J. A. Chesnut, wrote to Whig politician Richard Yates asking him to speak at a temperance meeting. He advised that Yates's opponent suffered from a "known proclivity to *spiritual indulgence*" yet also said that did not necessarily guarantee Yates the votes of the temperance men. Apparently even temperance men in southern Illinois did not vote on that issue alone. In contrast, the Erie County, Ohio, sheriff objected to the appointment of a justice of the peace who was, among other things, intemperate. The sheriff felt this disqualified the man for public office. Just as many associated temperance reform with Yankees, Chesnut associated liquor with extreme Southernness. "Down with rum sellers & fillibusters is my doctrine," he told Yates on another occasion. Illinois temperance legislation was further proof that temperance was not a powerful political issue in the Southern-dominated parts of the Midwest. The Whig- and Anti-Nebraska-dominated Illinois legislature passed a Maine law in 1855. Temperance forces carried most of the northern counties in the referendum on the law, but the southern counties provided enough votes to defeat it by a narrow margin. A southern Illinois man wrote that he did not want the Maine law passed, "for it will be a bad chance to get any liquor . . . unless we can get Linseed oil to answer the same purpose."[8]

Southerners saw drink as a personal, rather than a political, evil despite alcohol's ubiquity at the polling places of the South. General James Wilkinson advised that to win elections in Kentucky, "the way to men's hearts, is, down their throats."[9] The same tactics prevailed in Illinois:

"Treating" as it was called was an indispensable element of success at elections. In many counties the candidates would hire all the groceries in the county seats and other considerable villages, where the people could get liquor without cost for several weeks before election. The voters in all the neighboring country turned out every Saturday to visit the towns, see the candidates and hear the news. The candidates came also, and addressed the people from wagons, old logs or stumps newly cut. . . . The speeches being over, then commenced the drinking of liquor, and long before night a large portion of the voters would be drunk and staggering about town, cursing, swearing, halloing, yelling, huzzaing for their favorite candidates.[10]

Despite Upland Southern acceptance of liquor as part of political life, the language of the temperance debate had little to do with the transition from agriculture to industry but instead focused on the rhetoric of liberty.

To temperance reformers there was often no such thing as temperate drinking. The president of the Total Abstinence Society of Gustavus, Ohio, wrote that any "use of these liquors, as a beverage, infalliably creates a morbid appetite for them, which, at last nothing can satisfy; and that thus what is called a '*moderate or temperate* use' of inebriating drinks is precisely *the* way, and the *only* way in which men become drunkards, and consequently are ruined both for this world and the next." Drink "enslaved," unfitting men for the duties of life. The citizens of Richmond, Indiana, and its environs remonstrated that selling liquor was "the greatest curse that can befall a people; especially a free people." Obviously the addiction to liquor warred with the independence of republican citizens. Liquor sellers controlled the man of "depraved appetite" and "too feebly formed resolutions of reform." Indiana State Senator James P. Millikan, born in Maine, saw that control at work as the state legislature considered a temperance bill: "The rumsellers always have a set of dupes whom they have stupefied and dragged down to a state of acquiescence in their will, who attend all the primary political meetings. These men get all their political news from the dramseller, and are entirely influenced by him. . . . the dramseller and his dupes are making nominations for all classes to support." This explained the strong popular opposition to the bill.[11]

Intemperance also destroyed a republican society by undermining the virtue necessary to its survival. Drinkers lost their love of freedom "and prefer[red] a luxurious, vicious slavery, to virtuous, temperate liberty." "Adolescentia" wrote that liquor's effect on the political and national character was to lessen one's love of country, of independence, and of liberty. The Mass Temperance Convention meeting in Columbus, Ohio, in February 1852 noted that the happiness of the citizens of a free society depended on the "morality, intelligence and industry of the people," all of which liquor subverted. Therefore the manufacture and sale of liquor should be considered "crimes against society, and ought to be suppressed by law."[12]

Temperance advocates repeatedly compared the struggle against intemperance to the struggle for freedom during the Revolutionary War. "Uncle Adam" reported that a "respectable" hotel in Richmond, Indiana, served liquor. "Uncle Adam" advocated persuading the owner, by force if necessary, to close:

> Supposing our forefathers had suffered the *tea* brought over from England, to be landed without resistance, might we not to day have Victoria's little feet upon our necks? Had the citizens of Richmond been as watchful of their best interests as those who lived and acted in the days that tried men's souls, they would have met this fellow . . . promptly, and pitched his *tea,* if not into a harbor, into the gutter. . . . It would be doing this agent of King Alcohol a kindness for which he should be forever grateful, in helping him out of a most disgraceful traffic. It would doubtless save wives and husbands of our best citizens and most promising youth from being lured into his "parlors," like the fly into that of the spider, and where a sure destruction awaits them.[13]

Both tea and liquor had become symbols of tyranny. There was no compromise with the liquor trade—one drink, it seems, would lead to drunkenness, dependence, and the fall of the republic.

Abraham Lincoln compared the temperance revolution to the political revolution of 1776 in an address to the Springfield Washingtonian

Society. In fact, Lincoln seemed to find the temperance revolt of more lasting significance: "In *it,* we shall find a stronger bondage broken; a viler slavery, manumitted; a greater tyrant deposed. . . . By *it,* none wounded in feeling, none injured in interest. Even the dram-maker, and dram seller, will have glided into other occupations *so* gradually, as never to have felt the shock of change."[14] Just as the political rhetoric of the American Revolution emphasized the colonies' enslavement to the British, the bottle enslaved the drinker and the dram seller, the dram drinker. Lincoln's feeble attempt to deny that anyone would be hurt by the new legislation was a rare affirmation of the liquor seller's humanity. In Lincoln's scenario, alcohol was the tyrant; its sellers merely ordinary men trying to make a living.

Temperance opponents replied in the same vein that they were merely preserving their rights and their liberty against the oppressive tendencies of the temperance men. "Bacchus, Jun." called a bill to prevent drunkenness "subversive of natural Rights and Republican Liberty." A long poem in the same paper used as its refrain "Huzza, for Grog and Liberty." "Scioto" argued that what a man did with his time and money was his business alone. He also held up a previous protemperance correspondent to the scorn of all men "who have a proper appreciation of the rights and privileges of unoffending gentlemen, in this free country, whose constitution guarantees to all alike, to consult their own good judgement and preferences in the pursuit of life, liberty and the means of happiness."[15]

The methods to enforce temperate behavior could become dangerously oppressive. William Sawyer, delegate to the Ohio constitutional convention of 1850, wondered how the General Assembly would regulate intemperance: "Is there to be an inquisition established to learn who gets drunk?—a set of inquisitors to stop the works of the distiller?—a third to arrest the farmer on his way to a distillery to sell a load of corn?—another to establish and enforce a code of excise regulations?" Such regulations would, Sawyer contended, be the death knell of the new constitution, for "the independent republican freemen of the State—the Whig freemen— the Democratic freemen—the men who do not want you or the Constitution to say when they shall drink or when they shall not drink" would oppose the document.[16]

The argument to rights was a powerful one—even temperance reformer Calvin Fletcher admitted that, in a less enlightened period, many now temperate men "would have felt your rights infringed to be urged to sign a temperance pledge." Another temperance man tried to counter the argument from rights by maintaining that "the mass of people who form any government have the right, and an equal and justifiable right, to exercise that free moral agency which all enjoy in the passage of laws for the suppression of evil." Still another found the protests of endangered liberties to be the "childish cry" of demagogues and those profiting from the traffic.[17]

The temperance cause was hurt by its association with other reforms. The *Illinois State Register* objected that self-aggrandizing types with political ambitions seized upon temperance as a cause. These men allied themselves with the other "isms" of the day, notably abolitionism. But the *Register*'s central complaint was the danger these men posed to liberty: "It is plain that in the United States, where the people are accustomed to the largest liberty, no arbitrary law in violation of the sentiment of the people will long be borne with."[18]

Upland Southerners valued their liberties as much as Northerners valued morality and social order. One man's moral reform was another man's oppression. Drinking was an accepted part of Upland Southern culture; Southern religion did not effectively proscribe it, and efforts to root it out were too closely related to unpopular Yankee reform movements. Temperance had some appeal to an industrializing middle class, including some of the Southern born. It had little popularity, however, in the less developed parts of these Midwestern states, dominated by the Southerners. The North Carolina Quakers around Richmond, Indiana, favored temperance, and so did men like Abraham Lincoln, the corporate lawyer striving to put his rural origins behind him and succeed in the new market society where temperance equaled respectability. But while reformers argued that drink destroyed the republic, the Southern born saw the reformers themselves as the threat to the republic.

Land, like temperance, involved republicanism's definition of virtuous and independent citizens. Land established a man's status in society. Therefore, to deny some men land would lead to their landless dependence and the creation of a landholding aristocracy. In the year Indiana achieved statehood, a Memorial to Congress by the Inhabitants of Indiana Territory bemoaned that "many poor men unable to purchase land, have sought an assylum in the forests of our country . . . for the sake of a precarious independence; and in the hopes that a few years industrious perseverance, would enable them to become masters of that soil."[19] Like temperance, land became the subject of a sectional quarrel. First, the debate pitted Westerners against an Eastern government that often seemed unresponsive to Western needs. Secondly, Westerners found themselves united against the hated, and stereotypically Eastern, speculator.

The federal government's land policy moved, under pressure from settlers, toward more liberal measures: smaller tracts, lower prices, and a more forgiving stance toward squatters and debtors. From the passage of the Land Ordinance of 1785, government policy progressed toward lower prices and smaller lots. Preemption acts ended the presumption that people should stay off the public lands until after surveyors completed their task. By the Jacksonian period, all Westerners shared a rhetoric that praised the settler, cursed the speculator, and demanded access to the public domain. The half century culminated in the Republican Party's policy of homesteading settlers on free public land.[20]

From the first, Northerners and Southerners held conflicting views on the mechanics of settling the public lands. The 1785 ordinance's provision for orderly survey and settlement was a Northern preference. Southern settlers moved onto the lands according to their custom of "indiscriminate location and subsequent survey," which had the advantage of allowing them to select irregularly shaped parcels including the best lands. But the Southerners' preferred method led to uncertain land titles which drove many of them out of the Upland South in the first place. Southerners in Congress, aware of these patterns, favored the sale of smaller parcels of land. Northern congressmen, equally aware that many New Englanders settled in groups, favored sale of larger areas. Eventually the Northerners conceded that it would be as easy for their people to buy a set of sections as to buy a whole township.[21] A sectional rift along North-South lines thus failed to develop.

Squatting on the public lands pitted Southern settlers against the government located in the East. The Congress of the Confederation had issued proclamations and laws against squatting north of the Ohio River during the Revolutionary War, but to no avail. In 1785 the Congress of the new republic sent troops to clear out the squatters. Ensign John Armstrong was given this unpleasant task and found the illegal settlements to be more extensive than the government had imagined. He also found the squatters to be persistent, returning and rebuilding after he burnt them out. Albert Gallatin recalled that some people had had three successive cabins burned.[22]

Southern settlers believed the land could not be kept from them. John Amberson called an election to choose delegates for a constitutional convention, which was to meet at the mouth of the Scioto in April 1785. In his public notice for the election, he spoke of the people's "undoubted right to pass into every vacant country." He claimed Congress could neither forbid their movement nor sell the uninhabited land. Rufus Putnam complained that the number of squatters, mainly Kentuckians, on the public land was increasing and that although their avowed purpose was to buy the land when it came up for sale "the more lately arrived emigrants from Kentucky ... Say they mean to hold the Lands by Settling or without purchasing provided their numbers Should increase So far as to give them a prospect of Succeeding in a measure of that kind." John Cleves Symmes also complained of the arrogance with which backcountry Kentuckians, Virginians, and Pennsylvanians assumed control of the land: "[H]undreds are running into the wilderness west of the Great Miami, locating and making elections of land. They almost laughed me full in the face when I ask them one dollar per acre for first-rate land, and tell me they will soon have as good for thirty cents."[23] Symmes's problems with the settlers reveals their assurance that they had a right to the land and that it would pass to them at a nominal price.

The settlers assumed "the land was there to be taken." The government's responsibility was to oversee the formal transfer of title to the settlers. Government bureaucracy, interested in the orderly transfer of the land, ran head on into "a rough and ready land-taking tradition already two centuries old." Given this tension it was not surprising that the tradition of the frontier often triumphed over the "bureaucratic procedures devised by a distant national government." Squatters were only the most obvious evidence of the frontier impatience with government's ability to parcel out the land fairly.[24]

Land quickly became a Western issue. Representatives from the Western states spoke out on behalf of the squatters, arguing that they would buy the land; it was only the government's tardy surveys that prevented them from doing so. Congress was reminded that the settlers had endured Indian threats and other dangers to settle the frontier and ought to be rewarded for their courage. During the 1820s and 1830s, as Westerners forced concessions from the federal government, their congressmen defended them from the charge of wanting "to live by the bounty of the General Government." Congressmen argued that the settlers were poor but honest, had risked their lives in moving to the Indian frontier, and deserved to be rewarded for their sacrifices. Congressmen who opposed land laws that favored the settlers were accused of being anti-Western.[25]

Westerners also saw themselves as struggling with an evil force known as speculation, which had its base in the East. William Henry Harrison took special pride in enabling "every industrious man" to purchase land by introducing a bill in 1800 making it easier for settlers to meet payments. Forty years later, Harrison's bill was cited as a reason to vote for the old hero for president. "A Squatter" claimed that Harrison's bill prevented speculators from buying up large tracts and driving the price up, thus preventing settlers from buying the land. John Tipton of Indiana denied that squatters were "lawless rabble." In Tipton's analysis squatters were merely "industrious and enterprising citizens" who had acted somewhat ahead of the law. Although they arrived before the surveyors, they intended to pay the government for the land. It had been Congress's practice to protect "the actual settler from the iron grasp of the speculator."[26]

Long after the initial period of settlement and statehood, Western politicians agreed that the federal government's best interest lay in having the land "settled by a hardy, independent, industrious yeomanry, at low prices, than holding it up to be carved into principalities for the rich." In the 1840s, an Illinois Whig paper lamented that "land monopolists," i.e., speculators, thwarted the government's intention to sell to settlers. These speculators deprived the poor of homes, retarded settlement, and forced thousands into tenantry. "Does not this land holding threaten to subvert civil and religious liberty, by creating an aristocratic power that will in a coming generation, identify themselves by legislative classification?" From economic and political domination it was only a short step to the wrong, as described by Abraham Lincoln, of "grasping up the new lands of the continent, and keeping them from the settlement of free white laborers."[27] The people came to hate speculators; the invidious land monopolists became the focus for popular dislike and hatred because they made it impossible for settlers to achieve economic independence.

Settlers vastly overrated the actual presence and power of speculators. Both the wealthy speculator who bought large tracts to sell in smaller parcels and the squatter who expected to sell his improvements at a profit practiced speculation. An Indiana pioneer remarked, "The love of speculation seems inherent in the minds of men, and there has been no greater field for its operation than land sales in new districts and in and about towns and cities." Yet condemnation of the speculator was a staple of all public discussion of land policy. "A Bystander" accused an Illinois man of lying when he claimed to be a farmer. "Bystander" said General Duncan McArthur had not raised enough grain since he came to Illinois to feed an old cow for a month, rather "he has dashed about, and bought and sold and speculated, and probably, like other men of this description, run into debt."[28]

Southerners possessed a divided consciousness on speculation. While David Davis, Illinois politician, talked freely in his private correspondence about his speculations and his expectations for profit from those speculations, the criticism of General McArthur indicated general public condemnation of such behavior. Men hoped to profit from dealing in land, but the culture demanded sympathy for the "actual" settler and a policy that made land available to all. If the government stepped in with its rules about survey and sale, the local populace had rules of its own. A Wayne County, Indiana, politician was accused of speculating in land. Not only did he deny the charges, but he offered to sell the land, at its purchase price, to the accuser in order to prove the lack of speculative motives.[29]

In 1833, a southern Illinois church congregation voted that it was not right to buy public lands without paying the squatter for his improvements. Claim associations or clubs protected the settler's right to the land. Mutual agreement existed that when public lands finally came on the market, buyers would defer to the occupant of a particular tract. An article in the *Daily Chicago American* related with sympathy the plight of Colonel Beaubien, an early settler of the area. The colonel had been outbid on the lot containing his own house and now intended to bid on another. The paper called down curses and a "water-lot" in Tartarus on the man who would outbid the old frontiersman, and it urged others not to bid against the colonel. The author believed the auctioneer would respect the "rights of settlers" by accepting the colonel's bid and asserted that the loss of a few hundred dollars could not mean so much to the United States government as to prevent justice and humanity from being done to the colonel.[30] Obviously, the concern was not for the legal technicalities but for higher rights that settlers possessed to the land because they had braved the difficulties and dangers of the frontier.

Although the initial conflict involved Upland Southern squatters and the federal government, land quickly became an issue which united all Midwesterners both against a government which had to be cajoled into making land easier to acquire and against speculators, usually depicted as wealthy Easterners. When the land issue intersected with slavery, Northerners in the Midwest feared that the "slavocracy" would cut off the Northern population from those avenues of wealth and upward mobility offered by the Western territories. Perhaps this is why the Republican Party's emphasis on "Free Soil," so well articulated by Eric Foner,[31] had so much resonance for Abraham Lincoln, and other sons of Southern settlers in Indiana and Illinois.

In a society that trumpeted the need for equal rights and equal privileges, it seems odd that one portion of the population should have been consistently denied anything approaching equality of rights. Upland Southern Midwesterners were ambivalent about slavery, but unambivalent about free blacks. In each of the three states, free blacks operated under formal disabilities. In all three states, formal or informal barriers to voting, intermarriage, schooling, serving on juries, or testifying in court existed. State constitutional conventions of the period debated whether blacks should be allowed to emigrate into these states at all. In each state, the trifling numbers of blacks (around 1 percent of the population) makes it difficult to understand why the subject provoked such intense reactions. Blacks' low social status as slaves and as free menial laborers seemed to unfit them for republican citizenship. This ideological rationale combined with a race prejudice so visceral and powerful that it often required no justification, no supporting reasoning, at all.[32]

Southerners carried racism into the Midwest. While Illinois Upland Southern backwoodsmen could be described as a "determined set of republicans," insisting on absolute social and political equality, that did not prevent them from holding blacks in "the utmost contempt; not allowing them to be of the same species of themselves, but look on negers, as they call them, and Indians, as an inferior race of beings, and treat them as such." Some Southerners reserved "white folks" for Southerners only; Yankees, Indians, and blacks fell outside that group.[33]

In 1828 the Indiana Quaker Levi Coffin traveled through Ohio and Virginia with a free black, Ellis Mitchell. Also with them was Coffin's business partner, Dr. Henry H. Way. The trio found that Midwestern treatment of blacks followed Southern customs closely. At a tavern in Eaton, in southern Ohio, the landlady set the table for two and when reminded that there were three in the party, announced "we don't admit niggers to our table to eat with white folks. I will give your servant his supper in the kitchen." Dr. Way told her that Mitchell was not their servant, "but a respectable gentleman, fully as worthy as we are, and nearly as white; he owns good property, and is really worth more money than either of us." Way seemed to feel that Mitchell's wealth, status in society, and relative lack of African blood were qualifications for him to sit at table with the "full-blooded" whites. He did not assert the equality of all men; either he did not believe such arguments, or he felt they would not impress the landlady. In any case she was unmoved. "I don't care," she answered, "he can't eat at my table with white folks." Way followed up with scriptural appeals, but to no avail. The same scenes, however, were repeated in Virginia and again, Mitchell ate his meals in the kitchens.[34]

Upland Southerners regarded free blacks in their midst much the same way as temperance reformers regarded the bottle. Despite the natural revulsion they insisted whites possessed for blacks, they assumed amalgamation would result from racial contact. One Ohioan described, in disgusted detail, the inevitable outcome of freeing the slaves and leaving them in the United States to achieve perfect equality:

> The lady of Anglo-Saxon origin, white as the snow, and beautiful, must give her tender hand in matrimony to the man of Congo jet, and if female delicacy should reluctate and recoil, she must be taught to believe, that this is the unhappy result of ungenerous prejudice. . . . The young man of English and Scotch blood, by his smiles must woo and win the heart of the maid of Ethiopia and the enjoyment of her *sweet scented amour*, he must learn to subdue the *eructations of his offended stomach*.[35]

Whites and blacks were not expected to live side by side without interacting; in fact the only way to prevent such intermarriage was to shun blacks entirely.

Some Republicans attempted to turn race prejudice to their own advantage. A citizen of Chester, Illinois, reported that "decent white men" with "a decided preference for their own color" had lost their admiration for Stephen Douglas because of "his incessant twattle about negroes." Another southern Illinois man reported the audience of Democratic candidate P. B. Fouke was disgusted with his raving about "niggers." "A man with a family of twenty daughters," the correspondent claimed, "all of whom had suddenly taken it in to their heads to marry 'niggers,' would not have appeared more excited!" Although not denying the inappropriateness of intermarriage, the correspondent exaggerated the situation so as to make Fouke's antiblack diatribe appear ridiculous and hysterical. Racism could be a powerful political tool. Stephen Douglas accused the Republicans of altering their principles so as to be "jet black" in the northern part of the states, while "in the center they are in color a decent mulatto, and in lower Egypt they are almost white." Democrats used the epithet "Black Republicans" as often as possible to libel the opposition, just as Republicans did by pointing out that Democrats talked too much about blacks. Nevertheless, the Democrats bore away the laurels for racist slander. A Hoosier Democrat was congratulated on his victory over the "*Black Sambo* Party" and a Shelby County, Indiana, man mocked the Republican Party motto by recasting it as "Fremont, free wool, and free negroes."[36]

While antiblack rhetoric may have been a knee-jerk political response for many, it assumed black inferiority. That inferiority justified the denial of political rights. Stephen Douglas advocated granting to every "man of inferior race," including the black, those privileges and rights, he was "capable" of exercising, intimating there were incapacities in the black race that would obviate some privileges. Indeed inferiority necessitated paternalistic care, perhaps the same care blacks received under slavery. An Illinois Democratic paper believed that abolitionism harmed blacks: "Feeble in intellect, repulsive in person, and addicted to improvidence and vice, they cannot but be overborne by the competition of white labor." Rather than release the black into a life for which he was unfit, government ought to concentrate on those who were capable of exercising political privilege, namely, whites. The Vigo County, Indiana, convention, addressed by the state's first Republican governor, Oliver P. Morton, resolved that "the white man is socially, politically and intellectually above and superior to the negro." The first goal of all legislation should be to help the free white laborer, "the only true wealth and strength of our Republic."[37] When Midwesterners accepted black inferiority, as the Upland Southerners did, then the denial of political privilege followed logically.

Perhaps Upland Southern Midwesterners disliked blacks so fiercely because black subservience was a vivid reminder of the real meaning of the powerlessness Southerners referred to often in their rhetoric. A

Chillicothe, Ohio, orator argued that black slaves served as a useful reminder to republican free whites: "Warned by the fate of these unfortunate fragments of the human family, let the contrast between your situation and theirs, teach you the value of a liberty you have inherited at the PRICE of your FATHER'S BLOOD."[38]

Indeed, Southerners in the Midwest found it impossible to speak of black equality and degradation without voicing their fear of losing white equality. The Orange County, Indiana, Democratic Convention believed placing blacks on a social and political level with whites was "degrading" for whites. The Sangamon County, Illinois, Democrats backed the *Dred Scott* decision as having defined "the true political condition of the negro," that is that the black man was "inferior to that of the white man." They professed to "abhor" the theories of the Republicans, "who would elevate the negro to be the equal, politically and socially, of the white man, degrade the superior to a level with an essentially inferior race, and contaminate the ballot box, the jury box, and marriage institution."[39] But republicanism forced Southern-born Midwesterners to confront the promises of the Declaration of Independence.

In Cincinnati, two ministers debated the morality of slavery and the meaning of the Declaration for blacks. Reverend J. Blanchard, arguing the institution's sinfulness, distinguished between different kinds of rights. Abolitionists argued for the "natural" rights of all men, according to Blanchard, including the right to be free. The black man should not automatically receive political rights such as voting or social rights such as intermarriage. How far could government go in restricting rights? Until they came to the "inalienable rights" of "life, liberty, and the pursuit of happiness." It was a commonly accepted notion that the community could restrict political rights; "is the Irishman a slave, after landing in this country, and before he obtains his right to vote? I think, if you were to tell the Irishman or honest German that he was a slave because not yet naturalized, he would be apt to show you a large pair of hands." Blanchard's opponent, the Reverend N. L. Rice, wondered how Blanchard could distinguish between rights to be withheld and to be granted. He accused Blanchard of abandoning the Declaration. Blanchard "quotes that noble instrument as declaring that 'all men are born free and equal.' How can he carry out this doctrine, and yet allow one class of men to impose laws and taxes upon another, without allowing them a voice?" The true import of Blanchard's doctrine would require not only immediate emancipation but full equality, placing the government in the hands of a degraded race.[40] Rice believed blacks to be inferior:

Liberty is, indeed, a blessing; but it is a blessing which all men are not prepared to improve. It is more than doubtful, whether, should a constitution, such as that of the U. States, be adopted to-morrow in Mexico, the condition of the people would be any the better for it. And why? Because they are not prepared to live under a government so free as ours. . . . Whether the immediate emancipation of the slaves, with their present character, habits, and circumstances, would prove a blessing to them, is, to say the least, a debateable question.[41]

For Rice, there could be no splitting of hairs about the Declaration. If one admitted that the Declaration included blacks in any way, one had to conclude that the principles of the U.S. government included blacks in all ways—voting, taxation, education, immigration, and so on. It would be far better to pronounce the Declaration and the government to be for whites only.

The disagreement over the meaning of the Declaration divided men according to their regional origins. English-born Norton B. Townshend, delegate from Lorain County, Ohio, to the state's 1850–1851 constitutional convention, adamantly insisted that *"all* men are created equal." Another Ohio constitutional convention delegate, from the Southern-settled portion of the state, argued that as regarded the black race, the Declaration "was not true—the doctrine of the equality of right contained in it referred . . . to the Anglo-Saxon race." A New Albany, Indiana, man even expressed the opinion that so long as the U.S. government worked for whites, what happened to blacks was unimportant: The "great American experiment of freedom" was reserved to the "white races," and "it matters little what becomes of a few negroes."[42]

Abraham Lincoln was among the few Upland Southerners willing to defend black rights, and he did so at great political risk. Lincoln argued that slavery violated the republic's promises of equal rights:

> *Most governments* have been based, practically, on the denial of equal rights of men . . . *ours* began, by *affirming* those rights. *They* said, Some men are too *ignorant,* and *vicious,* to share in government. Possibly so, said we; and, by your system, you would always keep them ignorant, and vicious. We proposed to give *all* a chance; and we expected the weak to grow stronger, the ignorant, wiser; and all better, and happier together.[43]

Lincoln believed blacks could improve themselves if removed from a degrading system. While Lincoln was willing to concede basic political and economic rights to blacks, most Upland Southern Midwesterners feared to give the black man even these small freedoms.

All three states debated provisions to exclude free blacks from immigrating to or residing in their states. Those debates reveal much not only about attitudes toward blacks and slavery but about Upland Southern Midwesterners' feelings for the South. Upland Southerners were united in their dislike of blacks and their association of pro-black sentiment with New Englanders, but they were divided in their loyalties to the South. Some condemned and others defended the slave and plantation system.

The debates reprised and reemphasized the Upland Southern conviction that blacks were incapable of exercising political rights. In Indiana, Edward R. May of northeastern Steuben County proposed a facetious compromise between those who felt the black would never be capable of exercising political rights and those who demanded equal rights for him. He argued that just as the government required foreigners to achieve a knowledge of U.S. customs and institutions before admitting them to full citizenship, government could set a point at which the black was ready for the full rights and responsibilities of citizenship. Perhaps twenty-one was the age. "But I say, that if the black man has not intelligence and discretion enough at the age of twenty-one, to make him worthy the experience of the elective franchise, then extend the prescribed age to thirty-one, or forty-one, or, if need be, to ninety-one." May's suggestion was greeted with laughter, but he recognized, in jest at least, the dichotomy between those who said blacks would never be equal and those who maintained that with time and training, they would be so one day. Lake and Porter Counties' Daniel Crumbacker was more serious in his avowal that those favoring black rights requested nothing more than what was accorded the foreigners whose native laws and customs had "degraded them to a level with the negroes themselves." Foreigners were welcomed, but blacks were not, an inconsistency Crumbacker found puzzling.[44]

Southerners also accused Northerners in their states of a misplaced sympathy that would harm the Upland Southern portions of these states the most. In the Ohio constitutional convention of 1850, Virginia-born John L. Green argued that northern Ohio delegates proposed to throw the state's doors open to the free blacks of the South, knowing full well that the southern counties of Ohio would bear the brunt of "the evil." Their misplaced charity would hurt others but not themselves. While Illinoisan David Davis found Upland Southern fears of black inundation unreasonable, he also noted, "There are many rabid abolitionists in the northern portion of the State." When a New England newspaper criticized Illinois's prohibition of black immigration as a "slave law," the Springfield Whig paper pointed out that it had been forced on the state by its southern half. Southern legislators agreed to vote to put an arsenal at Peoria if northern members would vote for the exclusion law.[45]

Upland Southerners complained that free black competition would degrade white labor. The Western Reserve's Jacob Perkins taunted the Southerners with their true fear. For all their braggadocio about Anglo-Saxon superiority, it would seem they dare not, with all their Anglo Saxon energies, to come into a competition with others upon equal terms for the right to labor and to acquire and possess property in this great State. They are afraid that this degraded negro, whom they so despise, will compete for and control the rewards of labor and industry among them.[46]

A Richmond, Indiana, man argued that to grant blacks equal political and social rights would be to so increase the black population of the state as to "leave no room for whites in Indiana"; not even established whites would be able to survive such an inundation by blacks. One Illinoisan approved Indiana's prohibition of free blacks and feared the social order might be reversed. "If the whites were to change positions with the blacks—and the blacks were to be the most numerous—far the most numerous race—the position of the whites might be equally servile, and equally undesirable as that now occupied by the blacks." The relative positions of the races were based on numerical superiority, not on any faith in the inherent superiority of a particular race.[47]

This great evil had its origins in the South, and Upland Southern Midwesterners felt some ambivalence about the role of the plantation South in causing their plight. In Ohio, Adams County's George Collings maintained that the slaveowner's code of honor would make forbidding black immigration unnecessary, for his honor and affection for his slaves prevented him from casting off his old and worn-out slaves. One southern Hoosier found it a "slander" on the slaveholders of Kentucky to believe that they would pursue "such a barbarous and heathenish course" as abandoning their aged slaves, but most Southern-born Hoosiers had little reliance on slaveholders' honor.[48]

Upland Southerners usually argued that they had left the South in order to escape slavery and resented its following them North, including the Southern planters' habit of using Northern laws to the advantage of the plantation system. David Davis wrote that "The Southern Counties— being surrounded by Slave States, . . . complain, that those States, throw their refuse population on them." David M. Dobson, of Owen County, Indiana, opposed slavery, its extension to the Western territories, and attempts to make Indiana "the receptacle for all the free negroes in the Union, and of all the broke down and worthless slaves of the South." Many other delegates to the 1850 constitutional convention feared that the South looked longingly on Indiana as a dumping ground for old, worn-out, and useless slaves. James G. Read of Clark County, on the Ohio River, feigned ignorance of how the refined sensibilities of northern Hoosiers would react to an influx of black neighbors, but assured his audience that southern Hoosiers "would feel themselves very much degraded and grossly insulted to be asked to electioneer among negroes at their polls." James Rariden of Wayne County argued that permitting black immigration strengthened slavery by allowing the slaveholder to increase the value of his human holdings by freeing them from the burden of aged and indigent property. Rariden's argument received loud cries of approval. Thomas W. Gibson of Clark County reported that the only man he had met in favor of black immigration to Indiana was a Virginia slaveholder traveling in the state, doubtless eager that Indiana remain a refuge for the slaves he no longer wanted. Thomas A. Hendricks of Shelby County maintained the question was not between Indiana and free blacks but between Indiana and the South—revealing an underlying fear among Upland Southern delegates that the planter class they had left behind would oppress them. Hendricks maintained that Indiana had an obligation to care for her poor. The South had a similar duty to her poor; let the South bear her own burdens. "We have none of the advantages of the institution, (if it have any,) and we ought to bear none of its burthens. Under the influence of the present Southern policy, the number of negroes and mulattoes coming amongst us is greatly increasing; and in a few years the North will be burthened with the whole black population of the United States, if we adopt no measure to prevent it." Upland Southern Midwesterners feared subordination to the needs of an aristocracy they had left behind.[49]

When the states voted in constitutional convention on the issue of free black immigration, it was clear that they had divided internally along sectional lines. When the final vote was taken in 1850, delegates from southern Indiana overwhelmingly supported, and delegates from northern Indiana almost as overwhelmingly opposed, prohibiting free black immigration. Delegates from Egypt unanimously supported the 1847 constitutional convention's proposed ban on free black immigration to Illinois. Delegates from the central part of the state split on the issue, but delegates from the extreme north unanimously opposed the prohibition. In Ohio, delegates to the 1850 convention voted first on an amendment "to discourage" free black immigration to the state. Delegates from the old Ohio Company grant and the Western Reserve opposed the amendment. Delegates from central and southeastern Ohio divided on the amendment. An analysis of the birthplace of delegates confirms that those with New England roots opposed the amendment, as did the majority of delegates from the Mid-Atlantic states. Delegates with Southern birthplaces split evenly on the issue. Those born in the Old Northwest states voted by a three-to-two majority against the amendment. While areas of Indiana and Illinois dominated by the Upland Southerners were unequivocal in their support for prohibiting free black immigration, the Ohio amendment advocating prohibition had been withdrawn in favor of one to discourage such immigration. That amendment was defeated by a solid New England and Mid-Atlantic vote and a divided Upland Southern vote.[50]

Behind Upland Southern racism lay ambivalence about the nature of blackness. There was no consensus that color contained any attribute of inferiority, that it made a man less than human. Some accepted blacks as a matter of course as inferior, others did not. For most Upland Southern Midwesterners equal rights did not create a desire to incorporate blacks into society as equals. It was too widely accepted that racial equality would threaten the position of whites in society. Rather, the way to evade this hypocrisy, their admitted failure to fulfill the Declaration, was to eliminate the element that reminded them of their hypocrisy: the blacks. Prohibit blacks from immigrating, deny that the principles of republican government applied to them in any way, and one could consider the problem solved, because it did not have to be confronted. This required Southerners not only to reject the arguments of New Englanders who tended to be sympathetic to blacks, but also to confront their own ambivalent feelings toward their native South.

Those who defended black rights argued that if one group of men, blacks, could be excluded from equal political rights, then groups of white-skinned men could also be excluded. An Illinois Whig objected to the treatment of alleged fugitive slaves on the grounds that "Every human being has rights that should be sacredly guarded and protected by the country in which he resides; and when a black man's rights can be thus invaded and trampled on, how long will it be before the white man may be placed in the same position?" Abraham Lincoln said that Democratic arguments for limiting black rights were "the arguments that kings have made for enslaving the people in all ages of the world." Making excep-tions to the Declaration of Independence, according to Lincoln, would not stop with the exception made for the black. Nevertheless Southern-born Midwesterners and the Democratic Party made an exception for European immigrants that they did not make for blacks. Democrats held to the doctrine of black inferiority and yet made themselves the champi-ons of the equal rights of the immigrants.[51] Upland Southern Midwestern-ers possessed deeply, though not always rationally, held opinions about the inferiority of blacks. Blacks would be unable to exercise the privileges of republican citizenship. Foreigners differed because, although they lacked acquaintance with republicanism, they could learn republicanism in a way blacks never could.

In addition, because foreign immigration did not have the sectional overtones slavery did, the debate proceeded on a partisan level without the reference to regions that marked debates over black rights. The influx of immigrants to Indiana, Illinois, and the Southern-dominated portions of Ohio, with the exception of Hamilton County, was never large. Foreigners preferred northern Illinois, Ohio's Western Reserve, and the area around Toledo.[52] Much of Southern-born fear or acceptance existed in a vacuum. The Upland Southerners lacked the intimate acquaintance of foreigners that they possessed of blacks.

Antiforeign rhetoric among Southern-born Midwesterners revealed their fear of a conspiracy against republicanism. Suspicious of Europe, the Southern born looked at the influx of immigrants as "emissaries" of the kingdoms of the Old World sent to spread atheism and undermine America's free institutions with the purpose of bringing the United States back into "bondage" to Europe. When Irishman Allen Hamilton ran for state representative against native-born Anthony L. Davis, a Fort Wayne merchant reported that the people wanted "no Irish fugitive no foreigner who has not yet forgot how to bow to crown[d] heads, to represent nor *make laws for them,* they have asked for a native born citizen of the United States, a true American, one who could not be purchas[d] with Toys, one whose integrity was not doubted, who had never betray[d] his friends." Irishmen had not yet learned republicanism, their integrity was doubtful, and they had no principles, only a price. The Irish were not inherently inferior, merely untutored in the ways of republicanism and in the virtue necessary to sustain it.[53]

Since immigrants overwhelmingly supported the Democratic Party, more than a tinge of party animosity colored the nativism of Whigs and Republicans. An Indiana paper of the 1850s reported that foreigners of the prowhiskey and proslavery party were going to be shipped into the state to ensure the success of the "Church," the Democratic Party. To the Democrats' chagrin, the paper claimed, they would find that "Indiana is too far advanced in republicanism . . . to elevate to place and power a sett of men that would tear down the very bulwarks of Protestantism to make way for the reign and rule of free whiskey, tolerated slavery and intolerant Popery."[54] Republicanism was a learned ideology, and people would not so quickly unlearn it by succumbing to the appeals of Catholicism and Democracy. A man reared in the habits of monarchy, however, would need a period of adjustment to be inculcated in the ways of republicanism.

Midwesterners resented most the failure of immigrants to assimilate. An old man in Ohio's Western Reserve wished that "these old country people would bear in mind that they come here for their own benefit and not for ours, and that they must be humble to us about manners and customs, and not we to them." The Southern born hardly ever suggested that anyone should be "humble," but they shared the sentiment that "it was not wise to cultivate" the ways of the Old World when in the New, as suggested by an Ohio Whig.[55] A writer to the *Daily Scioto Gazette* was pleased to see the German volunteer militia company marching in American uniforms:

The change in uniform is especially gratifying, for the old . . . had a foreign look about it which did not accord fully with the idea that the wearers had wholly given up their fatherland, and were not only *among us,* but were indeed *a part of us.* But their present outward appearance suggests the fact, that though they may still entertain fond recollections of their old homes, yet they are now Americans in heart and soul, and ready to battle for their adopted country, and to shed their blood in defence of her honor and her rights.[56]

A Fourth of July orator in Jackson County, Illinois, believed that the United States should not exclude those seeking refuge from oppression. He did not, however, think foreigners ought to be granted office until they had become acquainted with republican government. When James Shields's Irish birth was held against him in his campaign for the U.S. Senate, a defender argued that once a man had adapted to a country, had made its interests his own, the incidence of his birth should be ignored. "Gen. Shields came to this state many years since—he has grown up with it—he has an intimate knowledge of all its wants and interests."[57] For the Upland Southerners, acceptance of the foreign born was contingent upon the immigrants' demonstrated knowledge of and commitment to republicanism.

Indeed, part of the resistance to granting equal political privileges stemmed from fear of the immigrants' effect on the political realm. As early as 1835, Whigs in Indiana were complaining that foreigners, little used to the privileges of a republican country, would become the tools of parties. Their numbers, their "clannishness," and their unfamiliarity with liberty and republican government combined to make their influence in politics a "baneful" one. The panic was most apparent in urban areas with growing immigrant populations. One Chicagoan was dismayed at the boast of an Irish candidate that the Irish alone could provide enough support to elect him without the aid of either Whigs or Democrats. The correspondent asked American citizens if they were ready to submit to such "dictation" from the foreign born. An Ohioan was disgusted by the city council's decision to give in to threats from Catholics who held "the balance of power" in the town. He asked whether Catholics could not live under the same laws as everyone else or whether "we must kiss their big toes, and legislate especially for them?"[58] Since the foreign-born voting bloc most often sided with the Democratic Party, the Whigs most often seemed to oppose equal rights for all white men.

Whigs protested that they were not antiforeign; they merely believed "that a man should know something of the country, and its institutions before he should undertake to govern it."[59] The resolutions Lincoln drafted following the 1844 anti-immigrant riots in Philadelphia embodied these principles:

> *Resolved,* That in admitting the foreigner to the rights of citizenship, he should be put to some reasonable test of his fidelity to our country and its institutions; and that he should first dwell among us a reasonable time to become generally acquainted with the nature of those institutions; and that, consistent with these requisites, naturalization laws, should be so framed, as to render admission to citizenship under them, as convenient, cheap, and expeditious as possible.[60]

Citizenship should not be difficult to acquire; in fact, it was to be quick and cheap once the foreign born had acquired the ways of a republican society.

Although Lincoln had no intention of completely denying the foreign born the rights of citizenship or of forcing them into a sort of second-class citizenship, Democrats accused him of having a "holy horror of all Irishmen and other adopted citizens." Lincoln had commented, on seeing some Irishmen on the levee at Naples, Illinois, during the senatorial campaign of 1858, that they had been transported there for the express purpose of defeating him. Democrats converted Lincoln's fears about fraudulent voting into attempts to deprive foreign-born citizens of their rights. But the use of foreigners, especially the Irish, as tools of the Democratic Party was a reality with which Whigs in Illinois were familiar. "Fair Play and No Gouging" reported that the Democrats were sending the Irish in groups of fifteen to twenty from the northern part of the state south to help turn the 1858 election. Lincoln spent much time and energy worrying about how Republicans could keep Irishmen from Chicago from voting farther south in the state. But Illinois was not alone in having problems with illegal voting. In Indiana during the 1850s, vote buying, ballot box stuffing, and the transportation of voters between polls were prevalent methods of vote fraud.[61] When immigrants overwhelmingly supported one party, the opposition party naturally suspected their ability to wield their new political rights wisely.

Despite immigrant support for the church of Democracy, Whigs and Republicans doubted that Democrats sincerely wished equality for foreigners. An Indiana Whig paper dismissed a candidate's chances of obtaining appointive office because "unfortunately, he is an Irishman and the Sham-Democracy have an idea that they do very well to vote—but not to hold office. He, therefore, stands no chance." An Illinois paper compared the Democratic control of the immigrants to Southern control of slaves. The Democratic Party was itself contributing to an unrepublican practice. Instead of enlightened free men making the best possible choices for the public interest, Democrats controlled droves of unthinking foreigners who cast their votes with no concern for the republic's good.[62]

Democrats, of course, interpreted as oppression any hesitance to grant aliens full rights. When Whigs spoke of the immigrants' potential political power and the potential damage to a republic, those who defended the immigrants heard a refusal to grant equal rights to all. Governor Ashbel P. Willard of Indiana accused nativists of trying to recreate in America the religious intolerance and wars of Europe: "You should regard that man who deprives a legal voter of his suffrage as an enemy to liberty," Willard warned, "as a tyrant not satisfied that man should be free." Whigs maintained that they protected the rights of naturalized citizens, not in return for their votes, but to preserve "the great cause of civil and religious liberty."[63]

Those who favored foreigners' rights found it difficult to believe that the man oppressed in his own land would feel anything but a deep and abiding love for his new land of freedom:

> Of what order is that intellect which could imagine that a poor wretch, Catholic though he be, who flies to this country as to a land of promise, from oppressions of all kinds, who embarks his *all* in our common ship, for good or for evil; who loves our institutions from report, and loves them still more fervidly, when the protection of their aegis is thrown around him; how, we ask, could any American suppose that such a man could become a traitor to his adopted country—the only country which he could call his own, and sell his dear-loved freedom—his all—to a foreign power or potentate.[64]

Simply having left behind the oppression of Europe proved the integrity of one's republicanism. Fondness for the homeland could even be evidence of patriotism toward the new home, for "The breast that is cold to its native land can never be *warm* to that of its adoption." Many agreed with the Southern-born Richard I. Hamilton that U.S. policy should be "let the gallant sons of Erin come—let the persecuted Pole, the honest industrious German, the generous Frenchman, the oppressed of nations, ... come and partake of the rich blessing of the institutions of freedom."[65]

Both parties were, no doubt, highly influenced by their ability or inability to attract the support of the immigrants. While the Southern-born Democrats proved unwilling to accord to blacks the status of equals, they largely assimilated the foreigners into the ideology that governed their lives. If foreigners could prove their willingness to become good republicans (unlike blacks, their ability to do so was not in doubt), they could quickly become part of that republican society. Both Upland Southern Whig/Republicans and Upland Southern Democrats first insisted on the necessary assimilation, the melding of interests so that the interests of the foreign born became identical to those of the native born. Although Whigs occasionally compared the foreigners the Democrats trotted to the polls to slaves, no systematic sectional rift held on this issue.

Upland Southern Midwesterners talked, often loosely, about their rights. They resisted the cultural tyranny of those who wished to deprive them of the "right" to drink. They asserted a right to land they had settled, land that was essential to a man's ability to establish economic and thus political independence. Racism, however, caused Southern-born Midwesterners to deny the equality of blacks. Some based these denials on the belief in black inferiority. Others simply argued that black equality would mean a degradation of the white race. This would not happen with foreigners—they were not racially inferior and could learn to be good republicans. So Upland Southern Midwesterners asserted their rights and rationalized the denial of political privilege to one group of men while, for the most part, they bestowed those privileges on another group.

Southerners in the Midwest shared with other Americans a republican philosophy within which they debated the issues of the antebellum period. When their Southernness was not an issue, Southerners in the Midwest were able to work through the second-party system, arguing its issues in much the same way other Americans did. Although they differed over policy, tending to be more resistant to parties, banks, manufacturing, education, temperance, and black rights than other Midwesterners, the rifts were not serious and did not take on virulent sectional overtones. In fact, on certain issues they perceived themselves as Westerners, united with Northerners to defend the interests and rights of the West. But sectionalism became a decisive factor when slavery extension emerged as the dominant political issue of the 1850s. No friends to slavery or the planter class, Southerners in the Midwestern states nevertheless fiercely resented the attacks on the South that were a part of the antislavery movement.

SEVEN

❧✿❧

Sectionalism Reborn

"THE TIMES ARE SQUALLY," a Hillsboro, Ohio, man wrote in 1856. The 1850s were indeed difficult times for Upland Southerners and all Midwesterners. With cultural and economic ties to the South, the states of Ohio, Indiana, and Illinois wished devoutly for the slavery issue to disappear.[1] No other issue of antebellum life so challenged the cohesiveness of the new region and the new nation. In one way, the sectional crisis strengthened Westernness by forcing Upland Southerners in the Midwest to search for the middle ground that lay between the extremes of abolitionism and secession. Yet even as they condemned New England fanaticism and planter-class intransigence, their own sense of Southernness was reinvigorated, weakening the bond with other settlement groups, especially the New Englanders.

Reactions to the Compromise of 1850 reveal the complex sectional and party loyalties within the Midwest. Some of the compromise measures provoked a clear response. On the two patently Northern measures, congressmen from the Old Northwest voted unanimously in favor of admitting California as a free state and abolishing the slave trade in Washington, D.C. Only congressmen from the South voted against these measures. The three other compromise measures provoked a mix of sectional and party loyalties from Northwesterners. All three of the remaining compromise measures (the Texas boundary bill, the Utah territory bill, and the Fugitive Slave Act) were solidly opposed by Whig congressmen from the Old Northwest, Southern born as well as those from other states. Democratic congressmen from Ohio, Indiana, and Illinois, although leaning toward the measures, split their ranks far more deeply than did the Whigs. But Southern-born Democrats did not. Only on the Fugitive Slave Act did Upland Southern Midwestern Democrats, two of eight, vote against the mainstream Democratic position. Clearly, all Midwesterners rejected the extreme Southern stance on California and slave sales in the capital but regarded the other measures with a mix of sectional and party views. Midwesterners of Southern background were particularly loyal to the Democratic ideology, especially as expressed in the provisions of the Utah territory bill, which left the decision about slavery open to the residents of the territory. Only the Fugitive Act was sufficiently repugnant to cause Southern-born Democrats to break ranks.[2]

Much as they wished to put the issue away, to hide behind the "finality" of the 1850 compromise, Upland Southern Midwesterners found that the "eternal Negro question" reappeared wherever they turned. Lincoln's law partner, Billy Herndon, satirized the problem and revealed the pleasure blacks took in shaking the U.S. political edifice to its foundation:

> My Colored brethren here say—'Why-Good Lord-a-massy Billey—de nigger am de great object of the American Gobernment—day am always de talk—Can't legislate for mail bags: but that de nigger am in de threads—in de whole bag massa—What am you going—you white folks—to do with the darky'; and . . . I must Confess that I can't answer the poor Sambo's simple question—. . . 'The Niggers' (as they themselves say) are America's great home-made institution.[3]

The Republican Party gained strength in some parts of the Midwest, but remained weak in the area dominated by the Southern born. Upland Southern Midwesterners had no particular liking for slavery and no wish for its expansion, but they disliked outsiders interfering with the institution and resented Republican condemnations of the South. Sectional hostility to Republicans was rooted in long-standing, though submerged, sectional animosities. Busybody Yankees were once again engaged in a conspiracy to order the lives of Southerners.[4] Yankees, abolitionists, and Republicans came to occupy a common niche in Upland Southern thinking. The Upland Southerners virulently resented the Yankee moralism of the abolition crusade and were pushed by it into greater sympathy for their native South.

This sympathy, however, was offset by the yeoman South's distrust for the planter aristocracy. The idea of a "slave power conspiracy" had meaning for Upland Southern Midwesterners who had personal experiences of a planter class that they felt attempted to oppress white nonslave-holders. Men who had doubted the motives of the planter aristocracy, who had left the South rather than be a part of its class and economic structure, were deeply suspicious of a South that wanted to spread that structure to Kansas. Buffeted by these competing pressures, many of the Upland Southerners found that the Democratic Party offered an attractive alternative to choosing between North and South. Popular sovereignty, traditionally associated with democracy and the will of the people, became in Stephen Douglas's reformulation, a way to avoid painful decisions while leaving the ultimate decision on slavery in the territories in the hands of the people of the territories themselves. Popular sovereignty was, however, also consistent with values that the Southern born held dear. The liberty of white settlers would not be infringed since they would make the decisions about the society in which they were to live. Neither Northern nor Southern fanatics would force a way of life on them. Popular sovereignty was also consonant with Upland Southern racism, which cared little about the fate of the black race as long as white liberties were secure.

Whenever the abolitionists went into the Southern-dominated sections of the Midwest, they faced hostility and even violence. The good Quaker folk of Wayne County, Indiana, were startled by an attack on a Milton congregation during an antislavery lecture and even more surprised when the local law officers refused to bring the perpetrators to justice. The same violence that led to the death of abolitionist Elijah Lovejoy in Alton, Illinois, and the tarring and feathering of Marius Robinson in Trumbull County, Ohio, was capable of breaking out any place Upland Southerners met abolitionist doctrine. The papers of Kentucky-born abolitionist James G. Birney are replete with accounts of such attacks, including the July 1836 destruction of Birney's press in Cincinnati. Birney felt the attacks originated with "gentlemen of property and standing, who are interested in Southern commerce, and have large southern connexions." A handbill, entitled "ABOLITIONISTS BEWARE," which appeared after his press was wrecked, bore out Birney's suspicions. It advised abolitionists to cease "the unholy cause of annoying our southern neighbors" and accused them of "undermining the business and property" of every citizen of Cincinnati by their "wicked and misguided operations." The agitation was so severe that Birney was advised to sneak in and out of Cincinnati at odd hours to avoid being lynched. Other mobbings occurred in Dayton and Cincinnati in the 1830s and 1840s, including the destruction of the *Philanthropist,* an abolitionist press, and an attack on black neighborhoods in Cincinnati. A Columbus, Ohio, man wrote Birney that the soldiers called out to quell the mob had "so little sympathy for the Abolitionists that they refused to fire on the mob." When an egg-throwing "drunken rabble" in Granville, Ohio, assaulted Birney, his "Kentucky connexcions" found the mobbing to be "greatly undignified on *my part.*" Birney's son, William, seemed to feel being attacked was an abolitionist rite of passage. He wrote his father that a Liberty Party candidate's speech in Mt. Vernon, Ohio, had been interrupted by boys throwing eggs. Young Birney was hit by an egg and reported, "This is the first time I have had the honor of being egged."[5]

A humorous piece printed in an Ohio newspaper reveals the depth of hostility toward abolitionists. Two men, P. and W., chanced to meet upon the street during the anxious winter of 1861. P. had been searching his mind for some further compromise that would appease the South. He could think of nothing "that we have not done, and overdone," for "We have conceded everything demanded and everything imaginable. We have granted all they have asked of us politically, and as social compromises, we have sent them preachers to tar and feather—we have shipped them 'schoolmarms' to insult and even imprison." Much to P.'s relief, W. proposed a possible further concession. Having seen a story in the morning paper describing how some Southerners "banded up an Abolitionist and rolled him into the Mississippi," W. proposed to provide the South with sufficient barrels and thus spare them the cost of cooperage.[6] Although revealing considerable frustration with Southern intransigence, the story suggested that the Midwest found abolitionism as objectionable as did the South. Even more startling than this hostile attitude toward abolitionists is the fact that the anecdote ran in a Republican newspaper.

Abolitionists acknowledged that their survival often rested on a compromise of principle: If they did not challenge the status quo they could hold their obnoxious opinions in peace. Samuel Galloway, an abolitionist living in southeastern Ohio, claimed, with the optimism many abolitionists felt for their cause in the 1830s, "that the good is progressing astonishingly" in places such as Dayton, Springfield, and Oxford, some of the same places which experienced anti-abolition violence. Some of the adherents to abolitionism were "of the first respectability." Yet the key to their ability to move unmolested was their reticence: "They say nothing upon the subject in public; yet they are free to express their opinions, privately. There is no unreasonable opposition, manifested to the cause." Galloway himself was known by all as an abolitionist yet found that "some of my warmest friends are Southern Students."[7] Gamaliel Bailey, writing from Cincinnati, told James G. Birney that Cincinnati abolitionists were trying to raise the three hundred dollars necessary to fulfill their pledge to the state antislavery society. "But, what a hard place this is!" Bailey lamented,

And what a curious sort of abolitionists we have got! One man told me with a grave face, that it would not do for him to take an *active, open* part in the cause, for it would injure his business! He is a member of the society, and professes to be a strong abolitionist. We are going to make great efforts to get up an abolition revival—it is hardly worth while to get men to join us, who are not *"powerfully converted,"* as the Methodists phrase it.[8]

Although this gentleman may have feared abolitionists' depredations on his purse more than attacks on his peace, abolitionists felt frustrated by the lack of commitment from even sympathetic Upland Southerners.

Abolitionists wisely assumed that Upland Southerners regarded them with anger and suspicion. The Kentucky-born politician, John M. Palmer, managed to win over a hostile southern Illinois crowd come to listen to, or harass, the abolitionist Owen Lovejoy, brother of the martyred Elijah. Palmer took an ax and knocked away the boards forming the sides of a speaking platform, telling the crowd, "Gentlemen, we have with us to-day the wonderful abolitionist, Owen Lovejoy. You have seen that he has neither horns nor tail, and now I will allow you to see that he has no hoofs." Palmer was credited with lightening the audience's mood and defusing their hostility. Yet Upland Southern Midwesterners still had trouble seeing abolitionism as a respectable cause. Palmer himself, although evidently sympathetic to the abolitionists, refused to join the movement out of "respect for the law."[9]

That Upland Southern Midwesterners abjured the abolitionist movement did not mean that they harbored any love for slavery. James G. Birney wrote that he had decided to move from Kentucky to Illinois because of the "corrupting influence of *slavery* on the character of the *young* . . . especially those of our sex—and six of my seven children are boys." Peter Cartwright, the itinerant Methodist minister born in Kentucky, called slavery "a domestic, political, and moral evil." Yet he had never found an abolition or free soil society he could join, because they used "unjustifiable agitation" which threatened the Union.[10]

Upland Southerners associated abolitionists with New England fanaticism. Governor John Reynolds of Illinois admitted that abolitionist fervor had its roots in "the finest sentiments of the human heart," yet he found them "misguided" and "fanatical." Reynolds likened abolitionism to the witch hunts of early New England. The Indiana Democratic paper agreed, stating that abolitionists were Puritans who believed themselves to be eradicating some grave national sin. Indiana would never side with the fanaticism of New England with its *"passionate attraction"* for blacks. Stephen Douglas was supposed to have warned his Chicago paper, "You are to be 'Yankeened'—in other words abolitionized, by means of abolition schoolteachers and abolition preachers." Even Upland Southern antislavery forces were wary of the New England versions of antislavery. Ohioan Samuel Galloway had made a trip into Kentucky to retrieve a horse and found that Kentuckians identified "all antislavery action with Oberlinism—that focus of folly & fanaticism." Galloway also found the Oberlin school too extreme and recommended that antislavery societies send out speakers from other locations.[11]

Southerners in the Midwest believed the Northerners living among them had themselves rejected the unifying bonds of Westernness by making sectional moral appeals. It was bad enough that an Illinois Democratic candidate for office solicited the vote of an abolitionist, but he further infuriated others by soliciting the abolitionist's vote with an appeal to their common Yankee birth. Godlove S. Orth, an Indiana Whig, advised that accusations of abolitionism during the gubernatorial campaign "ought not to be too strongly contradicted in the Northern or *infected* portions of Indiana." An Indiana Democrat described abolitionists as "all backbone, and no brains. They had rather see the Union dissolved than give one inch of territory to slavery." "Is the country to be ruined by such impractible fools?" he asked.[12]

In an exchange of letters in the *Indiana Daily State Sentinel,* the Democratic paper, "Publius" argued with the Reverend Mr. Simmons over the Biblical basis of slavery. The minister had preached that the Bible did not sanction slavery and that therefore his conscience would not allow him to obey the fugitive law. "Publius" argued Scripture to the contrary but concluded with a plea for the preservation of the government:

> You should have been sure, that you were not willing to set a ball in motion, whose revolutions would crush the Confederacy. You should have kept in mind, that this is the last experiment of man, to solve the problem of self-government; that the eyes of the whole world were watching the solution of this problem, with an agonizing earnestness; before you counseled that, which would rub out the solution, yet incomplete, in blood, you should have felt the last throb of the great heart of liberty, as it sunk in despair and death, before you pronounced your ideas right, and the assembled wisdom of our fathers wrong. You should have pictured to yourself the long, dark, dismal, despairing, ages of universal oppression, now hid in the womb of Time, which should follow the overthrow of the free institutions of this nation, before you suffered a lisp to escape your lips, that could be construed rebellious.[13]

Publius saw civil disobedience, not as a tolerable expression of disagreement with government policy, but as defiance that threatened the very survival of the republican experiment. Concerned with the fragility of this experiment in republicanism, Upland Southern Midwesterners were particularly frightened by the rumblings of sectional discontent.

John Brown's raid on the federal arsenal at Harpers Ferry, Virginia, confirmed Upland Southern Midwesterners' worst fears that abolition led to a disregard for the law, to disunion, and even to murder and insurrection. The Harpers Ferry plot proved to one Hoosier that abolitionists had no respect for the law and condoned not only the "butchering" of slaveowners but also of "helpless women and children."[14] Another Indiana man believed the South to be overreacting to Harpers Ferry, acting as if

> the whole North sanctioned and knew of it when perhaps not 500 men in all the Free States knew of Brown's designs and not one man in 5000 sanctions his bold but wicked design—the great mass of the people in the Free States are on this very question of slavery, perfect non Interventionists—they neither want to steal the negroes, or catch them that has run away, their sentiment is "hands off with the nasty thing."[15]

He condemned the raid yet could not keep from describing it admiringly as "bold." Another reaction to John Brown's raid reflected Midwestern ambivalence. A Hendricks County, Indiana, man said that while everyone "censured" John Brown, most "really admire the man." "He is looked upon as a martyr in a cause not legal but just. The public will be glad when the law is satisfied with the blood of the remaining prisoners, and quietude is again restored to the affrighted Virginians."[16]

In an attempt to defuse the sectional situation, Midwesterners proclaimed that their region had both Northern and Southern roots and was thus acutely sensitive to sectional crisis. Governor Joseph A. Wright of Indiana ended the tumultuous year of 1850 with a message to the legislature that stressed the necessity of adhering to the compromise: "There is no safety for property, for liberty, nor for life, except in the absolute supremacy of the law." He closed by denying that sectionalism had any relevance to Indiana: "Indiana takes her stand in the ranks not of *Southern Destiny,* nor yet of NORTHERN DESTINY. She plants herself on the basis of the constitution, and takes her stand in the ranks of AMERICAN DESTINY." In 1850, a Wayne County, Indiana, delegate introduced a resolution during the Indiana constitutional convention expressing approval of the compromise. One delegate expressed the view that Indiana, like the Union, had a North and a South with differing sentiments. The resolution, he felt, could only cause more "sectional heart-burnings." Indiana's Lt. Governor Abraham A. Hammond pointed out that the state lay geographically midway between North and South— belonging to neither region—and prayed "may we live to witness that political death of Northern and Southern Fanaticism upon the subject of slavery, and when that event shall happen, let a monument be erected to its memory, and inscribe on it 'Died in a vain attempt to dissolve the

Union.'" Yet in a few months he was objecting to Republican Party claims that Northern rights were being violated: "The States of the North, as well as the States of the South, have their rights, privileges and immunities under the Constitution. The North has no special rights in contradistinction to the *South.*"[17]

The Republican Party in Illinois strove to find a gubernatorial candidate who could draw votes in the southern part of the state, rather than one popular only in the northern section. Yet such a strategy bore its own punishments. In 1860, Allan Tomlin advised gubernatorial candidate Richard Yates, the candidate picked to appeal to both northern and southern Illinois, that he had lost his last election by not coming out strongly enough against the Fugitive Slave Act. Tomlin continued, "I know that Lincoln lost very many votes by courting Egypt—a radical candidate would take nearly all the votes north of the Illinois River & would take more south of that than a temporizer or compromiser." Attempts to bridge sectional differences may have lost as many friends as it gained. In the end, Yates's victory did not mark a lessening of Egypt's allegiance to the Democratic Party. In Yates's own words, however, it did mark a transfer of power within the state from "Egypt to Israel." An Illinois Whig proposed avoiding a sectional split in the national election by relying on a Western candidate, Lincoln. Lincoln would appeal to Upland Southern voters because of his Kentucky birth and to Easterners because of the principles he had voiced in his debates with Douglas, but most of all he would stand for the interests of a distinct section, the West. The writer specifically noted that the West's interests differed from those of the South: "The man who would run best in the West, is one who is familiarly known to our people, and whose interests and feelings are identified with our own."[18]

At the same time that they condemned New England fanaticism, Upland Southerners reassessed their relationship to the South. Upland Southern Midwesterners particularly disliked the provisions of the fugitive law that called for Northerners to be part of slave-catching posses. David Kilgore in the Indiana constitutional convention of 1850 protested "against the doctrine that the slaveholders of Kentucky and other Southern States had the right to use the freemen of Indiana like blood-hounds to catch their slaves." He insisted that those Hoosiers who favored the law lived in the extreme southern part of the state, had married Kentucky women, and had an interest in or expected an inheritance of slave property. They had become part of the plantation system. A man in Brazil, Indiana, wrote his congressman that the fugitive law was seen as "converting the Freemen of the North into a gang of Slave catchers for the South."[19] Upland Southern Midwesterners feared the stresses being exerted on the Union, yet they could not approve of all the measures undertaken to reduce those stresses. The Fugitive Slave Law benefited the planter class, whose oppression they had fled, and seemed once again to make them an appendage of that class. When the South appeared to threaten their liberties, they resisted it just as they resisted abolitionist fanaticism.

Southerners were themselves active in resisting the fugitive law and even in aiding fugitive slaves. A Virginia-born Ohioan called the bill "odious" and felt it had been deliberately designed to be so. In the 1840s, Salmon Chase defended a Kentucky-born Ohioan who had given a group of escaped slaves a ride in his wagon and was sued by their owner for harboring and concealing the slaves. In the early 1850s, slave catchers attempted to claim three black boys, who were being cared for by a local white while their father was away. The white man drove the men off at gunpoint and threatened, if the boys were disturbed, to kill "fifteen such worthless vagabonds as you . . . fugitive law or any other law." The people of Gibson County, Indiana, seemed to approve of his actions, for his political opponents found it impossible to use the issue against him when he ran for the legislature. When a long-lost son returned to visit his Pike County, Indiana, family, the neighbors suspected the stranger was a slave hunter. He might have been physically hurt if his sister had not revealed his identity.[20]

Some of the most powerful rhetoric about an iniquitous slave power conspiracy came from Upland Southerners themselves. James G. Birney had been a slaveowner, then an advocate for the American Colonization Society, and finally an abolitionist and presidential candidate of the Liberty Party. His conversion from colonization to abolitionism resulted from his perception that gradualism would never move the conscience of slaveowners and end slavery. Birney argued that the slaveowner would willingly admit the advantages of free labor and the resulting superiority of the free states and yet still refuse to give up his slaves. Birney condemned the "system" "by which the *majority* are to be made poor and miserable that the *few* may spend their useless lives in indolent volup-tuousness," that denied "the laboring man" a place in the political life of the country, that taught that "the *employer* ought to own the *employed*," and that offered itself as "the true 'corner-stone of the republican edifice.'" Birney addressed many of the same themes as Lincoln: that the South intended to impose an inferior labor system on the country; that such a labor system degraded all those who worked; and that it would establish an aristocracy inimical to true republicanism. The South asked the common people of the North to surrender their rights and their liberties and "lie down at the foot of the Southern Slaveholder 'like whipt and trembling Spaniels.'" Slavery was a "despotism," and the South an "oligarchy" made up of "petty despotisms, acting on the principle that men are *not* created equal—that a favored *few* are born, ready booted and spurred to leap into the saddles with which the backs of the *many* are furnished by *nature.*" Even the most ardent of fanatical New England abolitionists would have been hard-pressed to surpass Birney's denunciations of his native South.[21]

The sectional crisis forced all Midwesterners to rethink their loyalties. Northerners reaffirmed their connection to the North, and Southern-born Midwesterners became more strongly aware of their ties to the South. The Whigs of St. Joseph County, Indiana, bordering Michigan, ordered their legislators to instruct newly elected senators "to represent the North and not the South." The Democrats of Monroe County, Illinois, on the Missouri border south of St. Louis, resolved four years later, "that our brethren of the slave states have no just cause of alarm, for whatever be the dreams of a faction, such is the overwhelming current of popular opinion in the free states, that for the sake of the Union, they would peril all their resources, if necessa[r]y, in defence of the rights of the south." An Illinois Democratic paper noted that the migration of Puritan and Cavalier had created a new western region that contained incompatible elements. Just as the abolition instincts of the New Englanders were appearing in the Republican Party, so would the natural conservatism of the Southerners reawaken and strengthen their allegiance to the Democracy.[22] Despite its mention of the West, the resolutions actually chronicled the disintegration of Westernness as a binding force among disparate settlement groups.

Renewed loyalties became even more apparent when the Kansas-Nebraska Act of 1854 completely shattered the shaky political calm produced by the Compromise of 1850. Upland Southern Democrats came to link the agitation over slavery with an attempt to destroy the Democratic Party. Democrats claimed that their enemies "would vote for the devil . . . for the purpose of defeating the Democracy."[23] The indomitable Jeptha Garrigus was dismayed to find his old friend, John G. Davis,

> voting with a set of black hearted abolitionist[s] to the destruction of the democratic Party. . . . the black party are Exulting at your course. . . . I shall never live long enough to see things restored again, we are sure to lose our state tickets. The government will go into the hands of the abolitionist, then a Division of the union, so much for one wrong step. . . . it sorely grieves Me whe[n] I think how anxious I was to help put you Where you are, and now you have help to destroy our Party.[24]

In Garrigus's scenario the destruction of the Union would be less a calamity than the destruction of the Democracy. Another of Davis's correspondents objected that even though Democratic policy in Kansas was wrongheaded there was no reason for people to go "horsefoot and Dogory over to the *nigerites* with all their heresies." A correspondent of Richard Yates found all the parties to be dissolving: "Whig Democrat & free Soil are now all 'obsolete ideas,' and all bygones are gone forever."[25]

Despite the upheaval within the Democracy, Republican politicians found it difficult to recruit adherents in Southern-dominated regions, for they inherited the mantle of antislavery reform and thus the reputation for "unpardonable fanaticism" that would destroy the country's "free and well arranged institution." The new Republicans found their appeal to the Southern born limited, although many of them had Southern roots. A correspondent of Richard Yates, Kentucky born and the first Republican governor of Illinois, despaired that the light would ever break through the "Egyptian darkness." Indeed, a southern Illinois man vowed in 1856, "Let the north vote as she may, one thing is certain, Egypt will stand as firm as the hills, giving a heavier democratic vote than she has ever done, in behalf of the constitution and the Union." In 1860, Republicans reported hopefully that the party's "light" was illuminating Egypt's "clouded land." Their optimism was misplaced, for Lincoln received less than a quarter of southern Illinois's vote while getting nearly three-quarters of the vote in northern Illinois.[26]

Upland Southern Republicans, however, rejected a South they felt had become tyrannical in its behavior and demands. Richard Yates insisted that no one with any manhood would make a compromise with the South again—a compromise that would only be broken. Yates expressed the belief that if the Southern born could be wooed from their prejudices to see the real issue as slavery expansion rather than amalgamation or disunion, they would turn against an oppressive South. Yates failed to appreciate the lost feeling of Upland Southerners who saw party lines crumbling. One of Lyman Trumbull's correspondents captured that feeling: "[O]ne by one, the ties of party will give way in the north, under the unreasonable exactions of the south till we shall be led—God knows where."[27]

As parties weakened, many Upland Southern Midwesterners returned to older ties that still retained meaning for them. They resurrected their distrust of sneaky and conniving Yankees and aligned themselves in sympathy with the South. Among the Southern born, abolition helped to stimulate a feeling of solidarity with the South. One Illinoisan reported his intention of addressing a convention in Tennessee at the time of the 1850 crisis. There he planned to speak of Illinois's, especially southern Illinois's, "punctilious respect" for Tennessee's constitutional rights. He intended to tell them how Illinois had "put down the bad men in our own part of the State" and "had kept the abolitionists off Tennessee & the South." He called Illinois an "adamantine wall against every aggression upon Tennessee & the South." Among the evils caused by antislavery, Indiana Democrats included the assertion that "It has made the press of our Northern and Western States to groan with the most infamous falsehoods against the South."[28]

Stephen Douglas evidently found his Yankee birth a handicap during the sectional crisis, for he went to great lengths in his debates with Abraham Lincoln to deny that all Yankees were abolitionists and that all the Southern born opposed abolition. He asserted his love for his birthplace but also explained that his emigration to Illinois as a boy had "liberalized" his mind and "enlarged" his opinions. Lincoln, on the other hand, was attempting to "cover up" his abolition sentiments by harking back to his Southern birth and his boyhood in Indiana. This counted for nothing, according to Douglas:

> The worst Abolitionists I have ever known in Illinois have been men who have sold their slaves in Alabama and Kentucky, and have come here and turned Abolitionists whilst spending the money got for the negroes they sold, and I do not know that an Abolitionist from Indiana or Kentucky ought to have any more credit because he was born and raised among slaveholders. I do not know that a native of Kentucky is more excusable because raised among slaves, his father and mother having owned slaves, he comes to Illinois, turns Abolitionist, and slanders the graves of his father and mother, and breathes curses upon the institutions under which he was born, and his father and mother bred.[29]

Douglas attempted to turn the tide of Lincoln's appeal to a common Southern heritage by portraying Lincoln as a traitor to that heritage.

Even when Upland Southern Midwesterners denied that they possessed sectional bias, they often revealed a tilt toward the South. A Greencastle, Indiana, man of Southern origin felt that if Southern leaders became familiar with abolitionists they would be more cautious about furnishing them ammunition. While not denying Southern misbehavior (he blamed it on "moments of Excitement"), he saw it as most dangerous for the aid it gave to Northern abolitionists. Candidate Jehu Baker, born and raised in the South, avowed no sectional feeling. Baker pointed out that extremism had developed in both North and South, yet he seemed to find more Northern acts against the South than the reverse: resistance to the fugitive law, attempts to dissolve the Union, and anti-Southern propaganda. A Clay County, Indiana man felt that leaders of both sectional factions lacked "reason, philosophy, statesmanship, and patriotism." He compared them to the religious fanatics of medieval Europe. Still, he felt abolitionists plotted to exploit Southern fanaticism and to "press the whole South to the wall and force them to do the overt act of severing the union." An Ohio politician ridiculed Free-Soilers as being from "the land of constitutional scruples and pumpkins, freedom, philanthropy and cheese." Stephen Douglas accused Lincoln of not answering a question but rather turning "Yankee-fashion" to attack Douglas instead. The Jennings County, Indiana, Democratic Convention even went so far as to endorse the acquisition of Cuba, aligning itself with Southern fire-eaters and filibusterers, as "eminently desirable for the safety and prosperity of this Republic."[30]

At their most evenhanded, Southerners in the Midwest equated the "fanatical hordes of abolitionists in the north" with the "secessionists of the south." Both seemed intent on disunion. Parading Indiana Democrats carried a sign that depicted Abraham Lincoln and secessionist William Lowndes Yancey trying to divide the Union. In the picture, Lincoln attempted to split a log labeled "Union," with a wedge in the shape of a black baby. Yancey stood in the background with another black infant. Lincoln told Yancey, "I'm afraid I can't split this knotty log with my free nigger wedge." Yancey replied, "Then try my slavecode wedge, and I think by our united exertions we can separate it."[31] In this portrait, Northern and Southern extremists acted together, using different aspects of the slave question to destroy the Union.

For all their regional pride, Upland Southern Midwesterners nevertheless maintained a healthy mistrust of Southern motives. The Upper South yeomen who settled the Midwest had more than a passing acquaintance with the "slave power" or "slavocracy" so reviled in the abolitionist press. Sidney Breese invoked images of Southerners as minor despots when he accused Stephen Douglas's followers of responding to "the crack of his whip, as readily as his slaves on his Southern plantations, obey the lash of their overseer." Breese tried to paint Douglas as a "lazy slave-holder" who oppressed others. A Jeffersonville, Indiana, man explained that tyrants always waited for the people to be less vigilant: "Hence that South, ever watchful and stretching forward for position under the pretence of self defence have struggled to bring the doctrines of J.C. Calhoun . . . into practical working in our system of government."[32]

In this period of deepening sectional antagonisms, one proposition seemed to offer a middle ground for Upland Southerners. As they thought more about their attachments to the South and as the "west" as much as the Union seemed increasingly in danger of disintegrating, they turned to the solution offered by the senator from Illinois. Popular sovereignty promised to end sectional antagonisms by returning the nation to first principles, adherence to the will of the people.

Many Midwesterners no doubt ended the 1850s agreeing with the words of an Indiana man, "Damn Kansas let her go to the Devil where she belongs." At one point the Kansas-Nebraska Act's fundamental principle of popular sovereignty had seemed to hold out the promise of resolving the slavery controversy. Once simply an expression that meant self-government, popular sovereignty became, especially under the aegis of Stephen Douglas, a particular way of handling the problem of slavery in the territories. Rather than continue the geographic or political exclusions of slavery that had been the basis of previous compromises, Douglas proposed to let the people of the territories decide the issue with their votes. What ensued was a race for control of the territories and a bloody civil war in Kansas. Back in the East, however, popular sovereignty offered a refuge for Upland Southern Midwesterners from the pressures of conflicting loyalties. Rather than be forced into a condemnation of the South's attempts to spread an abhorrent institution, they found in popular sovereignty an excuse for doing nothing about the problem on the grounds that the settlers should decide. Those who objected to popular sovereignty objected that it was a fraud, mere squatter sovereignty to use the derisive term, and a cover for the South's true agenda, slavery expansion. Some historians have called popular sovereignty a "fudge" and a "nondecision" that allowed the Democratic Party to avoid the fatal splintering that overcame the Whigs.[33] Certainly, its adherents may have felt relief at being offered an alternative that was in agreement with their basic beliefs and required no painful, Union-threatening choices. Popular sovereignty appealed to the Southern-born because it emphasized the core of their political creed: the freedom of white men to decide their own fates.

Much has been made of Douglas's motive in pushing for a repeal of the Missouri Compromise. What seems clear is that Douglas, as David Potter pointed out, cared little about slavery as a moral issue. Indeed, Douglas avowed, "I do not believe that those people who are so loud in their opposition to slavery are honest. I do not believe that they really dislike slavery *per se.*" Rather they seemed more concerned with limiting white men's liberties than with expanding those of blacks. Douglas mocked objections to popular sovereignty by arguing that critics felt it perfectly all right for residents of the territories to govern themselves on all issues except slavery. These people "seem to think it requires a higher degree of civilization and refinement to legislate for the negro race than can reasonably be expected the people of a Territory to possess." He asserted that he had not left Kansas and Nebraska open to slavery but had left them open "to *freedom* by leaving the people *perfectly free* to do as they please." Douglas's complete preoccupation with the rights of white men left no room for consideration of the repercussions of his actions. He simply failed to understand what the fuss was all about.[34]

Was Douglas a traitor to the North and a tool of the "slave power" as his critics maintained? There can be no question that Douglas was sincere in his devotion to the principle of popular sovereignty. Again and again he maintained that the only goal of the Kansas-Nebraska Act was to secure to the people the right to "regulate their own institutions in their own way." His opposition to the Lecompton constitution, at great political cost, proved that his devotion was to popular sovereignty, not to slavery extension or to the South. Lecompton, by its refusal to submit the question of slavery to the people of Kansas, was to Douglas a heresy, a violation of the people's right to decide. Others in the Northwest were willing to force the pro-Southern Lecompton constitution down the Kansans' throats. William English, congressman from Indiana, proposed a compromise that was in reality a bribe. If Kansas accepted Lecompton, the state would receive a generous portion of government land. Kansans rejected the English compromise. One of Douglas's biographers argues that the Kansas-Nebraska Act was not a response to Southern dictation but was rather a Western measure. This interpretation asserts that Douglas believed the bill would secure the territories against slavery since he assumed that slavery could not compete with free labor and hence would die out in the West.[35]

Whatever Douglas's motives, the passage of the Kansas-Nebraska bill left politicians scrambling for secure footing during an upheaval of unprecedented dimensions. The vote on the bill itself gave hints of the party divisions within the Midwest. All the Whig congressmen from the region voted against Kansas-Nebraska, whereas Democrats split, fourteen supporting Douglas and ten rejecting the bill. As a result, in the 1854 elections in Indiana, the Democrats lost control of all but the southern portion of the state. In the 1856 race for governor, the Republican candidate, accusing his opponent of favoring slavery, came within 6,000 votes of victory. Democratic Congressman John G. Davis of Indiana, representing a Southern-dominated district, received conflicting reports about his constituents' reactions. From Indianapolis he heard, "The people with great unanimity are for the Nebraska bill. All the Democrats and a majority of the Whigs. The abolitionists are *howling*." From the campus of DePauw University in Greencastle, he heard that things were in a "calm" and that abolitionists were keeping a low profile. "The compromise of 1850 unfettered by the act of 1820 or none seems to be the maxim of all." Yet another correspondent reported that Democrats as well as Whigs were signing Anti-Nebraska petitions. Should Davis support Douglas, reelection by his district would be "thorny." Another man hoped that people would support popular sovereignty but found many who preferred to leave the Missouri Compromise in place.[36]

Illinois was less ambivalent toward Douglas. A Democratic Party newspaper believed the Southern born supported the law. While Abraham Lincoln claimed there were only three Democratic legislators in Illinois who favored Kansas-Nebraska, the Democrats followed Douglas's instructions to pass resolutions endorsing it. The only Democratic legislators to oppose the bill were from northern Illinois. The *Chicago Democrat* and other northern and central Illinois papers moved into the Anti-Nebraska column. Anti-Nebraska men argued that the legislature's actions did not reflect the general feeling. A correspondent of Lyman Trumbull reported that Anti-Nebraska sentiment was "becoming stronger and stronger every day" throughout the state. Clearly Kansas-Nebraska had produced a profound sectional split in Illinois. While conventions in southern and central Illinois accepted the Kansas-Nebraska doctrine, the *Chicago Democrat* pointed out that in northern Illinois not a single pro-Nebraska candidate had been elected. Far from providing a middle ground on which all Americans could safely agree, Douglas had split not only the nation, but also the Midwest, along sectional lines.[37]

But many Upland Southern Midwesterners found popular sovereignty a palatable, if not welcome, means of ending the agitation of the "abolition fanatics." Conventions throughout the Southern-dominated areas of the Midwest endorsed popular sovereignty as "a republican truth as old as the institution of American liberty." Christian County, Illinois, Democrats even asserted a Western dislike of Eastern interference by pronouncing "that we have greater confidence in the frontier man governing himself properly than we have in any one else governing him."[38]

Like Douglas, most Upland Southern Midwesterners were comfortable with Kansas-Nebraska because they spared little thought for the plight of the black man. One Hoosier wrote that the true understanding of the principles of popular sovereignty was "that in leaving to the people of a territory the settlement of the 'domestic institutions,' something more is understood than mere *niggers.*"[39]

Many argued that the only fair course between the two regions was popular sovereignty. Fayette County, Indiana, Democrats felt it was the only policy that gave "equal justice to both North and South." A Spencer, Indiana, man agreed that popular sovereignty was the only principle that granted all sections "equal justice" on the slavery issue. Another Hoosier wrote that it was "the only principle upon which the North & South can ever amicably settle the slavery question." The Kansas-Nebraska bill was popular around the man's Rockville, Indiana, home for that reason.[40]

Those Southern-born Midwesterners who opposed popular sovereignty did so for the very reasons others supported it: a fear that the middle ground between North and South had been lost, not found, and that self-government was threatened, not strengthened. One Illinois man reported that people were convinced "that no good will arise from [Kansas-Nebraska] but a great deal of harm." David Davis was torn between his dislike of Kansas-Nebraska and his fear that the Whig Party would be "abolitionized." "There never had been in my opinion any thing so ill timed and disastrous to the good feeling of this Country," Davis lamented. The Ross County, Ohio, Anti-Nebraska meeting viewed with "contempt and loathing" the overturning of the "happy settlement" of the slavery question provided by the compromises of 1820 and 1850. A friend of Sidney Breese reported that southern Illinois was restless at Douglas's attempts to force "nauseaus doses" of "pure Democracy" on them.[41]

Douglas's critics insisted that instead of providing self-government for the territories, he had introduced new forms of tyranny. Abraham Lincoln argued that a proper understanding of Douglas's popular sovereignty, which Lincoln called "squatter sovereignty," would bring the realization that slavery could not be kept out of the territories. Squatter sovereignty meant "That if any *one* man choose to enslave *another*, no *third* man shall be allowed to object." Lincoln adhered to the principle of self-government, which he called "absolutely and eternally right."[42] The crowd in Springfield cheered Lincoln's ridicule of Douglas for supposing that anyone opposed popular sovereignty: "Does he expect to stand up in majestic dignity, and go through his *apotheosis* and become a god, in the maintaining of a principle which neither a man nor a mouse in all God's creation is opposing?" When the result of Kansas-Nebraska proved to be a bloody civil conflict in which Missourians crossed the border to vote illegally for slavery in Kansas, popular sovereignty took on darker meanings. An Ohio Republican equated popular sovereignty with ballot box stuffing.[43]

If to Douglas, and to many of the Southern born, there was not enough humanity in the black to warrant such a fuss over his condition, to Lincoln and others of the Southern born, popular sovereignty's treatment of blacks made the policy a travesty of self-government. Popular sovereignty might work very well, Lincoln argued, if blacks were not human and the trade in slaves could be treated identically with the trade in any other commodity. Lincoln, however, insisted on the black man's humanity and therefore that popular sovereignty in the traditional sense did not apply. Lincoln argued that the Democrats had perverted the meaning of popular sovereignty so that "the right of people to govern niggers was the right of people to govern themselves." Douglas had "discovered that the right of the white man to breed and flog niggers in Nebraska was POPULAR SOVEREIGNTY!" Obviously, true popular sovereignty was not what Douglas intended at all. The intent of the "humbug," according to Lincoln, was to nationalize slavery, revive the African slave trade, and spread slavery throughout the territories. Lincoln insisted that if popular sovereignty meant a man could have slaves if he wanted them, it also meant that he could import them from Africa if he wanted to do that. In part, Lincoln was stressing the most radical and obnoxious extremes to which popular sovereignty as a pro-Southern position could be taken. Underlying Lincoln's discomfort with popular sovereignty, however, was a dislike of any policy that "acknowledges that slavery has equal rights with liberty."[44]

Others in the Midwest agreed with Lincoln that popular sovereignty was nothing but a cover for attempts to enslave the territories. An Ohio Republican newspaper defined it as "the sovereignty of the slave power, the rights of a slaveholder to take his slaves into a Territory and hold them there in defiance of the will of the people." Governor Salmon P. Chase's inaugural address called popular sovereignty "nothing but the right of a portion of the community to enslave the rest." Such a policy would subvert "the fundamental principles of American institutions" and would replace "a free and independent people," with "a community of masters, dependents, and slaves." E. W. Downer explained to Lyman Trumbull that, although he had been a lifelong Democrat, "after Douglass turned Traitor to freedom & I Plainly saw that either Slavery or Freedom had to become *National* . . . I took an active Part in the Anti-Nebraska League." If Democrats called the opposition "Black Republicans," some Republicans began to call their opposition "the slave democracy."[45]

After 1854, popular sovereignty superseded slavery as the issue foremost on Upland Southerners' minds. For some, popular sovereignty did become a formula by which they could avoid making the painful choice between siding with the planter aristocracy or backing the rabid abolitionists. At the same time, they could comfort themselves with the belief that they acted according to the principles of the republican experiment. The fate of the black race was inconsequential. In fact, black insignificance came through in the racist words of an Evansville, Indiana, man frustrated with the sectional conflict: "This infernal negro question stinks in my nostrils—as bad as Cuffey himself—with the thermometer at 90°."[46] Some Upland Southern mavericks such as Lincoln, however, refused to abide by that rationale. To these men, the humanity of blacks made it impossible to relegate the question of slavery to such a formula. Douglas, himself a slave to his presidential ambitions and to the Southern votes he needed to fulfill that ambition, had fashioned a slavery-extension proposal hidden in the false promise of self-government offered by the phrase "popular sovereignty."

Popular sovereignty did not save the Democratic Party in the Midwest. A Greencastle man wrote to Congressman Davis of Indiana that Douglas had to be the party's nominee in 1860 if the Democracy was to carry Indiana: "Indiana is doubtful to us, and more than doubtful, unless we have at our masthead 'popular sovereignty' and the captain of the ship must be its principal defender." Yet although Douglas ran as the candidate of his party, at least in the North, Indiana went Republican, as did Illinois and Ohio. The portions of those states inhabited by the Southern born still preferred the Democratic Party and Douglas's popular sovereignty formula to Lincoln and the party associated with fanatical abolitionism.[47] It remained to be seen, however, what the election would mean for Midwesterners and for the nation. Upland Southern Midwesterners felt renewed loyalty to their Southern heritage, and a renewed dislike for New Englanders. However their ambivalence about the Southern elite and their attachment to the Union which made possible a free and republican society made it unclear which side they would choose during the approaching crisis and whether the West, as well as the Union, would survive.

EIGHT

❦

Disunion

"[A]LL MY SYMPATHIES are with that south," wrote a Terre Haute, Indiana, man to his congressman in 1858, "what little of this wo[r]ld's goods I own are in the south or nearly so all my Kindred, I have no relatives elsewhere . . . but I know they are [w]rong and must soon see if they do not already see their danger." This plaintive lament echoed the feelings of many Midwesterners torn between the South and the Union. Divided loyalties shaped the choices Midwesterners made in the crisis years of 1860 and 1861. Anguished, they spoke of the claims of ancestral Southern homes. But again and again, they were forced to articulate the simple truth that they were no longer Southerners. Generations with memories and values drawn from the South had been born, been raised, lived, and died outside it. Thus it was that Midwesterners first turned for help to a Western solution. Then, that failing, most chose the Union, either actively by marching off to war, or passively, by refusing to support a Republican Party which seemed to use the cloak of war to label all dissent treason.[1]

As secession grew imminent, Upland Southern Midwesterners believed that if they strengthened their ties with the border South, a united West might counteract the extremism of both North and South and thus stave off disaster. In January 1860, in Louisville, Kentucky, Governor Ashbel P. Willard of Indiana spoke at a banquet attended by Kentucky, Tennessee, and Indiana government officials. Willard's theme was that the two sections could continue to live together if each section would allow the other to live in peace. The only question that endangered the Union, Willard asserted, was "the relation that exists between the white man and the black man." To the sound of cheers, Willard proposed, "Kentucky has no right to say to Indiana, you shall be a slave state; Indiana has no right to turn upon the other side and say Kentucky shall be a free State." But the problem did not originate with Kentucky and Indiana or the other border states. According to Willard, relations along the border were amicable. "They know full well that Kentucky blood has been poured out as water upon Indiana soil." The speech was well received, according to newspaper reports, and frequently interrupted with cheers, applause, and cries of "good, good."[2] Willard proposed that Indiana's true loyalties lay with neither North nor South but with the border South from which the state derived its heritage. Emphasizing Indiana's roots in Kentucky, and distinguishing between the border South and the deep South, made it possible for Hoosiers to remember their Southernness but, by emphasizing their Westernness, disassociate themselves from that South which clamored for disunion.

A year later, a meeting of the Indiana Democracy repeated the same theme of commonality along the border. Speaker after speaker argued that although the extreme North and extreme South were strangers to each other, the borders mingled. Therefore the border must resolve the crisis. Joseph E. McDonald argued that Indiana should try to restrain the North while the border slave states restrained the lower South. Indiana, with its citizens bound by ties of "consanguinity and commerce" to the South, would be duty bound to mediate the conflict. An Ohio Democrat at a Union meeting "avowed his attachment to the Union, dreaded civil war and thought the North ought to make such concessions as would satisfy the South. With South Carolina and Georgia he would have nothing to say or do—regarding them as traitors to the government, but he was willing to concede *all* the border slave States ask, and in doing so he conceded but what was right." Even during the war itself, an appeal for unity with the border South had its uses. Governor Oliver P. Morton of Indiana used such an appeal to rally Hoosiers to the support of Kentucky Unionists. He too referred to Kentuckians who had rescued Indiana in her "infancy" from "the scalping knife of the savage." Not to help Kentucky repel a Confederate invasion was "base ingratitude and criminal folly."[3]

Upland Southern Midwesterners desperately hoped for compromise even if it involved concessions to the South. The brother of an Indiana politician believed that overwhelming support existed in Indiana for any "honorable compromise." A letter from a Spencer, Indiana, man to his congressman indicated southern Indiana politicians were correct in their measurements of the procompromise sentiment of their region. George

W. Moore lamented that neither the South nor the administration would compromise. The dismal prospects caused him to wonder "is all the true patriots of Seventy Six dead, this government was formed by compromises and in the name of god cant there be anough of true [illegible] men to Save this glorious government we cry one and all Save our common country."[4]

From the border state of Kentucky came the winter's most widely supported proposal for compromise. Kentucky Senator John J. Crittenden called for a constitutional amendment to protect slavery in territories south of the Missouri Compromise line. The Crittenden Compromise had wide appeal among the Upland Southerners. A correspondent of Congressman William English believed that it would pass by a large majority in Indiana and relied on the border states to implement it. "Our only hope now is that the border states may agree on the Crittenden proposition and save the center, and that finaly, the extremes may come back to us, if this fails all is lost, & night is set in, and no one can tell the end." He appealed to English to "do all you can to give us another chance to speak, through the ballott box, before we resort to the cartridge box."[5]

Union meetings, which erupted all over the Midwest in the months after Lincoln's election, revealed Upland Southern Midwesterners' attempts to find common ground. Even the name "Union meeting" avoided the issue of slavery and tried to focus on that which Midwesterners held in common; as such it could mean different things to different men. But so innocuous a title did little to conceal the renewed sharpness of sectional discord in the Midwest. Most meetings ended by endorsing the Crittenden Compromise. Many of the meetings also offered sympathy and admiration to Southern Unionists and denied the constitutionality of secession.[6]

As part of the effort to solidify the Western border, Upland Southerners rejected the extremes of secession and abolition as equally obnoxious and dangerous to the Union. According to Governor Willard of Indiana, the problem, rather, lay with the "far North, where many men never saw four negroes in their lives . . . and down in the extreme South some great men— Southern men—are not satisfied with the present condition of the government." The Indiana Democracy included in their resolutions a plank blaming civil war extremists in the Republican Party, the South, and the federal government. John M. Palmer blamed the admittedly "unconstitutional and revolutionary" actions of the Southern states on the provocations of Northern abolitionists. He came close to charging a conspiracy between abolitionists and secessionists to dissolve the Union. War could have been avoided if the Republican Party had exuded the "proper spirit of compromise." The Ohio legislature by large margins passed resolutions, proposed by the senator from Madison County, part of the old Virginia Military District, that both denied the legality of secession and yet offered concessions to the South. The Ohio resolutions expressed fear that "revolutionary" principles such as nullification or secession would disrupt "the best and wisest system of Government in the world." Yet in veiled references to slavery and the fugitive slave law, Ohioans opposed interference in the internal affairs of another state and pledged to fulfill their obligations under the Constitution. They also expressed their gratitude to pro-Union men in the South.[7]

Some Upland Southerners shifted the balance of the blame to the North. Sensing Republican alienation from the South, an Indiana Democrat lamented the fact that Republicans felt "no kindred blood" with the South: "They can see no slavery in the bound apprentices, and in the busy din of *fourteen hours* in the factories of the North. But the poor negro of the South, who is well fed and clothed, should not be in bondage, but on an equal footing with his 'white brother,' with the same privileges of the most intelligent." Racism had long been used to solidify the cracks in Southern white society. Among the Republicans' crimes was their preoccupation with an alien race when their first loyalties should have been to other whites. Clement L. Vallandigham lamented the Republican refusal to compromise. "I fear that civil war is inevitable—though the united action of all the South *may* avert it. The Black Republican traitors & disunionists have done the work, & now they would *war* to all else."[8] Vallandigham shared with many others a refusal to acknowledge the South's responsibility for the crisis and a dislike for Republican intransigence.

In some cases, Upland Southern identification with the South extended beyond the firing on Fort Sumter. Editorially, some Democrats asserted that South Carolina's actions had been provoked and that an attempt to provision Fort Sumter constituted coercion. An Indiana Democratic newspaper insisted that Lincoln had intended war and that the expedition to Fort Sumter had been military in purpose: "It was an expedition intended to convince the people of the Southern States, in Republican language, that we have a government. It was known that a demonstration would be regarded as an act of war and the men of the South would have been regarded as mere braggarts if they had not resisted unto death. Their honor was at stake. If they had yielded without resistance they would have stood disgraced before the world." According to this interpretation, the Lincoln administration, if it had truly desired peace, would have found a face-saving way for the South to back down. That Lincoln offered confrontation instead was a symptom of his dishonest intentions.[9]

But many felt almost as frustrated with the South as did the Republicans. A Union meeting in Shawneetown, Illinois, resolved that South Carolina was guilty of treason, that President James Buchanan deserved hanging, and that military action was warranted against the South. A

Republican in Harrison County, Indiana, inadvertently indicated that Union meetings had some appeal to members of his party. The Democrats, he wrote, had called a Union meeting, but many Republicans attended—out of curiosity, of course. He called the organizers of the meeting "slave coders" and "devout worshippers at the Southern shrine," who came out for the Crittenden Compromise. He went on to explain Republican curiosity about their activities: "for you must know, Mr. Editor, that we are all anxious to know how many and who were willing to eat South-dirt." With so many virtuous Republicans there it might have been hard to tell them apart from those intent on "kneeling at the feet of Southern traitors, asking for peace even at the price of manhood."[10]

Republicans of Southern heritage, unlike other Upland Southern Midwesterners, had little love for the Old South and little hope for compromise. Their reasons reveal a deep alienation from the South itself. An editorial in a southern Ohio Republican paper scoffed at secession as South Carolina "bluster." The paper's sociological analysis of the South divided the nonslaveholding white population into three categories. A pro-Union majority that was usually "silent and submissive to the slaveholders," a minority "with more manhood and ambition" who "chafe under the rule of the oligarchs," and a tiny minority of "fanatical shouters for the slavery which degrades them, and the slaveholders on whom they are dependent." The slaveholders, lacking popular support, nevertheless threatened disunion because the tactic had been successful in the past. A weak South would be forced into the arms of pro-black foreigners. The southern Ohioans maintained that white Southerners need not fear Republicans who as fellow whites would ensure white control of the South. The point of difference lay in the territorial issue, and even that was another example of white solidarity, for Republicans wanted to keep the "common inheritance, the public lands," for whites and not for slaves or slaveholders.[11] The authors again and again showed contempt for the South: its lack of resources to carry off its bluff; the cowardice and subservience of the bulk of its white population; its probable union with outsiders even to the point of sacrificing the racial purity it presumably wished to defend.

Upland Southern Republicans saw themselves as the repository of conservatism in the face of this Southern extremism. An Indiana editor felt that the South had gone insane but also rejected the thought of provoking her: "While I would not yield one hair of principle to the madmen of the South, I would not do any act that might be regarded as a menace or threat."[12] John J. Janney of Ohio represented another conservative Upland Southern Republican viewpoint. Responding to a New York newspaper, Janney replied that if the South resisted Lincoln's election as president, that would be treason. He denied that Lincoln or the Republican Party were abolitionists. The word "abolitionist" was used "as a scarecrow, to frighten the timid and sensitive." At most, he conceded, some Northerners had striven for justice for the blacks and rebelled at being made slave catchers under the Fugitive Slave Law. He inveighed against the South for not guaranteeing the rights of all citizens; he pointed out that if he were to express out loud in a Southern city the sentiments he was committing to paper, he would be in physical danger. He pleaded with the good sense of the South to see the Republican Party as he saw it:

> As a Southerner, as a Virginian by birth and education, I have an abiding faith that you have among you, in the South I mean, patriotism enough to put down any attempt at insurrection, without the aid of a single northern man.
>
> But you mistake entirely the spirit of the Republican Party. There is no party in the land that will be less reluctant to infringe one of your constitutional rights. All they ask of you is to keep your slaves and your slavery at home.
>
> I am a warm Republican, but at the same time ardently attached to my native state and her people, and would resist to the last any attempt to deprive them of any constitutional right trusting that the good sense, and love of country that has heretofore characterized the Southern people may now govern and control them, and render any appeals to the terrors of the law unnecessary, and that the election of Abraham Lincoln may prove to you that the Republican party is the only truly conservative one.[13]

Despite his appeal to a Virginia heritage, Janney distanced himself from a South he obviously did not comprehend. He did not say that "we" in the South have patriotism enough to avoid insurrection but spoke of "you," Southerners, "your slaves and slavery." For all his references to his native state, Janney spoke as an outsider who wished to reassure the South that it had little to fear from another outsider: Lincoln.

Janney possessed warm feelings for the South that other Republicans did not share. One Indiana Republican ridiculed Southern discontent with Lincoln's election by describing the consequences of the 1860 election in the far southern county of Posey:

> You have went and gone and done it, haven't you? You have elected Lincoln, and, I 'spose, feel mighty good over it. But have you ever considered the awful consequences to result from that one rash act? Did it ever occur to you that Posey county, the home of the free and unterrified— the residence of those who imbibed, as if it were whiskey, that inordinate love of country and bombast, that is so apparent in Gov. Wise—wouldn't

stand the election of a sectional President? If not, learn from me that such is the case. Hear the truth and tremble.

The news came by grapevine telegraph that all the States with the exception of South Carolina (which was considered doubtful) had gone for Lincoln, and the greatest consternation was everywhere visible. Business was at a standstill. The store keeper informed me that he had sold nothing but one plug of tobacco and three barrels of red-eye for two days. Something was evidently 'to be did.' The little cloud, at first no bigger than a man's hand, gradually swelled and finally 'bust.' Posey county was about to *secede from the Union.!!*

A meeting was called, committees appointed, and resolutions adopted denouncing the election of Lincoln as destructive to the rights of Posey; also one appointing a committee to borrow $10,000,000 Boone County money with which to carry on the new government. All this being accomplished, this afternoon at precisely half past 2 o'clock Posey county took up its hat and walked out of the Union. The Kingdom of Posey is now a fixed fact. Will South Carolina, Delaware, Long Island, Coney Island and other States and Territories whose rights have not been respected by these Lincolnites follow suit?

What will become of you now? Indiana, heretofore a great and happy sovereignty, has lost her Posey county. The Union will lose its South Carolina, and the affairs of the nation and of the world are gone to everlasting smash.[14]

Southerners, like Southern Hoosiers, responded with exaggerated and unnecessary fear and bombast to the imaginary threats to their freedom. The author exaggerated Southern extremism and Republican popularity by depicting only South Carolina and Posey County, Indiana, as opposed to Lincoln's election. The South's tendencies were toward monarchy, according to the author's picture of a "Kingdom of Posey." Nor would the South provide a reputable government and economy, for the reference to borrowing money from Boone County alluded to a bank fraud currently under investigation there. Even if South Carolina did secede, it would be no more a loss to the Union than if Indiana lost the small extreme southern county of Posey or the country lost such insignificant places as Coney Island. Obviously, South Carolina vastly overestimated its importance.

Republicans even doubted the South's commitment to republicanism. To Ohio governor William Dennison, slavery was a moot question, which had been settled by climate and Lincoln's election. In fact, the election was only a pretense for secession. The crisis arose because the intriguing men who always existed in a republic had at last found a pretext for their disunionist plans. The South had declined in economic and political strength because of slavery while the North grew. The plotters capitalized on "a narrow, mistaken, yet honest patriotism for the locality of its

birth." Southern extremists were antirepublicans who had found themselves deprived of political power in the nation because of the inherent
disadvantages of their slave institutions. Ousted from political power,
they attempted to exploit a legitimate regional loyalty to regain that
political power. The power they sought, however, was inherently undemocratic because it could only be acquired by ignoring the wishes of the
majority in the free states. Lincoln's election merely provided the opportunity for "the explosion of a plot long maturing for the establishment of
a Southern confederacy."[15]

Abraham Lincoln passed through Indiana en route to his inauguration
"looking care worn and haggard as if he was conscious that he had a hard
road to travel," according to an observer. Repeatedly Lincoln asserted his
devotion to preserving the Union and "every star and every stripe of the
glorious flag." By contrast, his characterization of his native South
revealed little fondness. He compared the Union to a marriage. The South
wanted the marriage to be based on "free love" and "passionate attraction."[16] Obviously the South's "attraction" to the Union was fickle and
transient, not based on commitment, responsibility, and respect, those
things that contribute to a marriage of long duration. For Lincoln, the
South had rendered its devotion to the Union suspect and had placed itself
in the position of a partner who deserts his spouse for light and frivolous
reasons. Still, fidelity was not all that was at issue. If any candidate
appeased his opponents and accepted conditions in return for his elevation to an office he had fairly won,

> this government, and all popular government, is already at an end.
> Demands for such surrender, once recognized, and yielded to, are without
> limit, as to nature, extent, or repetition. They break the only bond of faith
> between public, and public servant; and they distinctly set the minority
> over the majority. Such demands acquiesced in, would not merely be the
> ruin of a man, or a party; but as a precedent they would ruin the
> government itself.[17]

Surrender to the South would end the republican experiment.

Ironically, however, the secession crisis caused even Republicans to
reaffirm their Southernness. No Southerners, they argued, could tolerate
the concessions the South asked. Lincoln drew on his Southern heritage
when he appealed against secession. In a fragment intended for a Kentucky audience, Lincoln placed the matter of federal sovereignty in the
context of personal honor. He assumed that Southerners would "die by
the proposition" that no other conditions should be placed on the
inauguration of their successful candidate than those already imposed by
the Constitution and laws of the lands. "What Kentuckian," Lincoln

asked, "worthy of his birth place, would not do this?" Having established appeasement of the South as outside the bounds of Southern honor, he affirmed, "Gentlemen, I too, am a Kentuckian."[18] Other Upland Southern Midwesterners agreed that to give in to the South's demands would be to succumb to bullying. C. A. Trimble, representative from Ohio, objected to the Crittenden Compromise as excluding his constituents from moving south of the extended Missouri Compromise line, altering the Constitution, and denying the power to exclude slavery from the territories. He concluded with an appeal to the values he had absorbed as an Upland Southern Midwesterner:

> I object again, because it is in violation of the principles of all free government; and lastly, sir, because it demands a sacrifice of my convictions of right, and of my principles, inherited from a Virginia ancestry and strengthened by the teachings of Southern Statesmen. I believe slavery to be an evil; and I believe it now more firmly than ever before. I believe too, that it is a local institution, and wholly dependent upon local law for its maintenance. I cannot, then, consent to provide [illegible] constitutional amendment for its nationalization, and for the acquisition of territory into which this evil is to be extended and perpetuated.[19]

Trimble asserted that it was precisely the Southern values of honor he had inherited that made it impossible for him to sacrifice the Union to the South.

Some of those who vowed loyalty to the border South, vowed also not to bear arms against it. A disgruntled Indiana Democrat, who blamed the crisis on the bungling of abolitionists and Republicans, scoffed at the idea that Republicans expected Northern Democrats to help them subdue a South, which the Republicans had forced into secession. Republicans, having created the mess, should face the consequences of their own actions. Part of his refusal to help resolve the conflict stemmed from a reluctance to subjugate a South with which Indiana had close historical connections. "They expect the Democracy of Indiana to go with them to invade Kentucky. Kentucky, that, in our infancy, when we were weak and few, sent her veteran warriors here to defend us from the tomahawk and scalping knife of the savage. Kentucky, whose gallant sons, upon the bloody field of Tippecanoe, rolled back the tide of war, and rescued the women and children of Indiana from the massacre and debaucheries of Indian warfare!" A Union meeting, in far southern New Albany, Indiana, dissolved into a struggle between Southern sympathizers and pro-Union forces. One speaker, Judge Thomas L. Smith, asked the assembly if they should "tie ourselves to the tail of stunny Yankeedom, or go with the South with whom are all of our interests?" The judge vowed to plunge his bayonet into the hearts of Hoosiers before he would let them march across the Ohio to "crush the seceding states." Joseph E. McDonald, speaking at a meeting of Indiana Democrats went so far as to make an impassioned plea based on the brotherhood of Indiana and Kentucky. McDonald "would take no part in arms to make inroad upon the institutions of Kentucky. Kentucky and Indiana had been brothers in other days. Kentucky had proved to us an elder brother." McDonald pointed to the Kentuckians who had fought and died at Tippecanoe and concluded that "if the day ever comes that Kentucky and Indiana should be aliens to each other, if he were a Kentuckian he would ask to visit these shores once more, not as an armed host, but in the funeral garb, and gather from the battle fields of Indiana the bones of her patriotic dead, and bury them on a friendly soil where they could rest in peace."[20]

Pro-Southern sympathizers did exist. Union men in Londonderry, Ohio, claimed to have been threatened by pro-Southern mobs. Londonderry Confederate sympathizers were said to have procured a "palmetto flag," responded with public approval to a man wearing "a secession cockade," declared their intention to fight for the South, celebrated the secession convention and the fall of Fort Sumter with toasts, and proclaimed themselves as good traitors as anyone in the South. In southern Illinois, Southern sympathizers tried to take over the telegraph office in Carbondale, and young Marion County men were said to be hiding arms to use against Union troops scheduled to move into southern Illinois to prevent its secession. A Lynchburg, Illinois, man wrote Governor Richard Yates that secessionists were "thickly interspersed" with Union men. A relative of Jefferson Davis was said to be telling volunteers to go home, insulting "the aged matrons because their Patriotic sons has turned out to defend the Stars and stripes," and trying to "influence his more illiterate neighbors to turn in favor of the south."[21] Many were convinced the southern counties of Indiana or Illinois merely awaited a signal from the Confederacy to rise up in arms.

Some Upland Southern Democrats gave credence to such fears. A southern Indiana politician wrote in early April that not only was he ready to recognize the Confederacy, but "as a last resort I would divide the State & if possible Ills. and out of the Southern portion of each I would form a new State and call it Jackson." He believed this to be the course his constituents wanted but professed an inability to foretell the "destiny of Indiana." He concluded, "I cannot obliviate the fact that our interest is with the South, and I can not reconcile the Separation, and it will be the last day in the evening before I consent to fight there." Some were even willing to pledge themselves to a Southern confederacy. "M.," writing from Cannelton, Indiana, believed the local Union meeting was a "Democratic swindle." He accused southern Indiana Democrats of wanting "the dismemberment of the state and a union with the Southern Confederacy." He reported that southern Indiana Democrats had refused to endorse the Crittenden resolutions and resolved that "if a line is to be drawn between the North and South, that line shall be found North of us." Another Indiana politician, Daniel W. Voorhees, provided a letter of introduction for a military man traveling in the South and informed the letter's recipients that the bearer's sympathies as to "the disturbing questions of the day" were with the South. Voorhees professed to be in "close harmony" with the officer's views.[22]

After the firing on Fort Sumter made war a reality, Upland Southern Midwesterners reacted, as they had talked, in divided ways. While some extremists still pledged loyalty to the South, the actions of many showed their willingness to rally to the central government. Not only did meetings, including Democratic ones, resolve that it was the duty of all citizens to support the government regardless of party, but scores of young men from Upland Southern–dominated areas enlisted as well. Reports in an Indiana Republican newspaper described the recruitment of troops and requests for weaponry, which came from all over the state. Putnam, the county that had pledged, "Not one dollar, and not one man from Indiana with which to subjugate the South and inaugurate civil war!," raised three companies to fight for the Union. Illinoisans also rallied to the flag. A Union meeting in Springfield called the firing on Fort Sumter an act of treason and asked patriotic Illinoisans to support their country's cause while seeking a peaceful solution. The Democratic politician, John A. McClernand, spoke in Jacksonville, Illinois, and urged the audience to support the Union, regardless of party. The meeting resolved to preserve the Union peacefully if possible but forcibly if necessary. A Hillsboro, Illinois, man wrote to deny rumors of his secessionist leanings. He had favored a peaceful resolution of the difficulties, "But we have reached a point of actual conflict. In such a conflict I am for maintaining and defending the government with all the force necessary for that purpose."[23]

A southern Illinois congressman, John Logan, also denied charges that he was a secessionist and favored southern Illinois's joining the Confederacy. He claimed the rumors stemmed from articles in southern Illinois newspapers "suggesting that Egypt would secede." He had seen such articles, "But the impossibility and absurdity of such secession were so palpable that I viewed the suggestion as a broad burlesque upon the illegitimate and unconstitutional action of the south in this matter of secession, and I gave the subject no second thought, knowing that however it might become true that the Union could be and would be dissolved, the unity of Illinois never could be disturbed." He pointed out that the number of young men enlisting from the Ninth District proved Illinois's loyalty. Logan's plight was related to the events in Williamson

County, Illinois, some of whose residents had gone south to fight for the Confederacy. Federal court judge William P. Allen wrote a letter, similar to Logan's, denying secessionist leanings. Allen maintained that only twenty-two men left to fight for the South and that they did so without the knowledge of others in the county. He too pointed out the patriotism of those fighting for the Union as proof of southern Illinois's loyalties despite their overwhelmingly Democratic partisanship. "In this war," he wrote, "everybody in Southern Illinois, so far as my knowledge extends are for the Union, the Constitution and the enforcement of the laws, without regard to past party predilections." Citizens of Williamson County also responded with a letter to the Springfield Democratic paper. Some fifteen or twenty "misguided" men had gone to fight for the Confederacy, the letter explained, and the rest of the citizenry felt the need to discountenance their actions. An accompanying editorial defended Egypt: "While the people of southern Illinois are mostly of Southern birth, they are none the less loyal and true to the Union, as is shown, if proof were necessary, by the alacrity with which they have filled up the regiment in the ninth district." Despite the protestations of loyalty and nonpartisanship in the Union cause, Williamson County's loyalties were divided. "A.B." reported that both Logan and Allen, although they had tried to discourage the men from volunteering for the Confederacy, had known of their intent. How could they not, when Logan's brother-in-law was one of the company?[24]

Throughout the spring of 1861, the Illinois Republican paper in Springfield received regular dispatches from a correspondent in Cairo. "Juvenis" reported on the number of Southerners fleeing north and the number of Midwesterners traveling south. The latter he maintained dwindled in number from around one hundred a day to ten or twelve per day in the month after Fort Sumter. He reported the public's enthusiastic reception of the first troops to reach Cairo, the numbers of troops being raised in Egypt, and the widespread rumors of imminent invasion, and he expressed optimism that "Egypt will support the *Stars and Stripes.*" Prominent local politicians made Union speeches and encouraged recruiting. The few remaining secessionists in Egypt ("Juvenis" predicted their number had dwindled from half a dozen to one) were under close supervision.[25]

While Upland Southern Midwesterners often felt pangs of unhappiness over the split between North and South, many were prepared to take vigorous action against secessionists and their sympathizers. A man from Greene County, Indiana, believed most residents there advocated flogging the secessionists. He admitted to the existence of a "few sympathizers with the South, who clearly exhibit by their disloyalty that they have sprung forth from their ancestral tories in South Carolina and other States of the South; but they have to keep pretty mute. Sea grass and hemp is unreservedly talked of as an effectual remedy for such diseases." "D. H. R." reported from Union City, Indiana, that a pro-Southern man had been "drummed" out of town. The Southern sympathizer had evicted a woman and her child after her husband enlisted, on the assumption that without her husband's financial support, she would be unable to pay the rent. When the alleged Southern sympathizer, or hard-headed business-man, came to town to sell a load of hams, he found himself without customers. When he declined to contribute to the relief fund for the families of enlistees, he was forcibly evicted from town. An Indianapolis man of Kentucky birth urged Kentucky to come out strongly for the Union as the war began. "I WAS a Kentuckian," he told the Republican newspaper, "but when to be a Kentuckian is to be a *traitor* to my country, and her glorious old flag, I am no longer a Kentuckian—henceforth I am an AMERICAN." At the same time, he recognized the loyalty of Upland Southern Midwesterners to the South, writing that "The thousands of Kentuckians in the Northwest cannot look upon these degenerate sons of noble sires, but with mingled feelings of pity, contempt and loathing." Nevertheless, he called for action against the South, saying there was no time to be wasted in lamenting the sad state of the nation's affairs.[26]

This Hoosier's sentiments indicated that a decade-long conflict had reshaped regional identity in the Midwest, rejuvenating a sense of Southernness and its anti-Northern side. The sense of Westernness, though fractured somewhat by older ties to South or North, retained enough integrity so that Midwesterners looked for common ground in such Western solutions as the Crittenden Compromise. Moreover, the majority of Midwesterners, despite the sectional pro-Southern rhetoric, marched off to fight for Uncle Abe and the Union. During the war, despite occasional scares, there was no significant anti-Union danger in the Midwest. Decades and generations in the Midwest had not entirely eradicated Midwesterners' ties to the South, but they were no longer Southerners.

⚜

Conclusion

IN THE ELECTORAL CAMPAIGN OF 1886, Ohio Senator John Sherman made a circuit in support of Republican candidates. In speeches in Virginia and Kentucky, Sherman commented on the relationship between Ohio and these two Upland South states. In Virginia, denying accusations that he had waved "the bloody shirt" of sectional recrimination, he swore, "I never uttered an unkind word about the people of Virginia that mortal man can quote. I have always respected and loved the State of Virginia, its memories, its history, its records, and its achievements." He further claimed never to have heard an Ohioan denigrate a Confederate soldier's bravery. Of his speech in Louisville, Kentucky, Sherman recalled, "I referred to the long and intimate association of Ohio and Kentucky since the days of the Indian wars, when Kentucky sent her best and bravest men to fight the battles of Ohio." He appealed to the Kentuckians "not for the purpose of reviving past controversies, but to see whether, after all, the people of Ohio and Kentucky ought not now to stand side by side in their political action, as they did in days of old."[1]

Sherman's remarks reveal much about what had changed and what had not in regional sentiments. He spoke of respect for the South, of old alliances, even of love but not of brotherhood and the fellowship of kindred ties, themes that would have appealed to earlier Midwestern politicians on similar occasions. He acknowledged the close historical ties of Kentucky and Ohio but seemed unaware of Kentucky's contributions to Ohio's population or that Kentuckians, in the days of the Indian wars, might have viewed those battles as self-protection. Sherman's Ohio was strangely detached from Kentucky and Virginia just as his political interests, financial policy, were detached from the overriding issues of the antebellum era. Sherman's comments were echoes of a sectional politics that no longer existed in the Midwest.

In the aftermath of the Civil War, both the nation and the Midwest faced painful choices about regional identities. The Union's triumph did not destroy regional loyalties, yet regionalism no longer threatened the nation's survival. In the Midwest, an emerging sense of Westernness increasingly subsumed sectional identities, encompassing them within a Western identity. Ultimately this Western, or Midwestern identity, became the nation's identity.

Union victory signaled the dominance of one interpretation of the Constitution and American nationalism. Many Upland Southern Midwesterners objected to the use of the war crisis as a pretext for implementing the Whigs' economic program and reordering race relations. They asked for "the Constitution as it is and the Union as it was," charging that Republican efforts to reinterpret the nation's political philosophy were unacceptable. The Republicans cried "Copperhead conspiracy" and treason. The argument made clear that although the political philosophy of republicanism had provided the framework for Midwestern and national discourse, disputes continued over the proper meaning of republicanism.[2]

The finer points of constitutional arguments over republican ideology, however, were lost in vigorous partisanship. For a generation after Appomattox, the Civil War, and the third-party system it created, shaped political loyalties. Before and after the war, Midwesterners operated within a national party system. Since the Democratic Party retained a substantial base within the Midwest, Republicans had to choose many of their national candidates from those states. Only twice between 1860 and 1912 did the Republican Party choose presidential candidates from states other than Ohio, Indiana, and Illinois.[3] James G. Blaine, Republican candidate for president, discovered the vigor of partisanship during the presidential election of 1884. The Democratic paper in Indiana, the *Indiana State Sentinel,* countering accusations that Grover Cleveland had fathered a bastard child, printed charges that Blaine's oldest child had been born a bare three months after Blaine's wedding. The paper ignored an earlier wedding, a full year before the child's birth. Blaine intended to sue the paper for libel but withdrew the suit after being informed that the judge and bailiff would be Democrats. Reluctantly he informed his lawyers,

When I visited Indiana in October I was repeatedly advised that six Democrats could not be found in the state who in a political suit would give a verdict against their leading party organ. This did not necessarily convey an imputation upon their personal integrity as citizens but simply that the blinding of party prejudice would prevent an impartial consideration of the evidence submitted.[4]

Having survived the Civil War, the two-party system remained the primary means by which Midwesterners formed a political identity. The party system continued, after the war, to unify Midwesterners.

In the latter part of the nineteenth century, national party candidates, including those from the Midwest, sought to promote national reconciliation by moderating the sectional quarrels that had led to war. In doing so, they deemphasized regional identities. Rutherford B. Hayes commented to his diary that a Grand Army of the Republic meeting in Steubenville, Ohio, was marred by "the disposition of one or two men to scold the South—to discuss irritating topics in an ill-tempered way. . . . The Southern people are our countrymen. They displayed great endurance and courage, great military traits of character during the war. Let us now as soon as possible bring them into good relations with those who fought them. Let us become one people." Thirty years after the war's beginning, its causes were dismissed as "irritating topics." Hayes was not alone in his desire for reconciliation. Even Memorial Day services for the Civil War dead became occasions for preaching reunion. Poetry, much of it bad, written for the occasion featured such themes as mothers weeping over the graves of two sons—one buried in a gray uniform, the other in a blue. As potent a force as the "bloody shirt" may have been, equally potent was the refrain that sectional differences must be suppressed. Even Oliver P. Morton, Republican governor of Indiana during the Civil War, and master of the bloody shirt rhetoric said, "let by-gones be by-gones" on Memorial Day.[5]

Subtle regional differences nevertheless continued in the Midwest. An Eastern traveler commented that Midwesterners were likely to inquire, "How do you like it here in the West?" and to condemn the East as weak and effeminate, exemplifying the sectional stereotypes of the pre–Civil War period.[6] Another editorialist, having entitled a concluding chapter, "The Spirit of the West," argued that the charge that his definition of "folks" bore a Kentucky stamp

> does not distress me a particle, for are not we of Ohio, Indiana, and Illinois first cousins of the people across the Ohio? At once some one will rise to declare that all that is truly noble in the Middle West was derived from the Eastern States or from New England, and on that question I might with a good conscience write a fair brief on either side.[7]

Identification with the West had not ended other regional identifications. But as in the early nineteenth century, loyalty to New England or to the

South were no longer the most important regional identities. Claims to Puritan or Upland Southern ancestry were something in which to take pride, but they did not merit genuine divisiveness within the Midwest. The author would cheerfully "write a fair brief on either side."

As sectional issues ceased to trouble the nation's peace, sectionalism in the Midwest yielded once again to the sense of Westernness. Unlike that of the pre–Civil War period, however, this Westernness would become the dominant regional, and even national, identity. An Englishman contemplating the Midwest after World War II lamented the difficulty of pinpointing what made the Midwest Midwestern, of discerning "how much is more, or less, American; more, or less, peculiar to the Midwest." The twentieth-century novelist Sinclair Lewis began his story of Gopher Prairie, Minnesota, by affirming the cultural homogeneity of the United States. Gopher Prairie's Main Street "is the continuation of Main Streets everywhere. The story would be the same in Ohio or Montana, in Kansas or Kentucky or Illinois, and not very differently would it be told in Up York State or in the Carolina hills." One Midwestern town could be any other Midwestern or American town. The literature of Midwestern authors such as Booth Tarkington and Theodore Dreiser of Indiana, Sherwood Anderson of Ohio, and Edgar Lee Masters of Illinois embodied, so critics argued, the typical Midwestern, and hence American, experience. In the decades after the Civil War, Midwesterners and most Americans came to see the Midwest as a uniquely American region typified by the dominance of the middle class and its business culture. When the sociologists Robert and Helen Lynd sought out the "representative" American city, a city "in that common-denominator of America, the Middle West," they chose Muncie, Indiana.[8]

The political issues of the first half of the nineteenth century had sometimes strengthened and sometimes weakened this growing sense of Westernness. Shared republicanism, shared political partisanship, and shared Westernness had enabled Midwesterners before the Civil War to overcome regional animosities and join forces as Westerners and as Americans. They enabled Midwesterners to do the same when the war was over. The sectional issue of slavery came closest to sundering entirely the Midwest's common bonds. The Midwest emerged from war, as did the country, shaken but intact. Animosities lingered, but enough common ground existed to justify one Upland Southern Midwesterner's hope that a nation conceived in liberty and dedicated to equality could long endure.

NOTES

Introduction

1. Godlove S. Orth to Schuyler Colfax, Aug. 16, 1845, J. Herman Schauinger, ed., "The Letters of Godlove S. Orth, Hoosier Whig," *Indiana Magazine of History,* 39 (Dec. 1943), 365-500, esp. 367; William Oliver, *Eight Months in Illinois* (1843, reprint, Ann Arbor, 1966), 29.

2. Clifford Geertz, *The Interpretation of Cultures* (New York, 1973), 5, 144; George Peter Murdock, "How Culture Changes," in *Man, Culture, and Society,* ed. Harry L. Shapiro (New York, 1960), 247-60.

3. Sidney Verba, "Comparative Political Culture," in *Political Culture and Political Development,* ed. Lucian W. Pye and Sidney Verba (Princeton, 1965), 512-60, esp. 521; Gabriel A. Almond, "Comparative Political Systems," *Journal of Politics,* 18 (Aug. 1956), 391-409, esp. 396.

4. Lucian W. Pye, "Introduction: Political Culture and Political Development," in *Political Culture and Political Development,* ed. Pye and Verba, 3-26, esp. 7. See also Gabriel A. Almond and Sidney Verba, *Civic Culture: Political Attitudes and Democracy in Five Nations* (Princeton, 1963); Gabriel A. Almond, "The Intellectual History of the Civic Culture Concept," in *The Civic Culture Revisited,* ed. Gabriel A. Almond and Sidney Verba (Newbury Park, 1989), 1-36; Walter A. Rosenbaum, *Political Culture* (New York, 1975).

5. Wilbur Zelinsky, "General Cultural and Popular Regions," in *This Remarkable Continent: An Atlas of United States and Canadian Society and Culture,* ed. John F. Rooney, Jr., Wilbur Zelinsky, and Dean R. Louder (College Station, Tex., 1982), 3-24. Frederick Jackson Turner, *The Significance of Sections in American History* (Gloucester, Mass., 1959).

6. Andrew R. L. Cayton and Peter Onuf, *The Midwest and the Nation: Rethinking the History of an American Region* (Bloomington, 1990).

7. John D. Barnhart, *Valley of Democracy: The Frontier versus the Plantation in the Ohio Valley, 1775–1818* (Bloomington, 1953); Richard Lyle Power, *Planting Corn Belt Culture: The Impress of Upland Southerner and Yankee in the Old Northwest* (Indianapolis, 1953); L. C. Rudolph, *Hoosier Zion: The Presbyterians in Early Indiana* (New Haven, 1963); Richard J. Jensen, *Illinois: A Bicentennial History* (New York, 1978).

8. For the ideology of republicanism, see Bernard Bailyn, *The Ideological Origins of the American Revolution* (Cambridge, Mass., 1967); Gordon S. Wood, *The Creation of the American Republic, 1776–1787* (Chapel Hill, 1969); J. G. A. Pocock, *Virtue, Commerce, and History: Essays in Political Thought and History, Chiefly in the Eighteenth Century* (Cambridge, Eng., 1985); Drew R. McCoy, *The Elusive Republic: Political Economy in Jeffersonian America* (Chapel Hill, 1980), 67-69. For parties, see Richard P. McCormick, *The Second American Party System:*

Party Formation in the Jacksonian Era (Chapel Hill, 1966); John Ashworth, *'Agrarians' & 'Aristocrats': Party Political Ideology in the United States, 1837–1846* (London, 1983); Ronald P. Formisano, *The Transformation of Political Culture, 1790s–1840s* (New York, 1983); Joel Silbey, *The Shrine of Party: Congressional Voting Behavior, 1841–1852* (Pittsburgh, 1967); Daniel Walker Howe, *The Political Culture of the American Whigs* (Chicago, 1979); Harry R. Stevens, *The Early Jackson Party in Ohio* (Durham, 1957); Roy F. Nichols, *The Invention of the American Political Parties* (New York, 1957); Jean H. Baker, *Affairs of Party: The Political Culture of Northern Democrats in the Mid-Nineteenth Century* (Ithaca, 1983). See also essays in *The History of American Electoral Behavior,* ed. Joel H. Silbey, Allan G. Bogue, William H. Flanigan (Princeton, 1978); *Essays on American Antebellum Politics, 1840–1860,* ed. Stephen E. Maizlish and John J. Kushma (Arlington, Tex., 1982); *The American Party Systems: Stages of Political Development,* ed. William Nisbet Chambers and Walter Dean Burnham (New York, 1967). For the influence of the idea of the West, see Frederick Jackson Turner, "The Significance of the Frontier in American History," *Proceedings of the Forty-First Annual Meeting of the State Historical Society of Wisconsin* (Madison, 1894), 79-112; and Patricia Nelson Limerick, *The Legacy of Conquest: The Unbroken Past of the American West* (New York, 1987).

1. North and South in the Midwest

1. For works comparing the North and South see Joseph L. Davis, *Sectionalism in American Politics, 1774–1787* (Madison, 1977); David M. Potter, *The Impending Crisis, 1848–1861* (New York, 1976), 9-13, 41-43; Charles A. Beard and Mary R. Beard, *The Rise of American Civilization* (2 vols., New York, 1927), II, 3-51; Avery Craven, *The Coming of the Civil War* (Chicago, 1957); Eugene D. Genovese, *The Political Economy of Slavery: Studies in the Economy & Society of the Slave South* (New York, 1967); Eric Foner, *Free Soil, Free Labor, Free Men: The Ideology of the Republican Party before the Civil War* (New York, 1970); Edward Pessen, "How Different from Each Other Were the Antebellum North and South?" *American Historical Review,* 85 (Dec. 1980), 119-49; Thomas P. Govan, "Was the Old South Different?" *Journal of Southern History,* 21 (Nov. 1955), 447-55; Carl N. Degler, *Place Over Time: The Continuity of Southern Distinctiveness* (Baton Rouge, 1977); William R. Taylor, *Cavalier and Yankee: The Old South and National Character* (Cambridge, 1979); W. J. Cash, *The Mind of the South* (New York, 1965).

2. Richard Lyle Power, *Planting Corn Belt Culture: The Impress of Upland Southerner and Yankee in the Old Northwest* (Indianapolis, 1953); Richard J. Jensen, *Illinois: A Bicentennial History* (New York, 1978). One recent exception to the emphasis on struggle is Andrew R. L. Cayton, "Marietta and the Ohio Company," in *Appalachian Frontiers: Settlement, Society, & Development in the Preindustrial Era,* ed. Robert D. Mitchell (Lexington, 1990), 187-200.

3. U.S. Bureau of the Census, *The Statistical History of the United States: From Colonial Times to the Present* (New York, 1976), 27; U.S. Bureau of the Census, *Mortality Statistics of the Seventh Census of the United States, 1850* (Washington, D.C., 1855), 38-39; Gregory S. Rose, "Hoosier Origins: The Nativity of Indiana's United States–Born Population in 1850," *Indiana Magazine of History,* 81 (Sept. 1985), 201-32, esp. 212.

4. R. Carlyle Buley, *The Old Northwest: Pioneer Period, 1815–1840* (2 vols., Indianapolis, 1950), I, 1-6; Wilbur Zelinsky, "Where the South Begins: The

Northern Limit of the Cis-Appalachian South in Terms of Settlement Landscape," *Social Forces*, 30 (Dec. 1951), 172-78. William T. Utter, *The Frontier State, 1803–1825* (Columbus, 1942); John M. Coggeshall, "Carbon-Copy Towns? The Regionalization of Ethnic Folklife in Southern Illinois's Egypt," in *Sense of Place: American Regional Cultures*, ed. Barbara Allen and Thomas J. Schlereth (Lexington, 1990), 103-19.

5. John Mack Faragher, *Sugar Creek: Life on the Illinois Prairie* (New Haven, 1986), 46. On cultural regions, see Fred Kniffen and Henry Glassie, "Building in Wood in the Eastern United States: A Time-Place Perspective," *Geographical Review*, 56 (Jan. 1966), 40-66; D. W. Meinig, *The Shaping of America: A Geographical Perspective on 500 Years of History*, vol. I: *Atlantic America, 1492–1800* (New Haven, 1986); D. W. Meinig, "The Continuous Shaping of America: A Prospectus for Geographers and Historians," *American Historical Review*, 83 (Dec. 1978), 1186-1205; Wilbur Zelinsky, "General Cultural and Popular Regions," in *This Remarkable Continent: An Atlas of United States and Canadian Society and Culture*, ed. John F. Rooney, Jr., Wilbur Zelinsky, and Dean R. Louder (College Station, Tex., 1982), 3-24, esp. 809; Terry G. Jordan, "Division of the Land," ibid., 54-70; James M. Bergquist, "Tracing the Origins of a Midwestern Culture: The Case of Central Indiana," *Indiana Magazine of History*, 77 (March 1981), 1-32; Henry Glassie, *Pattern in the Material Folk Culture of the Eastern United States* (Philadelphia, 1968); Donald A. Hutslar, *The Architecture of Migration: Log Construction in the Ohio Country, 1750–1850* (Athens, Ohio, 1986); John R. Stilgoe, *Common Landscape of America, 1580–1845* (New Haven, 1982); Wilbur Zelinsky, "Where the South Begins," 172-78; David E. Schob, *Hired Hands and Plowboys: Farm Labor in the Midwest, 1815–60* (Urbana, 1975). For the role of regions in U.S. history, see Frederick Jackson Turner, *The Significance of Sections in American History* (Gloucester, Mass., 1959); Joseph L. Davis, *Sectionalism in American Politics, 1774–1787* (Madison, 1977); Malcolm J. Rohrbough, "Diversity and Unity in the Old Northwest, 1790–1850: Several Peoples Fashion a Single Region," in *Pathways to the Old Northwest: An Observance of the Bicentennial of the Northwest Ordinance* (Indianapolis, 1988), 71-87; Jackson K. Putnam, "The Turner Thesis and the Westward Movement: A Reappraisal," *Western Historical Quarterly*, 7 (Oct. 1976), 377-404; James R. Shortridge, *The Middle West: Its Meaning in American Culture* (Lawrence, 1989); Stanley Elkins and Eric McKitrick, "A Meaning for Turner's Frontier. Part I: Democracy in the Old Northwest," *Political Science Quarterly*, 69 (Sept. 1954), 321-53; Stanley Elkins and Eric McKitrick, "A Meaning for Turner's Frontier. Part II: The Southwest Frontier and New England," ibid. (Dec. 1954), 565-602; Andrew R. L. Cayton, "'Separate Interests' and the Nation-State: The Washington Administration and the Origins of Regionalism in the Trans-Appalachian West," *Journal of American History*, 79 (June 1992), 39-67.

6. John McCardell, *The Idea of a Southern Nation: Southern Nationalists and Southern Nationalism, 1830–1860* (New York, 1979), 13; James B. Finley, *Autobiography of Rev. James B. Finley or, Pioneer Life in the West*, ed. W. P. Strickland (Cincinnati, 1856), 69-70; William R. Taylor, *Cavalier and Yankee: The Old South and American National Character* (Cambridge, Mass., 1979), 21.

7. J. P. Dunn, Jr., *Indiana: A Redemption from Slavery* (Boston, 1905), 453. *Webster's Third New International Dictionary*, 1986, has as its first definition for Hoosier "an ignorant rustic."

8. Warren R. Hofstra, "'A Parcel of Barbarians and an Uncooth Set of People': Settlers and Settlements of the Shenandoah Valley" (presented at the Conference

"George Washington and the Virginia Backcountry," April 21-22, 1989, Shenandoah College, Winchester, Va., copy in Nicole Etcheson's possession), 2, 14, 17-18. Virginia was the second most important source of immigrants to Indiana, after Kentucky, with most coming from the Shenandoah Valley. Southern settlers also came from the north central Piedmont area of North Carolina, the eastern uplands of Tennessee, and the north central part of Maryland where the Shenandoah Valley crosses the state. Gregory S. Rose, "Upland Southerners: The County Origins of Southern Migrants to Indiana by 1850," *Indiana Magazine of History*, 82 (Sept. 1986), 242-63, esp. 253.

9. Everett Dick, *The Dixie Frontier: A Social History of the Southern Frontier from the First Transmontane Beginnings to the Civil War* (New York, 1948), 321-39; W. J. Cash, *The Mind of the South* (New York, 1965), 31-58, 24-25; Grady McWhiney, *Cracker Culture: Celtic Ways in the Old South* (Tuscaloosa, 1988), 268, 253, xiv; Forrest McDonald and Grady McWhiney, "The South from Self-Sufficiency to Peonage: An Interpretation," *American Historical Review*, 85 (Dec. 1980), 1095-1118.

10. Edmund S. Morgan, *American Slavery, American Freedom: The Ordeal of Colonial Virginia* (New York, 1975); William J. Cooper, Jr., *Liberty and Slavery: Southern Politics to 1860* (New York, 1983); J. Mills Thornton, III, *Politics and Power in a Slave Society: Alabama, 1800–1860* (Baton Rouge, 1978); Albert H. Tillson, Jr., *Gentry and Common Folk: Political Culture on a Virginia Frontier, 1740–1789* (Lexington, 1991); Rachel N. Klein, *Unification of a Slave State: The Rise of the Planter Class in the South Carolina Backcountry, 1760–1808* (Chapel Hill, 1990).

For works on Southern nationalism, see William W. Freehling, *The Road to Disunion*, vol. I: *Secessionists at Bay, 1774–1854* (New York, 1990); Steven A. Channing, *Crisis of Fear: Secession in South Carolina* (New York, 1970); William L. Barney, *The Secessionist Impulse: Alabama and Mississippi in 1860* (Princeton, 1974); William Barney, *The Road to Secession: A New Perspective on the Old South* (New York, 1972); William J. Cooper, Jr., *The South and the Politics of Slavery, 1828–1856* (Baton Rouge, 1978); Jesse T. Carpenter, *The South as a Conscious Minority, 1789–1861* (New York, 1930); Clement Eaton, *The Growth of Southern Civilization, 1790–1860* (New York, 1961); John McCardell, *The Idea of a Southern Nation;* Kenneth S. Greenberg, *Masters and Statesmen: The Political Culture of American Slavery* (Baltimore, 1985).

11. William Perkins Cutler and Julia Perkins Cutler, *Life, Journals, and Correspondence of Rev. Manasseh Cutler, LL.D.* (Cincinnati, 1888), II, 399, 404-405. Peter S. Onuf, *Statehood and Union: A History of the Northwest Ordinance* (Bloomington, 1987), 42-43. "Unworthy" settlers were already moving into the Northwest. Some had defied Virginia's prohibition of settlement to come to Illinois during the American Revolution. In 1779, Bellefontaine, Illinois, became the first permanent village of English speakers north of the Ohio River. Clarence Walworth Alvord, *The Illinois Country, 1673–1818* (Chicago, 1965), 359. The Northern states delayed the organization of the Northwest Territory because of their knowledge that Southerners would be most likely to settle the area thus adding to Southern national political power. The Ohio Company's plan helped overcome Northern opposition to the organization. Ibid., 392-95. When the Congress lands were sold, a compromise was worked out whereby alternate townships were "sold entire" (thirty-six square miles) to accommodate the group settlement patterns of New Englanders and "by lots" of a square mile to accommodate the individual family farm favored by the Southerners. Meinig, *The Shaping of America*, I, 357.

12. Ray Allen Billington, *Westward Expansion: A History of the American Frontier* (New York, 1960), 218; Thaddeus Mason Harris, "The Journal of a Tour into the Territory Northwest of the Allegheny Mountains," in *Early Western Travels, 1748–1846*, ed. Reuben Gold Thwaites (Cleveland, 1904), III, 357-58; Beverley W. Bond, Jr., *The Correspondence of John Cleves Symmes, Founder of the Miami Purchase* (New York, 1926), 70-71.

13. Elias Pym Fordham, *Personal Narrative of Travels in Virginia, Maryland, Pennsylvania, Ohio, Indiana, Kentucky; and of a Residence in the Illinois Territory: 1817–1818*, ed. Frederic Austin Ogg (Cleveland, 1906), 223; William Oliver, *Eight Months in Illinois* (1843, reprint, Ann Arbor, 1966), 29; George W. Ogden, "Letters from the West, Comprising a Tour through the Western Country, and a Residence of Two Summers in the States of Ohio and Kentucky," in *Early Western Travels, 1748–1846*, ed. Reuben Gold Thwaites (Cleveland, 1905), XIX, 21-112, esp. 29; Tully R. Wise to John Laird, June 30, 1821, Vallandigham and Laird Family Papers, microfilm, reel 1 (Ohio Historical Society–Western Reserve, Columbus); *Supporter, and Scioto Gazette,* Aug. 5, 1824.

14. Wm. A. Trimble to John A. Trimble, Feb. 8, 1830, folder 2, box 1, John A. Trimble Papers (Ohio Historical Society, Columbus).

15. *Chicago Democrat,* July 16, 1834; *Scioto Gazette,* March 23, 1836; (Kaskaskia, Illinois) *Kaskaskia Republican,* April 6, 1824.

16. *Daily Chicago American,* Oct. 23, 1839.

17. *Scioto Gazette and Independent Whig,* April 23, 1834; Stephen A. Douglas to Julius N. Granger, in *The Letters of Stephen A. Douglas,* ed. Robert W. Johannsen (Urbana, 1961), 12; Rose, "Hoosier Origins," 231.

18. Rev. Wm. M. Daily to John G. Davis, Nov. 29, 1852, box 1, John Givan Davis Papers (Indiana Historical Society, Indianapolis).

19. Elisha M. Huntington to John Tipton, Jan. 11, 1834, *John Tipton Papers,* comp. and ed. Robertson and Riker, III, 10.

20. (Cincinnati) *Western Spy,* Nov. 28, July 4, July 11, 1817.

21. *Kaskaskia Republican,* Dec. 14, 1824. On Westernness, see R. Carlyle Buley, *The Old Northwest: Pioneer Period, 1815–1840* (2 vols., Indianapolis, 1950), I, 358-94; Power, *Planting Cornbelt Culture;* Arthur K. Moore, *The Frontier Mind: A Cultural Analysis of the Kentucky Frontiersman* (Lexington, 1957); Henry Nash Smith, *Virgin Land: The American West as Symbol and Myth* (New York, 1950).

22. (Springfield) *Illinois State Register,* Jan. 23, Jan. 30, Feb. 13, Feb. 20, 1846, Oct. 4, 1849.

23. Godlove S. Orth to Schuyler Colfax, Aug. 16, 1845, J. Herman Schauinger, ed., "The Letters of Godlove S. Orth, Hoosier Whig," *Indiana Magazine of History,* 39 (Dec. 1943), 365-400, esp. 367.

24. Howard Johnson, "At Home in the Woods: Oliver Johnson's Reminiscences of Early Marion County," *Indiana History Society Publications,* vol. XVI, no. 2 (Indianapolis, 1951), 135-234, esp. 226-27.

25. For the political history of the region, see R. Carlyle Buley, *The Old Northwest: Pioneer Period, 1815–1840* (2 vols., Indianapolis, 1950); Andrew R. L. Cayton, *The Frontier Republic: Ideology and Politics in the Ohio Country, 1780–1825* (Kent, 1986); Jeffrey P. Brown and Andrew R. L. Cayton, eds., *The Pursuit of Public Power: Political Culture in Ohio, 1787–1861* (Kent, 1994); James H. Madison, *The Indiana Way: A State History* (Bloomington, 1986); Theodore Calvin Pease, *The Frontier State, 1818–1848* (Chicago, 1922). See also Svend Peterson, *A Statistical History of the American Presidential Election*

(Westport, 1981), 128-29, 149, and Roy R. Glashan, *American Governors and Gubernatorial Elections* (Westport, 1979).

26. William P. Bryant to John G. Davis, July 19, 1854, box 2, Davis Papers; Richard Lyle Power, "The Hoosier as an American Folk-Type," *Indiana Magazine of History,* 38 (June 1942), 107-22, esp. 109; (Springfield) *Illinois Daily Journal,* Feb. 28, 1852, June 3, 1853, March 4, 1850. See also Foner, *Free Soil, Free Labor, Free Men,* 48-50.

27. *Report of the Debates and Proceedings of the Convention for the Revision of the Constitution of the State of Ohio, 1850–1851,* (2 vols., Columbus, 1851), II, 157.

28. Robert W. Johannsen, ed., *The Lincoln-Douglas Debates of 1858* (New York, 1965), 152.

29. Geo. Hawk to Alexander S. Boys, June 26, 1854, folder 4, box 1, Alexander S. Boys Papers (Ohio Historical Society, Columbus); Roy P. Basler, ed., *The Collected Works of Abraham Lincoln* (8 vols., New Brunswick, 1953), III, 396.

30. Frances Wright, *Views of Society and Manners in America,* ed. Paul R. Baker (Cambridge, Mass., 1963), 199.

2. Statehood

1. William Henry Smith, *The St. Clair Papers* (2 vols., Cincinnati, 1882), II, 588.

2. D. W. Meinig refers to this problem as the United States' "democratic dilemma," i.e., keeping government local and responsive to the people and yet aware of national needs. D. W. Meinig, *The Shaping of America: A Geographical Perspective on 500 Years of History,* vol. I: *Atlantic America, 1492–1800* (New Haven, 1986), 415-16. Peter S. Onuf, *Statehood and Union: A History of the Northwest Ordinance* (Bloomington, 1987), 4-7.

3. Acting Governor Sargent to Secretary of State, January 20, 1797, Clarence Edwin Carter, ed., *The Territorial Papers of the United States,* vol. II: *The Territory Northwest of the River Ohio, 1787–1803* (Washington, 1934), 587; Acting Governor Sargent to Secretary of State, August 14, 1797, ibid., 622.

4. Governor St. Clair to James Ross, Dec. 1799, Smith, *St. Clair Papers,* II, 482.

5. Beverley W. Bond, Jr., *The Foundations of Ohio* (Columbus, 1941), 406. Outsiders continued to rail against the tendency of Upland Southern Midwesterners to take justice into their own hands in later incidents, including the Massac County War in Illinois, when Regulators drove accused criminals out of the county, and the anti-Mormon violence in the same state. (Springfield) *Illinois State Register,* Sept. 18, 1846, Jan. 22, 1847, Nov. 6, Nov. 13, 1846.

6. Jeffrey Paul Brown, "Frontier Politics: The Evolution of a Political Society in Ohio, 1788–1814" (Ph.D. diss., University of Illinois, Urbana-Champaign, 1979), 54-55; Randolph Chandler Downes, *Frontier Ohio, 1788–1803* (Columbus, 1935), 142; Morris Birkbeck, *Letters from Illinois* (London, 1818, reprint, 1968), 97, 98.

7. Governor St. Clair to James Ross, Jan. 15, 1802, Smith, *St. Clair Papers,* II, 556. For other descriptions of the Chillicothe riot, see Beverley W. Bond, Jr., *The Civilization of the Old Northwest: A Study of Political, Social, and Economic Development, 1788–1812* (New York, 1934), 112-14; and Andrew R. L. Cayton, *The Frontier Republic: Ideology and Politics in the Ohio Country, 1780–1825* (Kent, 1986), 74.

8. *Western Spy and Hamilton Gazette,* July 24, 1802; (Vincennes) *Western Sun,* July 23, 1808. Some settlers did not chafe under territorial government, of course. St. Clair praised the New Englanders of Marietta for their love of liberty and "order." To them he could speak of the benefit of "wholesome and equal laws" to restrain "the passions of men," give their actions "proper direction" and perfect the "beautiful fabric of civilized life." Governor St. Clair's address at Marietta, July 1788, Smith, *St. Clair Papers,* II, 54. But the idea that the territorial government created by the Northwest Ordinance was a "necessary inducement to potential settlers" applied only to those settlers Congress wished to attract, New Englanders, not the "lawless banditti" of the South. Onuf, *Statehood and Union,* 58-59. (Vincennes) *Western Sun,* May 15, 1802.

9. Downes, *Frontier Ohio,* 128; Bond, *Civilization of the Old Northwest,* 56-57; John D. Barnhart, *Valley of Democracy: The Frontier versus the Plantation in the Ohio Valley, 1775–1818* (Bloomington, 1953), 4, 159. Andrew R. L. Cayton, "The Origins of Politics in the Old Northwest," in *Pathways to the Old Northwest: An Observance of the Bicentennial of the Northwest Ordinance* (Indianapolis, 1988), 59-69, esp. 65-66; Cayton, *Frontier Republic,* x-xi, 56-57, 82-83, 105-107; Andrew R. L. Cayton, "Land, Power, and Reputation: The Cultural Dimensions of Politics in the Ohio Country," *William and Mary Quarterly,* 47 (April 1990), 266-86. On the violence of political rhetoric, see John R. Howe, "Republican Thought and the Political Violence of the 1790s," *American Quarterly,* 19 (Summer 1967), 147-65; Lance Banning, *The Jeffersonian Persuasion: Evolution of a Party Ideology* (Ithaca, 1978), 17-18.

10. Ralph A. Wooster, *Politicians, Planters and Plain Folk: Courthouse and Statehouse in the Upper South, 1850–1860* (Knoxville, 1975).

11. Governor St. Clair to Oliver Wolcott, n.d., 1795, Smith, *St. Clair Papers,* II, 382-83; Bond, *Civilization of the Old Northwest,* 99-102; Ray Allen Billington, *Westward Expansion: A History of the American Frontier* (New York, 1960), 265-66; William Henry Harrison to Thomas Worthington, Jan. 22, 1802, William Henry Harrison Collection (Indiana Historical Society, Indianapolis); Onuf, *Statehood and Union,* 69-72, 91-92; Sears, *Thomas Worthington,* 57; *Western Spy and Hamilton Gazette,* July 9, 1800.

12. *Scioto Gazette,* June 12, 1802; William Goforth to President Jefferson, Jan. 5, 1802, Clarence Edwin Carter, comp. and ed., *The Territorial Papers of the United States,* vol. III: *The Territory Northwest of the River Ohio, 1787–1803 Continued* (Washington, 1934), 199.

13. *Scioto Gazette,* Feb. 12, 1801; Malcolm J. Rohrbough, *The Trans-Appalachian Frontier: People, Societies, and Institutions, 1775–1850* (New York, 1978), 383; William Goforth to President Jefferson, Jan. 5, 1802, Carter, comp. and ed., *Territorial Papers of the United States,* III, 198; Memorial to Congress from the Legislative Assembly, referred Feb. 14, 1816, Clarence Edwin Carter, comp. and ed., *The Territorial Papers of the United States,* vol. XVII: *The Territory of Illinois, 1814–1818 Continued* (Washington, 1950), 285-86; Address to Congress by Citizens of Jefferson County, Dec. 27, 1811, ibid., VIII, 154-55; Michael Baldwin to Thomas Worthington, April 2, 1802, quoted in Sears, *Thomas Worthington,* 86.

14. Thomas Worthington to Secretary of Treasury, Oct. 29, 1801, Carter, comp. and ed., *Territorial Papers of the United States,* III, 184; Thomas Worthington to Nathaniel Massie, March 5, 1802, Daniel Meade Massie, *Nathaniel Massie, A Pioneer of Ohio: A Sketch of His Life and Selections from His Correspondence* (Cincinnati, 1896), 201; Thomas Worthington to President Jefferson, Feb. 20, 1802, Carter, comp. and ed., *Territorial Papers of the United*

States, III, 212-13; Thomas Worthington to Nathaniel Macon, July 23, 1802 quoted in Sears, *Thomas Worthington,* 88.

15. Judge Symmes to President Jefferson, Jan. 23, 1802, Carter, comp. and ed., *Territorial Papers of the United States,* III, 205-206; Nathaniel Massie to James Madison, n.d., Massie, *Nathaniel Massie,* 184-87; Sears, *Thomas Worthington,* 50-52, 65-68, 64, 73-77; Bond, *Civilization of the Old Northwest,* 111-12, 114.

16. Abel Westfall to the Secretary of State, Dec. 15, 1807, Clarence Edwin Carter, comp. and ed., *The Territorial Papers of the United States,* vol. VII: *The Territory of Indiana, 1800–1810* (Washington, D.C., 1939), 500-502.

17. Petition to Congress by the People of the Illinois Country, referred April 6, 1808, ibid., 545-50; Jack Ericson Eblen, *The First and Second United States Empires: Governors and Territorial Government, 1784–1912* (Pittsburgh, 1968), 61-63.

18. James H. Madison, *The Indiana Way: A State History* (Bloomington, 1986), 46-50; John D. Barnhart and Donald F. Carmony, *Indiana from Frontier to Industrial Commonwealth* (4 vols., New York, 1954), I, 97-119; Logan Esarey, *A History of Indiana from Its Exploration to 1850* (Indianapolis, 1970), 126-80; Nathaniel Ewing to Secretary of the Treasury, June 26, 1810, Carter, comp. and ed., *Territorial Papers of the United States,* VIII, 25-26; Elias McNamee to the President of the Senate, Dec. 12, 1809, ibid., VII, 682-86; Jonathan Jennings to William Duane, Dec. 1809, in "Unedited Letters of Jonathan Jennings," *Indiana Historical Society Publications* (Indianapolis, 1933), X, 147-278, esp. 170-72; Secretary of the Treasury to the President, April 27, 1808, Carter, comp. and ed., *Territorial Papers of the United States,* VII, 562-63. Jonathan Jennings to David G. Mitchell, Jan. 16, 1820, "Unedited Letters of Jonathan Jennings," 172-74; Jonathan Jennings to John K. Graham, Jan. 16, 1811, box 1, John Kennedy Graham Papers (Indiana Historical Society, Indianapolis); Jo. Jennings to John K. Graham, Dec. 11, 1810, ibid.; Jonathan Jennings to John K. Graham, Jan. 16, 1812, ibid.

19. Petition to Congress by Citizens of Indiana Territory, referred Dec. 11, 1811, Carter, comp. and ed., *Territorial Papers of the United States,* VIII, 144; Jonathan Jennings to William Duane, Dec. 1809, "Unedited Letters of Jonathan Jennings," 170-72.

20. William Henry Harrison to Albert Gallatin, Aug. 30, 1809, Harrison Collection.

21. Petition to the President and Senate by Citizens of Harrison County, January 1810, Carter, comp. and ed., *Territorial Papers of the United States,* VII, 710-11; (Vincennes) *Western Sun,* June 1, 1816; Gov. Harrison to Sec. of State, Dec. 28, 1812, Carter, comp. and ed., *Territorial Papers of the United States,* VIII, 228; *Richmond* (Indiana) *Palladium,* Jan. 9, 1836; William Henry Harrison to Col. Thomas Worthington, Sept. 11, 1801, Harrison Collection; William Henry Harrison to W. G. Nicholas, Nov. 21, 1809, ibid.

22. Petition to Congress by Citizens of the [Illinois] Territory, n.d., 1812, Carter, comp. and ed., *Territorial Papers of the United States,* XVI, 205-207; Gov. Edwards to Richard M. Johnson, March 4, 1812, ibid., 199-202.

23. Frederic L. Paxson, *History of the American Frontier, 1763–1893* (Boston, 1924), 127; William T. Utter, *The Frontier State, 1803–1825* (Columbus, 1942), 15; Cayton, "Origins of Politics in the Old Northwest," 63-64; John D. Barnhart, "The Southern Influence in the Formation of Indiana," *Indiana Magazine of History,* 33 (Sept. 1937), 261-76, esp. 274; Daniel J. Elazar, *Cities of the Prairie: The Metropolitan Frontier and American Politics* (New York, 1970), 286-88; Isaac Franklin Patterson, *The Constitutions of Ohio* (Cleveland, 1912), 73-97;

Charles Kettleborough, *Constitution Making in Indiana: A Source Book of Constitutional Documents with Historical Introduction and Critical Notes*, vol. I: *1780–1851* (Indianapolis, 1971), 83-125; Emil Joseph Verlie, ed., "Illinois Constitutions," *Collections of the Illinois State Historical Library* (Springfield, 1919), XIII, 25-47; R. Carlyle Buley, *The Old Northwest: Pioneer Period, 1815–1840* (2 vols., Indianapolis, 1950), I, 79-80, 88, 90, 73.

3. Manliness

1. Roy P. Basler, ed., *The Collected Works of Abraham Lincoln* (8 vols., New Brunswick, 1953), I, 108-16, esp. 109.

2. *Western Spy and Hamilton Gazette*, July 16, 1800; *Richmond Indiana Palladium*, Sept. 30, 1837; *Richmond* (Ind.) *Public Leger*, April 16, 1825; *Scioto Gazette and Fredonian Chronicle*, Sept. 7, 1815.

3. Bertram Wyatt-Brown, *Southern Honor: Ethics and Behavior in the Old South* (New York, 1982), 34, 138; David D. Gilmore, *Manhood in the Making: Cultural Concepts of Masculinity* (New Haven, 1990), 12, 17, 110-16, 222-29. For the experience of Northern middle-class males, see E. Anthony Rotundo, *American Manhood: Transformations in Masculinity from the Revolution to the Modern Era* (New York, 1993); Mark C. Carnes, *Secret Ritual and Manhood in Victorian America* (New Haven, 1989); Mark Gerzon, *A Choice of Heroes: The Changing Faces of American Manhood* (Boston, 1992); and the essays in *Meanings for Manhood: Constructions of Masculinity in Victorian America*, ed. Mark C. Carnes and Clyde Griffen (Chicago, 1990). See also Peter N. Stearns, *Be a Man! Males in Modern Society* (New York, 1979); David Leverenz, *Manhood and the American Renaissance* (Ithaca, 1989); and Ted Ownby, *Subduing Satan: Religion, Recreation, and Manhood in the Rural South, 1865–1920* (Chapel Hill, 1990).

4. Julian Pitt-Rivers, "Honor," David L. Sills, ed., *International Encyclopedia of the Social Sciences* (New York, 1968), VI, 503-11, esp. 506; Wyatt-Brown, *Southern Honor*, 14; Clement Eaton, "The Role of Honor in Southern Society," *Southern Humanities Review*, 10 (Bicentennial Issue, 1976), 47-58. Honor in other cultures is also a matter of reputation. See Julian Pitt-Rivers, "Honour and Social Status," in *Honour and Shame: The Values of Mediterranean Society*, ed. J. G. Peristiany (Chicago, 1966), 19-77. John Tipton to Spear S. Tipton, Jan. 24, 1833, Nellie Armstrong Robertson and Dorothy Riker, comp. and ed., *The John Tipton Papers*, vol. II: *1828–1833* (Indianapolis, 1942), 790; John Tipton to Citizens of Harrison County, Aug. 3, 1821, Glen A. Blackburn, comp., *The John Tipton Papers*, vol. I: *1809–1827* (Indianapolis, 1942), 290-91; John Tipton to Editors of Indiana Gazette, Aug. 9, 1821, ibid., 291-92.

5. (Chillicothe) *Supporter*, Oct. 1, 1816; Robert W. Johannsen, ed., *The Lincoln-Douglas Debates of 1858* (New York, 1965), 42. Douglas recounted all this in the northern Illinois town of Ottawa, where emphasizing Lincoln's roots in southern Indiana and Illinois may have had a negative effect on the audience.

6. Peter Cartwright, *Autobiography of Peter Cartwright* (New York, 1956), 177-78.

7. Edward L. Ayers, *Vengeance and Justice: Crime and Punishment in the 19th-Century American South* (New York, 1984), 13-14; Pitt-Rivers, "Honour and Social Status," 29, 31; Elliott J. Gorn, "'Gouge and Bite, Pull Hair and Scratch': The Social Significance of Fighting in the Southern Backcountry," *American Historical Review*, 90 (Feb. 1985), 18-43; Grady McWhiney, "Ethnic Roots of

Southern Violence," in *A Master's Due: Essays in Honor of David Herbert Donald*, ed. William J. Cooper, Jr., Michael F. Holt, and John McCardell (Baton Rouge, 1985), 112-37; Jack Kenny Williams, *Vogues in Villainy: Crime and Retribution in Ante-Bellum South Carolina* (Columbia, 1959); Jack K. Williams, *Dueling in the Old South: Vignettes of Social History* (College Station, Tex., 1980); Raymond D. Gastil, "Homicide and a Regional Culture of Violence," *American Sociological Review*, 36 (June 1971), 412-27; Dickson D. Bruce, Jr., *Violence and Culture in the Antebellum South* (Austin, 1979); John Hope Franklin, *The Militant South, 1800–1861* (Cambridge, Mass., 1956); John Shelton Reed, *One South: An Ethnic Approach to Regional Culture* (Baton Rouge, 1982), 139-53; Sheldon Hackney, "Southern Violence," *American Historical Review*, 74 (Feb. 1969), 906-25. F. Cuming, "Sketches of a Tour to the Western Country, through the States of Ohio and Kentucky; a Voyage down the Ohio and Mississippi Rivers and a Trip through the Mississippi Territory, and Part of West Florida," in *Early Western Travels, 1748–1846*, ed. Reuben Gold Thwaites (Cleveland, 1904), IV, 137.

8. *Alton Spectator*, Nov. 20, 1832.

9. A. Lincoln to John T. Stuart, March 1, 1840, Basler, ed., *Collected Works of Abraham Lincoln*, I, 206; Abraham Lincoln to Elias H. Merryman, Sept. 19, 1842, ibid., 300-302; Lincoln to Joshua F. Speed, Oct. 5, 1842, ibid., 302-303.

10. *Belleville* (Illinois) *Advocate*, Aug. 22, 1840; *Alton Telegraph & Democratic Review*, June 12, 1841; *Belleville* (Illinois) *Advocate*, July 18, 1840; D. S. Gooding to John G. Davis, April 16, 1858, box 4, John Givan Davis Papers (Indiana Historical Society, Indianapolis); Robert Reddish to John G. Davis, April 3, 1858, ibid.; (Springfield) *Illinois Register*, July 14, 1843.

11. *Report of the Debates and Proceedings of the Convention for the Revision of the Constitution of the State of Ohio, 1850–1851* (2 vols., Columbus, 1851), II, 114; Basler, ed., *Collected Works of Abraham Lincoln*, II, 365; *Scioto Gazette*, June 12, 1802, April 4, 1808.

12. (Connersville, Indiana) *Fayette Observer*, July 28, 1827; (Jacksonville) *Illinois Patriot*, July 26, 1834.

13. "Communication to the Readers of *The Old Soldier*," Feb. 28, 1840, Basler, ed., *Collected Works of Abraham Lincoln*, I, 203-205; (Indianapolis) *Indiana State Journal*, July 18, 1849.

14. *Richmond* (Indiana) *Palladium*, July 4, 1848; *Indiana Daily State Sentinel*, Sept. 20, 1859; Speech at Springfield, Illinois, July 17, 1858, Basler, ed., *Collected Works of Abraham Lincoln*, II, 513.

15. (Vincennes) *Western Sun*, Feb. 9, 1808; Richard L. Bushman and Claudia L. Bushman, "The Early History of Cleanliness in America," *Journal of American History*, 74 (March 1988), 1213-38; Stow Persons, *The Decline of American Gentility* (New York, 1973); John F. Kasson, *Rudeness & Civility: Manners in Nineteenth-Century Urban America* (New York, 1990); Edwin Harrison Cady, *The Gentleman in America: A Literary Study in American Culture* (Syracuse, 1949); John Fraser, *America and the Patterns of Chivalry* (Cambridge, Eng., 1982); Norbert Elias, *The Civilizing Process: A History of Manners*, trans. Edmund Jephcott (New York, 1978). (Springfield) *Illinois Register*, July 30, 1841; *Richmond* (Indiana) *Palladium*, Oct. 9, 1856; *Decatur* (Illinois) *Daily Chronicle*, Sept. 25, 1856; David Davis to William H. Seward, March 29, 1861, folder A-31, drawer 1, case 4, David Davis Family Papers (Illinois State Historical Library, Springfield); (Chillicothe) *Supporter*, Aug. 4, 1810.

16. Thomas Corwin to Ballard Preston, n.d., VFM 391 (Ohio Historical Society, Columbus); Richard Yates to David Davis, May 21, 1849, folder A-14,

drawer 1, case 4, Davis Family Papers; David Davis to Julius Rockwell, May 28, 1850, folder A-16, ibid.; *Alton Weekly Courier,* Oct. 21, 1858; A. Lincoln to Thomas Ewing, May 20, 1849, Basler, ed., *Collected Works of Abraham Lincoln,* II, 47.

17. Logan Esarey, "The Pioneers of Morgan County, Memoirs of Noah J. Major," *Indiana Historical Society Publications* (Indianapolis, 1915), vol. V, no. 5, 225-516, esp. 360; Stephen B. Oates, *With Malice Toward None: The Life of Abraham Lincoln* (New York, 1978), 28.

18. Roger H. Van Bolt, "The Hoosier Politician of the 1840's," *Indiana Magazine of History,* 48 (March 1952), 23-36, esp. 23; Thomas D. Clark, *The Rampaging Frontier: Manners and Humors of Pioneer Days in the South and the Middle West* (Indianapolis, 1939), 127-28.

19. (Lawrenceburg, Indiana) *Oracle,* March 32, 1822; *Belleville Advocate,* July 9, 1846; Frederic L. Paxson, *History of the American Frontier, 1763–1893* (Boston, 1924), 195; *Report of the Debates and Proceedings of the Convention for the Revision of the Constitution of the State of Ohio, 1850–51,* II, 179.

20. *Belleville* (Illinois) *Advocate,* July 18, 1840; *Daily Chicago American,* May 22, 1840.

21. (Springfield) *Illinois Daily Journal,* April 23, 1849; *Western Spy and Hamilton Gazette,* May 13, 1801; Stephen A. Douglas to Gehazi Granger, Nov. 9, 1835, Robert W. Johannsen, ed., *The Letters of Stephen A. Douglas* (Urbana, 1961), 21; (Vandalia) *Illinois State Register and People's Advocate,* July 22, 1836.

22. *Chicago Democrat,* Jan. 21, 1834; *Chicago Daily Journal,* June 15, 1846; *Indiana Daily State Sentinel,* Aug. 2, 1858.

4. Interest

1. Thomas A. Flinn, "Continuity and Change in Ohio Politics," *Journal of Politics,* 24 (Aug. 1962), 521-44, esp. 525; Walter Dean Burnham, *Presidential Ballots, 1836–1892* (Baltimore, 1955), 176-80, 208-10; Charles Grier Sellers, Jr., "Who Were the Southern Whigs?" *American Historical Review,* 59 (Jan. 1954), 335-46; Thomas B. Alexander, "The Dimensions of Voter Partisan Constancy in Presidential Elections from 1840 to 1860," in *Essays on American Antebellum Politics, 1840–1860,* ed. Stephen E. Maizlish and John J. Kushma (Arlington, Tex., 1982), 70-121, esp. 75-76; John Davis to J. A. Wright, July 13, 1844, box 1, John Givan Davis Papers (Indiana Historical Society, Indianapolis).

2. *Chicago Democrat,* March 18, 1834, Dec. 17, 1833; *Chicago American,* July 18, Aug. 1, 1835, March 12, 1836.

3. *Western Spy and Hamilton Gazette,* July 9, 1800; (Springfield) *Illinois Register,* Dec. 3, 1841; (Vincennes) *Western Sun,* July 14, 1810, April 22, 1809; (Vincennes) *Indiana Gazette,* Aug. 21, [1804].

4. (Springfield) *Illinois State Register,* Nov. 23, 1839; John McLean to John Wallace, May 7, 1823, box 1, Wallace-Dickey Family Papers (Illinois State Historical Library, Springfield).

5. *Belleville Advocate,* June 13, 1840.

6. Jennings to His Constituents in *Western Clarion,* June 19, 1822, "Unedited Letters of Jonathan Jennings," in *Indiana Historical Society Publications* (Indianapolis, 1933), X, 147-278, esp. 232-33; William Henry Harrison to [torn], Nov. 9, 1835, M364, William Henry Harrison Collection (Indiana Historical Society, Indianapolis).

7. W. E. Little, to Sidney Breese, Feb. 12, 1848, box 1, Sidney Breese Papers (Illinois State Historical Library, Springfield); B. B. Hamilton to Richard Yates, April 17, 1854, box 1, Richard Yates Papers (Illinois State Historical Library, Springfield).

8. Samuel Milroy to John Tipton, Dec. 28, 1831, Nellie Armstrong Robertson and Dorothy Riker, comp. and ed., *The John Tipton Papers*, vol. II: *1828–1833* (Indianapolis, 1942), 483-85; David Davis to Julius Rockwell, April 24, 1849, folder A-13, drawer 1, case 4, David Davis Family Papers (Illinois State Historical Library, Springfield).

9. Isaac Trimble to John A. Trimble, April 5, 1830, folder 2, box 1, John A. Trimble Papers (Ohio Historical Society, Columbus).

10. William E. Gienapp, *The Origins of the Republican Party, 1852–1856* (New York, 1987), 6-7. Quoted in Joel H. Silbey, *A Respectable Minority: The Democratic Party in the Civil War Era, 1860–1868* (New York, 1977), 8. Joel H. Silbey, *The Shrine of Party: Congressional Voting Behavior, 1841-1852* (Pittsburgh, 1967); David J. Russo, "The Major Political Issues of the Jacksonian Period and the Development of Party Loyalty in Congress, 1830–1840," *Transactions of the American Philosophical Society*, 62 (May 1972), 1-51; Thomas B. Alexander, *Sectional Stress and Party Strength: A Study of Roll-Call Voting Patterns in the United States House of Representatives, 1836–1860* (Nashville, 1967). Richard P. McCormick, *The Second American Party System: Party Formation in the Jacksonian Era* (Chapel Hill, 1966), 4; Roy F. Nichols, *The Invention of the American Political Parties* (New York, 1967); Richard Hofstadter, *The Idea of a Party System: The Rise of Legitimate Opposition in the United States, 1780–1840* (Berkeley, 1959); Ronald P. Formisano, "Political Character, Antipartyism and the Second Party System," *American Quarterly*, 21 (Winter 1969), 683-709, esp. 686. John Michael Rozett, "The Social Bases of Party Conflict in the Age of Jackson: Individual Voting Behavior in Greene County, Illinois, 1838–1848 (Ph.D. diss., University of Michigan, 1974), 38; Ronald P. Formisano, "Deferential-Participant Politics: The Early Republic's Political Culture, 1789–1840," *American Political Science Review*, 68 (June 1974), 473-87; Herbert Ershkowitz and William G. Shade, "Consensus or Conflict? Political Behavior in the State Legislatures during the Jacksonian Era," *Journal of American History*, 58 (Dec. 1971), 591-621.

11. Noah Noble to John Tipton, Oct. 15, 1830, Robertson and Riker, comp. and ed., *John Tipton Papers*, II, 355-56; John Tipton to Calvin Fletcher, April 28, 1831, ibid., 406; Roy P. Basler, ed., *The Collected Works of Abraham Lincoln* (8 vols., New Brunswick, 1953), I, 21-22.

12. Richard Yates to Thomas Marshall, Jan. 18, 1860, microfilm, Richard Yates Correspondence (Illinois State Historical Library, Springfield).

13. (Kaskaskia) *Illinois Reporter*, Aug. 7, 1826.

14. (Chillicothe) *Supporter*, Aug. 4, 1810; (Indianapolis) *Indiana Journal*, June 28, 1825.

15. John Tipton to the People of the Representative District Composed of Harrison, and Part of Floyd and Crawford Counties, May 17, 1820, Glen A. Blackburn, comp., *The John Tipton Papers*, vol. I: *1809–1827* (Indianapolis, 1942), 194-95; John Tipton to Noah Noble, Jan. 14, 1838, Robertson and Riker, comp. and ed., *John Tipton Papers*, III, 504; "Voter" to Voters of Indiana, Nov. 1833, ibid., II, 849-50; John Tipton to Calvin Fletcher, Jan. 18, 1832, ibid., 508-10; Lucius H. Scott to John Tipton, Dec. 15, 1831, ibid., 465.

16. *Daily Chicago American*, July 17, 1840, March 26, 1836; John Dowling to John G. Davis, Aug. 4, 1855, box 3, Davis Papers.

17. (Vandalia) *Illinois State Register and People's Advocate,* March 29, 1839; (Cincinnati) *Western Spy,* Oct. 10, 1818, Oct. 9, 1813.

18. Frederick Grimke, *The Nature and Tendency of Free Institutions* (Cambridge, Mass., 1968), 177-88, esp. 173.

19. Edward Pessen, *Jacksonian America: Society, Personality, and Politics* (Urbana, 1985), esp. 197, 327; James Stanton Chase, "Jacksonian Democracy and the Rise of the Nominating Convention," *Mid-America,* 45 (Oct. 1963), 229-49, esp. 230-31; John Reynolds, *My Own Times: Embracing Also the History of My Life* (Chicago, 1879), 304-305; (Springfield) *Illinois Register,* June 9, 1843.

20. *Belleville* (Illinois) *Advocate,* April 13, 1843; To the Democratic Republicans of Illinois, Dec. 31, 1835, in *Letters of Stephen A. Douglas,* ed. Johannsen, 25; (Vandalia) *Illinois Advocate,* Oct. 14, 1835.

21. Ibid., June 3, Dec. 9, Nov. 11, 1835, Feb. 17, 1836; (Springfield) *Illinois State Register,* June 25, 1841.

22. (Springfield) *Illinois Register,* May 12, 1843, Sept. 8, 1848.

23. *Indiana Daily State Sentinel,* Aug. 4, 1860.

24. *Alton Telegraph & Democratic Review,* June 12, 1841.

25. Rollin C. Dewey to J. K. Graham, Sept. 28, 1825, box 1, John Kennedy Graham Papers (Indiana Historical Society, Indianapolis); Ing. L. Robinson to Wm. H. English, Nov. 2, 1842, folder 3, box 1, William H. English Collection (Indiana Historical Society, Indianapolis).

26. Alex Dunnington to John G. Davis, Dec. 31, 1852, Davis Papers.

27. J. N. McNamar to John G. Davis, Feb. 11, 1858, box 4, ibid.

28. *Belleville* (Illinois) *Advocate,* July 10, 1841; Thomas Corwin to Anson Burlingame, Aug. 21, 1848, VFM 391 (Ohio Historical Society, Columbus); *Indiana Daily State Sentinel,* July 9, 1860.

29. S. A. Douglas to Dean Richmond, June 22, 1860, in *Letters of Stephen A. Douglas,* ed. Johannsen, 493.

30. J. B. Otey to John G. Davis, Feb. 7, 1858, box 4, Davis Papers.

31. Ohio differs greatly from Indiana and Illinois for the simple reason that its first public works were begun earlier, were completed, and did bring a large degree of prosperity to the state. Harry N. Scheiber, *Ohio Canal Era: A Case Study of Government and the Economy, 1820–1861* (Athens, Ohio, 1969), 52, 156-57. See also Carter Goodrich, *Government Promotion of American Canals and Railroads, 1800–1890* (New York, 1960); Ralph D. Gray, "The Canal Era in Indiana," in *Transportation and the Early Nation: Papers Presented at an Indiana American Revolution Bicentennial Symposium* (Indianapolis, 1982), 113-34; and Ronald E. Shaw, "The Canal Era in the Old Northwest," ibid., 89-112.

32. *Scioto Gazette, and Fredonian Chronicle,* Jan. 7, 1820.

33. *Supporter, and Scioto Gazette,* July 12, 1823, April 8, April 9, 1850.

34. Edward Coles to James B. Ray, May 25, 1825, Evarts Boutell Greene and Clarence Walworth Alvord, "The Governors' Letter-Books, 1818–1834," *Collections of the Illinois State Historical Library* (Springfield, 1909), IV, 86.

35. (Indianapolis) *Indiana Journal,* July 31, 1827.

36. Ibid., Sept. 5, 1826.

37. Jonathan Jennings to His Constituents, April 16, 1829, "Unedited Letters of Jonathan Jennings," *Indiana Historical Society Publications* (Indianapolis, 1933), X, 147-278, esp. 268-70; *Report of the Debates and Proceedings of the Convention for the Revision of the Constitution of the State of Ohio, 1850–51* (2 vols., Columbus, 1851), II, 120.

38. *Indiana State Journal,* Jan. 31, 1828.

39. (Indianapolis) *Indiana Journal,* April 3, 1828.

40. Ibid., July 7, 1830.

41. Governor's Message, ibid., Dec. 7, July 20, 1839.

42. (Springfield) *Illinois State Register,* March 6, 1846.

43. *Annals of Congress,* 14 Cong., 2 sess., pp. 934, 190-91, 1062; ibid., 17 Cong., 1 sess., pp. 1734, 1874–75; ibid., 18 Cong. 1 sess., pp. 1468-69.

44. (Jacksonville) *Illinois Patriot,* July 12, 1834; Theodore Calvin Pease, *The Story of Illinois* (Chicago, 1925), 180; (Springfield) *Daily Register,* Jan. 3, 1849.

45. Ibid., April 10, 1849.

46. Ibid., May 18, May 22, 1849.

47. Ibid., April 14, April 18, April 24, May 9, 1849.

48. (Springfield) *Illinois Daily Journal,* Feb. 28, 1849; *Charleston Courier,* March 31, 1849; (Springfield) *Daily Register,* May 11, 1849; (Springfield) *Illinois Daily Journal,* Nov. 3, 1849.

49. Ibid., May 29, 1849.

50. (Springfield) *Daily Register,* June 6, July 19, 1849.

51. Ibid., July 26, 1849; (Springfield) *Illinois Daily Journal,* June 11, 1849; (Springfield) *Daily Register,* Sep. 4, 1849; (Springfield) *Illinois Daily Journal,* June 11, 1849; (Springfield) *Daily Register,* Oct. 8, Oct. 11, 1849.

52. (Springfield) *Illinois Daily Journal,* Dec. 18, 1849.

53. Ibid., Dec. 22, 1849; (Springfield) *Illinois State Register,* Oct. 27, Dec. 1, 1853; David Davis to [illegible], Feb. 15, 1854, folder A-22, drawer 1, case 4, Davis Family Papers.

54. (Indianapolis) *Indiana Journal,* July 11, 1825; R. Carlyle Buley, *The Old Northwest: Pioneer Period, 1815–1840* (2 vols., Indianapolis, 1950), II, 261, 282; Governor's Inaugural Address, (Indianapolis) *Indiana Journal,* Dec. 8, 1837.

5. Opportunity

1. Steven Hahn, "The Yeomanry of the Nonplantation South: Upper Piedmont Georgia, 1850–1860," in *Class, Conflict, and Consensus: Antebellum Southern Community Studies,* ed. Orville Vernon Burton and Robert C. McMath, Jr. (Westport, 1982), 29-56, esp. 45; William Oliver, *Eight Months in Illinois* (1843, reprint, Ann Arbor, 1966), 59-60; Daniel Wait Howe, "Making a Capital in the Wilderness," *Indiana Historical Society Publications* (Indianapolis, 1908), IV, no. 4, 299-338, esp. 337; Robert B. Duncan, "Old Settlers," ibid. (Indianapolis, 1894), II, no. 10, 375-402, esp. 396.

2. (Indianapolis) *Indiana Journal,* July 11, 1826; Rowland Berthoff, "Conventional Mentality: Free Blacks, Women, and Business Corporations as Unequal Persons, 1820–1870," *Journal of American History,* 76 (Dec. 1989), 753-84, esp. 757; John Ashworth, *'Agrarians' & 'Aristocrats': Party Political Ideology in the United States, 1837–1846* (London, 1983), 128; John Ashworth, "The Jacksonian as Leveller," *Journal of American Studies,* 14 (Dec. 1980), 407-21, esp. 412, 420-21; *Indiana Daily State Sentinel,* Dec. 18, 1857.

3. *Daily Scioto Gazette,* Sept. 25, 1855.

4. (Vandalia) *Illinois State Register and People's Advocate,* July 27, 1828.

5. William H. English, notebook, 1852, folder 12, box 1, William H. English Collection (Indiana Historical Society, Indianapolis); (Cincinnati) *Western Spy,* May 5, 1815; Julia Perkins Cutler, *Life and Times of Ephraim Cutler* (Cincinnati, 1890), 156.

6. (Indianapolis) *Indiana State Sentinel,* Dec. 7, 1841; *Charleston* (Illinois) *Courier,* March 31, 1849.

7. *Report of the Debates and Proceedings of the Convention for the Revision of the Constitution of the State of Ohio, 1850–51* (2 vols., Columbus, 1851), II, 631-32.

8. Eric Foner, *Free Soil, Free Labor, Free Men: The Ideology of the Republican Party before the Civil War* (New York, 1971), 38-39.

9. Jean H. Baker, *"Not Much of Me": Abraham Lincoln as a Typical American* (Fort Wayne, 1988).

10. Oliver, *Eight Months in Illinois,* 29; Robert McColley, *Slavery and Jeffersonian Virginia* (Urbana, 1973), 35.

11. Paul Finkelman, "Slavery and the Northwest Ordinance: A Study in Ambiguity," *Journal of the Early Republic,* 6 (Winter 1986), 343-70; Paul Finkelman, "Evading the Ordinance: The Persistence of Bondage in Indiana and Illinois," *Journal of the Early Republic,* 9, (Spring 1989), 21-51; J. P. Dunn, Jr., *Indiana: A Redemption from Slavery* (Boston, 1905), 245-46; United States Bureau of the Census, *A Century of Population Growth: From the First Census of the United States to the Twelfth, 1790–1900* (Baltimore, 1909), 133.

12. Peter S. Onuf, *Statehood and Union: A History of the Northwest Ordinance* (Bloomington, 1987), 114-15, 130-32; Dunn, "Slavery Petitions and Papers," 447-49, 455-57, 462-63.

13. *Western Spy and Hamilton Gazette,* Nov. 21, 1801.

14. (Kaskaskia) *Republican Advocate,* March 2, 1824, June 19, 1823.

15. Dunn, "Slavery Petitions and Papers," 476-77, 520; Clarence Edwin Carter, comp. and ed., *The Territorial Papers of the United States,* vol. VII: *The Territory of Indiana, 1800–1810* (Washington, D.C., 1939), 705-707; (Kaskaskia) *Republican Advocate,* Oct. 9, 1823.

16. (Vincennes) *Western Sun,* March 18, 1809.

17. John Rankin, *Letters on American Slavery, Addressed to Mr. Thomas Rankin, Merchant at Middlebrook, Augusta Co., Va.* (Westport, 1837, reprint, 1970), 70-72.

18. (Vincennes) *Western Sun,* Feb. 11, 1809; *Kaskaskia Republican,* July 6, 1824.

19. *Scioto Gazette, and Fredonian Chronicle,* Nov. 9, Dec. 7, 1820.

20. Theodore Calvin Pease, ed., *Illinois Election Returns, 1818–1848* (Springfield, 1923), 27-29.

21. Harry L. Watson, *Jacksonian Politics and Community Conflict: The Emergence of the Second American Party System in Cumberland County North Carolina* (Baton Rouge, 1981), 317-18.

22. On banks, see R. Carlyle Buley, *The Old Northwest: Pioneer Period, 1815–1840* (2 vols., Indianapolis, 1950), I, 567; William Gerald Shade, *Banks or No Banks: The Money Issue in Western Politics, 1832–1865* (Detroit, 1972), 21; James Roger Sharp, *The Jacksonians versus the Banks: Politics in the States after the Panic of 1837* (New York, 1970). See also Eugene H. Roseboom, *The Civil War Era, 1850–1873* (Columbus, 1944), and Donald R. Adams, Jr., "The Role of Banks in the Economic Development of the Old Northwest," in *Essays in Nineteenth Century Economic History: The Old Northwest,* ed. David C. Klingaman and Richard K. Vedder (Athens, Ohio, 1975), 208-45.

23. *Scioto Gazette and Fredonian Chronicle,* Jan. 4, 1816; (Indianapolis) *Indiana Journal,* Sept. 22, Oct. 27, 1832; John Tipton to Calvin Fletcher, Jan. 6, 1834, Nellie Armstrong Robertson and Dorothy Riker, comp. and ed., *The John Tipton Papers,* vol. III: *1834–1839* (Indianapolis, 1942), 9.

24. Allen G. Thurman to Friend Hughes, Jan. 4, 1839, folder 2, box 1, Allen G. Thurman Papers (Ohio Historical Society, Columbus); *Report of the Debates and Proceedings of the Convention for the Revision of the Constitution of the State of Ohio, 1850–51*, II, 791.

25. (Springfield) *Illinois Register,* Nov. 24, 1843, Dec. 21, 1839; *Scioto Gazette and Fredonian Chronicle,* Sept. 25, 1818.

26. *Western Spy and Literary Cadet,* Aug. 24, 1820; *Kaskaskia* (Illinois) *Republican,* June 29, 1824; (Springfield) *Daily Register,* Feb. 21, 1852; (Indianapolis) *Daily Indiana State Journal,* Feb. 25, 1852; Governor's Message, (Chillicothe) *Supporter,* Dec. 30, 1818; *Chicago Democrat,* Sept. 25, 1839; (Indianapolis) *Indiana Journal,* Jan. 8, 1834.

27. (Vandalia) *Illinois State Register and People's Advocate,* July 27, 1838.

28. (Indianapolis) *Weekly Indiana State Journal,* May 4, 1857; (Vandalia) *Illinois State Register and People's Advocate,* July 27, 1838; *Belleville Advocate,* July 3, 1841; (Indianapolis) *Indiana State Sentinel,* Sept. 7, 1841.

29. *Report of the Debates and Proceedings of the Convention for the Revision of the Constitution of the State of Ohio,* I, 282-83; Governor's Message, *Scioto Gazette,* Dec. 10, 1840; (Springfield) *Illinois Register,* Nov. 24, 1843; Allen G. Thurman to J. House, Feb. 5, 1836, folder 1, box 1, Thurman Papers.

30. Governor's Message, *Scioto Gazette,* Dec. 14, 1837; John J. Janney, untitled essay, 1842, folder 5, box 3, Janney Family Papers (Ohio Historical Society, Columbus).

31. *Annals of Congress,* 22 Cong., 1 sess., p. 3852; *Members of Congress since 1789* (Washington, 1977).

32. Ashworth, *'Agrarians' & 'Aristocrats,'* 34; John J. Janney, E. F. Drake Biography, pp. 3-4, n.d., folder 10, box 2, Janney Family Papers.

33. Harold E. Davis, "Economic Basis of Ohio Politics, 1820–1840," *Ohio State Archaeological and Historical Quarterly,* 47 (Oct. 1938), 288-318, esp. 300.

34. Toasts, Anniversary, May 13, 1811, Tammany Society Chillicothe Wigwam Records, microfilm, reel 1; *Western Spy,* July 6, 1811, July 28, 1815; (Charlestown) *Indiana Intelligencer and Farmers' Friend,* July 9, 1823; *Scioto Gazette, and Fredonian Chronicle,* July 9, 1819; (Cincinnati) *Western Spy and Literary Cadet,* Dec. 7, Nov. 16, 1822.

35. *Western Spy,* Jan. 29, 1814, Sept. 5, 1817; *Address of the Tammany Society, or Columbian Order to its Absent Members* (Cincinnati, 1819), 17, 20, 22, Tammany Society, Chillicothe Wigwam Records; Resolution on Domestic Manufactures, [1810], ibid.

36. Daniel Harmon Brush, *Growing Up with Southern Illinois, 1820 to 1861,* ed. Milo Milton Quaife (Chicago, 1944), 98-99; John J. Janney, Untitled Essay, 1842, folder 5, box 3, Janney Family Papers; (Springfield) *Illinois Daily Journal,* Aug. 21, 1849.

37. *Annals of Congress,* 20 Cong., 1 sess., pp. 2471-72; ibid., 22 Cong., 1 sess., pp. 3830-31; *Congressional Globe,* 34 Cong., 3 sess., p. 971; ibid., 36 Cong., 1 sess., p. 2056; *Members of Congress since 1789.*

38. (Springfield) *Illinois Daily Journal,* Dec. 11, 1851.

39. Ibid., May 10, 1850.

40. (Springfield) *Illinois State Register,* May 2, 1845, June 25, 1841, June 9, April 14, 1843; Governor's Inaugural Address, *Scioto Gazette,* Dec. 14, 1842.

41. *Daily State Sentinel,* April 15, 1861.

42. Joseph O. King to Richard Yates, Jan. 9, 1852, box 1, Richard Yates Papers (Illinois State Historical Library, Springfield); William T. Utter, *The Frontier*

State, *1803–1825* (Columbus, 1942), 319-21; Cutler, *Life and Times of Ephraim Cutler,* 174; Buley, *Old Northwest,* II, 348, 362; Frederick M. Binder, *The Age of the Common School, 1830–1865* (New York, 1974), 18-19, 91-92; Richard J. Jensen, *Illinois: A Bicentennial History* (New York, 1978), 43; Grady McWhiney, *Cracker Culture: Celtic Ways in the Old South* (Tuscaloosa, 1988), 214-15; Wayne E. Fuller, *The Old Country School: The Story of Rural Education in the Middle West* (Chicago, 1982), 31-38. See also Michael B. Katz, "The Origins of Public Education: A Reassessment," in *The Social History of American Education,* ed. B. Edward McClellan and William J. Reese (Urbana, 1988), 91-117.

43. Binder, *Age of the Common School,* 138; *Chicago Daily American,* Dec. 4, 1841; (Jacksonville, Illinois) *Western Observer,* June 5, 1830; (Connersville, Indiana) *Fayette Observer,* June 30, 1827; (Chillicothe) *Supporter,* Aug. 18, 1810.

44. *Daily* (Springfield) *Illinois State Register,* Dec. 10, Dec. 19, 1856.

45. *Alton Spectator,* July 13, 1837; Memorial to Congress from Indiana Legislative Assembly, in Charles Kettleborough, *Constitution Making in Indiana: A Source Book of Constitutional Documents with Historical Introduction and Critical Notes,* vol. I: *1780–1851* (Indianapolis, 1971), 69-72; ibid., art. VIII, sec. 1, p. 346.

46. *Richmond* (Indiana) *Palladium,* Jan. 9, 1850.

47. (Vandalia) *Illinois State Register and People's Advocate,* Aug. 3, 1838; (Cincinnati) *Western Spy,* July 11, 1818; "The Prospects and Obligations of Western Youth," by R. Yates, address delivered at Illinois College, 1834, box 1, Yates Papers; James B. Finley, *Autobiography of Rev. James B. Finley or, Pioneer Life in the West,* ed. W. P. Strickland (Cincinnati, 1856), 40-42; (Vandalia) *Illinois State Register and People's Advocate,* Aug. 3, 1838.

48. *Illinois Journal,* Jan. 26, 1861.

49. Thomas Worthington to Ohio legislature, Dec. 7, 1818, quoted in Alfred Byron Sears, *Thomas Worthington, Father of Ohio Statehood* (Columbus, 1958), 206-207; *Peoria Daily Democratic Press,* May 3, 1855; Governor's Message, *Peoria Daily Press,* Feb. 9, 1854; Governor's Message, (Chillicothe) *Supporter,* Dec. 16, 1818; Governor's Message, *Scioto Gazette,* Dec. 14, 1826; Governor's Inaugural Address, ibid., Dec. 28, 1836; (Vandalia) *Illinois Advocate and State Register,* Feb. 14, 1835.

50. (Springfield) *Illinois Daily Journal,* May 2, 1849; *Charleston* (Illinois) *Courier,* June 2, 1858.

51. Binder, *Age of the Common School,* 18-19; *Scioto Gazette,* Dec. 25, 1860; Charles Moores, *Caleb Mills and the Indiana School System* (Indianapolis, 1905), 528-31, 539-41, 401-402.

52. (Vandalia) *Illinois State Register and People's Advocate,* Jan. 11, 1839.

6. Rights

1. A. Lincoln to the Editor of the Sangamo Journal, June 13, 1836, Roy P. Basler, ed., *The Collected Works of Abraham Lincoln* (8 vols., New Brunswick, 1953), I, 48.

2. James B. Finley, *Autobiography of Rev. James B. Finley or, Pioneer Life in the West,* ed. W. P. Strickland (Cincinnati, 1856), 249-50, 245-47.

3. Charles E. Canup, "Temperance Movements and Legislation in Indiana," *Indiana Magazine of History,* 16 (March 1920), 3-37, esp. 8-9; Finley, *Autobiography,* 240-41, 248-49.

4. Ian R. Tyrrell, "Drink and Temperance in the Antebellum South: An Overview and Interpretation," *Journal of Southern History,* 48 (Nov. 1982), 485-510, esp. 507; Ian R. Tyrrell, *Sobering Up: From Temperance to Prohibition in Antebellum America, 1800–1860* (Westport, 1979), 5, 227; S. A. Douglas to Julius N. Granger, in *The Letters of Stephen A. Douglas,* ed. Robert W. Johannsen (Urbana, 1961), 19.

5. (Jacksonville, Illinois) *Western Observer,* Aug. 28, 1830; Tyrrell, *Sobering Up,* 232.

6. David E. Schob, *Hired Hands and Plowboys: Farm Labor in the Midwest, 1815–60* (Urbana, 1975), 121; Tyrrell, *Sobering Up,* 243-44; Tyrrell, "Drink and Temperance," 501-10.

7. William Cooper Howells, *Recollections of Life in Ohio, from 1813 to 1840* (Cincinnati, 1895, reprint, 1963), 125-26; Schob, *Hired Hands and Plowboys,* 98-100; (Lawrenceburg, Indiana) *Oracle,* Sept. 29, 1821.

8. J. A. Chesnut to Richard Yates, Sept. 18, 1852, box 1, Richard Yates Papers (Illinois State Historical Library, Springfield); Isaac Fowler to Governor Mordecai Bartley, Feb. 3, 1846, reel 14, Governor's Papers (Ohio Historical Society, Columbus); J. A. Chesnut to Richard Yates, June 18, 1853, box 1, Yates Papers; J. A. Chesnut to Richard Yates, Dec. 6, 1852, ibid.; Robert P. Howard, *Illinois: A History of the Prairie State* (Grand Rapids, 1972), 283; Tyrrell, *Sobering Up,* 262, 295-96; Robert W. Johannsen, *Stephen A. Douglas* (New York, 1973); Samuel Vinson to B. P. Hinch, Jan. 15, 1855, folder 2, SC 1763, Hinch Correspondence.

9. Allan M. Winkler, "Drinking on the American Frontier," *Quarterly Journal of Studies on Alcohol,* 29 (June 1968), 413-45. In Winkler's opinion temperance sentiment could only take hold when the loneliness and hard work of the frontier period had passed. Ibid., 433-35, 442. Tyrrell, *Sobering Up,* 227. Tyrrell sees treating at elections during colonial and early republican times as one of the ways that elites maintained control over the population. Ibid., 16. W. J. Rorabaugh sees the electorate's willingness to drink on election day as proof of feelings of frustration and powerlessness and resentment of their lack of real liberty in making their choice of candidates. W. J. Rorabaugh, *The Alcoholic Republic: An American Tradition* (New York, 1979), 151-55. General Wilkinson quoted in Rorabaugh, *Alcoholic Republic,* 20.

10. Governor Ford quoted in Winkler, "Drinking on the American Frontier," 437.

11. Geo. Herlep to Governor Thomas Corwin, [Nov. 1841], reel 12, Governor's Papers; *Scioto Gazette,* Jan. 23, 1850; *Richmond* (Indiana) *Palladium,* Feb. 2, 1839, Dec. 9, 1858, Feb. 20, 1850; (Indianapolis) *Daily Indiana State Journal,* March 1, 1852.

12. (Jacksonville, Illinois) *Western Observer*; *Western Spy and Hamilton Gazette,* March 26, 1800; *Daily Scioto Gazette,* Feb. 28, 1852.

13. *Richmond* (Indiana) *Palladium,* Jan. 6, 1859.

14. "An Address, Delivered before the Springfield Washington Temperance Society," Feb. 22, 1842, by A. Lincoln, Basler, ed., *Collected Works of Abraham Lincoln,* I, 278-79. Lincoln's assurance that no one would be hurt by temperance was belied by a liquor seller's impassioned plea to Congressman John G. Davis of Indiana: "Davis I don't know what I shall do the Corporation have repealed the license Ordinance, and now we cant retail and the Citizens are making a great fuss about selling whiskey and I will have to quit and what to do I dont know." Samuel A. Fisher to John G. Davis, Jan. 9, 1859, box 5, John Givan Davis Papers (Indiana Historical Society, Indianapolis).

15. *Supporter, and Scioto Gazette,* Jan. 4, 1827; *Daily Scioto Gazette,* June 2, 1853.

16. *Report of the Debates and Proceedings of the Convention for the Revision of the Constitution of the State of Ohio,* II, 713; *Richmond Indiana Palladium,* June 14, 1855.

17. Calvin Fletcher, "Address Delivered to the Temperance Society at Noblesville, June 20, 1848," *Recollections and Addresses,* Bound Volume 1880; *Daily Scioto Gazette,* Sept. 12, 1853; *Peoria Daily Democratic Press,* May 23, 1855.

18. (Springfield) *Illinois State Register,* March 23, April 23, 1853.

19. Clarence Edwin Carter, comp. and ed., *The Territorial Papers of the United States,* vol. VIII: *The Territory of Indiana, 1810–1816 Continued* (Washington, 1939), 392.

20. R. Carlyle Buley, *The Old Northwest: Pioneer Period, 1815–1840* (2 vols., Indianapolis, 1950), I, 95, 103, 133-36; Hildegard Binder Johnson, *Order upon the Land: The U.S. Rectangular Land Survey and the Upper Mississippi Country* (New York, 1976), 61, 65; Eric Foner, *Free Soil, Free Labor, Free Men: The Ideology of the Republican Party before the Civil War* (New York, 1971), 28-29.

21. Ray Allen Billington, *Westward Expansion: A History of the American Frontier* (New York, 1960), 207; John R. Stilgoe, *Common Landscape of America, 1580 to 1845* (New Haven, 1982), 103-104.

22. Malcolm J. Rohrbough, *The Land Office Business: The Settlement and Administration of American Public Lands, 1789–1837* (Belmont, 1990), 14-15.

23. Eugene Holloway Roseboom and Francis Phelps Weisenburger, *A History of Ohio* (New York, 1934), 80; Clarence Edwin Carter, ed., *The Territorial Papers of the United States,* vol. II: *The Territory Northwest of the River Ohio, 1787–1803* (Washington, 1934), 654; Beverley W. Bond, Jr., *The Correspondence of John Cleves Symmes, Founder of the Miami Purchase* (New York, 1926), 174-75.

24. Rohrbough, *Land Office Business,* 236, 110, xv, 76-78.

25. *Annals of Congress,* 16 Cong., 1 sess., April 19, 1820, pp. 1889-98; *Gales & Seaton's Register of Debates in Congress,* 21 Cong., 1 sess., Jan. 4, 1830, p. 9; ibid., 22 Cong., 2 sess., Feb. 20, 1833, pp. 1743-44; Rohrbough, *Land Office Business,* 76-78.

26. William Henry Harrison Circular, May 14, 1800, William Henry Harrison Collection (Indiana Historical Society, Indianapolis); *Annals of Congress,* 6 Cong., 1 sess., March 31, 1800, pp. 650-51; *Daily Chicago American,* Oct. 14, 1840; Speech on Pre-emption Bill, Jan. 27, 1838, in Robertson and Riker, comp. and ed., *Tipton Papers,* III, 519.

27. (Vandalia) *Illinois State Register and People's Advocate,* July 15, 1836; (Springfield) *Illinois Daily Journal,* Dec. 22, 1849; Basler, ed., *Collected Works of Abraham Lincoln,* II, 408.

28. Stanley Lebergott, "'O Pioneers': Land Speculation and the Growth of the Midwest," in *Essays on the Economy of the Old Northwest,* ed. David C. Klingaman and Richard K. Vedder (Athens, 1987), 37-57; Buley, *Old Northwest,* II, 151; Rohrbough, *Land Office Business,* 238; Logan Esarey, "The Pioneers of Morgan County: Memoirs of Noah J. Major," *Indiana Historical Society Publications* (Indianapolis, 1915), vol. V, no. 5, 225-516. (Kaskaskia) *Illinois Reporter,* July 31, 1826.

29. David Davis to [William P. Walker], Dec. 13, 1845, folder A-3, drawer 1, case 4, David Davis Family Papers (Illinois State Historical Library, Springfield); David Davis to Wm. P. Walker, July 1, 1837, folder A-1, ibid.; *Richmond Indiana Palladium,* Aug. 4, 1838.

30. Jensen, *Illinois,* 25-26; Allan G. Bogue, *From Prairie to Corn Belt: Farming on the Illinois and Iowa Prairies in the Nineteenth Century* (Chicago, 1963), 38; Johnson, *Order upon the Land,* 65; *Daily Chicago American,* June 18, 1839.

31. Foner, *Free Soil, Free Labor, Free Men.*

32. Leonard Erickson, "Politics and the Repeal of Ohio's Black Laws, 1837–1849," *Ohio History,* 82 (Summer-Autumn 1973), 154-75; Emma Lou Thornbrough, *The Negro in Indiana: A Study of a Minority* (Indianapolis, 1957), 58-59, 121, 125; Leon F. Litwack, *North of Slavery: The Negro in the Free States, 1790–1860* (Chicago, 1961), 75, 93-94, 154-55; United States Bureau of the Census, *A Century of Population Growth: From the First Census of the United States to the Twelfth, 1790–1900* (Baltimore, 1909, reprint 1970), 82; Rowland Berthoff, "Conventional Mentality: Free Blacks, Women, and Business Corporations as Unequal Persons, 1820–1870," *Journal of American History,* 76 (Dec. 1989), 753-84, esp. 757-58, 783-84.

33. John Woods, "Two Years' Residence in the Settlement on the English Prairie," in *Early Western Travels, 1748–1846,* ed. Reuben Gold Thwaites (Cleveland, 1904), X, 317; Christiana Holmes Tilson, *A Woman's Story of Pioneer Illinois,* ed. Milo Milton Quaife (Chicago, 1919), 24-25.

34. Coffin, *Reminiscences of Levi Coffin,* 120-25.

35. *Scioto Gazette,* July 20, 1836.

36. *Scioto Gazette,* Sept. 27, 1850; D. R. Eckels to John G. Davis, May 16, 1854, box 2, Davis Papers; *Alton Weekly Courier,* Oct. 21, 1858; Charles A. Church, *History of the Republican Party in Illinois, 1854–1912* (Rockford, 1912), 48; *Indiana Daily State Sentinel,* Sept. 23, 1858; Jas. K. O'Haver and F. M. Akin to John G. Davis, Oct. 16, 1856, box 3, Davis Papers; *Indiana Daily State Sentinel,* Sept. 21, 1858.

37. Speech at Chicago, July 9, 1858, *The Lincoln-Douglas Debates of 1858,* ed. Robert W. Johannsen (New York, 1965), 33; (Springfield) *Illinois State Register,* April 26, 1853; (Indianapolis) *Weekly Indiana State Journal,* March 4, 1858.

38. *Scioto Gazette,* June 14, 1830.

39. *Indiana Daily State Sentinel,* Sept. 15, 1857; *Daily* (Springfield) *Illinois State Register,* Oct. 6, 1857.

40. J. Blanchard and N. L. Rice, *Debate on Slavery: Held in the City of Cincinnati, on the First, Second, Third, and Sixth Days of October, 1845, upon the Question: Is Slave-Holding in Itself Sinful, and the Relation between Master and Slave, a Sinful Relation?* (Cincinnati, 1846), 43-44, 90-91, 52-53, 101, 33.

41. Ibid., 215-16.

42. *Report of the Debates and Proceedings of the Convention for the Revision of the Constitution of the State of Ohio,* II, 550-51, 13, I, 56-57; George A. Bricknell to Wm. H. English, June 1, 1860, folder 12, box 3, William English Papers (Indiana Historical Society, Indianapolis).

43. Johannsen, ed., *Lincoln-Douglas Debates,* 52-53.

44. (Indianapolis) *Indiana State Journal,* Nov. 5, 1850.

45. *Report of the Debates and Proceedings of the Convention for the Revision of the Constitution of the State of Ohio,* II, 337-38, 604; David Davis to [no name], June 25, 1847, folder A-7, drawer 1, case 4, Davis Family Papers; (Springfield) *Illinois Daily Journal,* April 2, 1853.

46. *Report of the Debates and Proceedings of the Convention for the Revision of the Constitution of the State of Ohio,* II, 601.

47. *Richmond* (Indiana) *Palladium,* Nov. 23, 1833; (Springfield) *Illinois Daily Journal,* Sept. 5, 1851.

48. *Report of the Debates and Proceedings of the Convention for the Revision of the Constitution of the State of Ohio,* II, 602-603; (Indianapolis) *Daily Indiana State Journal,* Jan. 3, 1852.

49. David Davis to [no name], June 25, 1847, folder A-7, drawer 1, case 4, Davis Family Papers; (Indianapolis) *Daily Indiana State Journal,* Nov. 5, Nov. 6, Nov. 18, Nov. 29, 1850; *Richmond* (Indiana) *Palladium,* July 10, 1850.

50. *Report of the Debates and Proceedings of the Convention for the Revision of the Constitution of the State of Indiana* (2 vols., Indianapolis, 1850), II, 1817; Arthur Charles Cole, ed., *The Constitutional Debate of 1847* (Springfield, 1919), 201, 250, 855, 863; *Report of the Debates and Proceedings of the Convention for the Revision of the Constitution of the State of Ohio,* II, 604-605.

51. *Illinois Journal,* Feb. 17, 1860; Basler, ed., *Collected Works of Abraham Lincoln,* II, 500; Ashworth, *'Agrarians' & 'Aristocrats,'* 223.

52. Robert P. Swierenga, "The Settlement of the Old Northwest: Ethnic Pluralism in a Featureless Plain," *Journal of the Early Republic,* 9 (Spring 1989), 73-105, esp. 83-87, 91.

53. (Jacksonville, Illinois) *Western Observer,* July 3, 1830; George W. Ewing to John Tipton, Feb. 27, 1829, Robertson and Riker, comp. and ed., *Tipton Papers,* II, 147-49. There were definite prejudices about national character. Germans, Scots, and Englishmen were considered to make very good citizens. An Irishman rarely was. Yet the "respectable and educated" of whatever country were welcomed. Richard Beste, *Wabash,* I, 318-19; (Springfield) *Daily Register,* July 9, 1849.

54. (Indianapolis) *Weekly Indiana State Journal,* April 3, 1856.

55. D. Griffiths, Jr., *Two Years in the New Settlements of Ohio* (1835, reprint, Ann Arbor, 1966), 70; John J. Janney, E. F. Drake Biography, n.d., p. 14, folder 10, box 2, Janney Family Papers.

56. *Daily Scioto Gazette,* May 21, 1853.

57. *Belleville Advocate,* Aug. 11, 1842; *Chester* (Illinois) *Reveille,* July 12, 1849.

58. *Richmond* (Indiana) *Palladium,* Oct. 24, 1835; *Alton Telegraph & Democratic Review,* May 29, 1841; *Daily Chicago American,* Aug. 3, 1839; Cullom Davis, "Illinois: Crossroads and Cross Section," in *Heartland: Comparative Histories of the Midwestern States,* ed. James H. Madison (Bloomington, Ind., 1988), 127-57, esp. 144; *Scioto Gazette,* Aug. 22, 1850.

59. (Springfield) *Illinois Daily Journal,* Nov. 12, 1850.

60. Speech and Resolutions Concerning the Philadelphia Riots, June 12, 1844, Basler, ed., *Collected Works of Abraham Lincoln,* I, 337-38.

61. Speech at Meredosia, Illinois, Oct. 18, 1858, ibid., III, 328-29; *Alton Weekly Courier,* Oct. 28, 1858; A. Lincoln to Norman B. Judd, Sept. 23, 1858, Oct. 20, 1858, Basler, ed., *Collected Works of Abraham Lincoln,* III, 202, 329-30. The legal case on alien voting came before the Illinois Supreme Court in 1840. Stephen A. Douglas was to defend the right of aliens to vote before a court dominated by Whigs. The court might have ruled against Douglas in time for the election of 1840 if Douglas's discovery of a clerical error had not forced the postponement of the case. Johannsen, *Stephen A. Douglas,* 83-84. Schob, *Hired Hands and Plowboys,* 186; Emma Lou Thornbrough, *Indiana in the Civil War Era, 1850–1880* (Indianapolis, 1965), 40.

62. *Daily Indiana State Journal,* Jan. 5, 1853; *Alton Weekly Courier,* Sept. 3, 1857. The Democrats also accused Republicans of courting as "intelligent, educated Germans," those they had once scorned as "Drunken Dutch" and "Cattle." *Joliet* (Illinois) *Signal,* Oct. 28, 1856. A. Lincoln to Anton C. Hesing,

Henry Wandt, Alexander Fisher, July 30, 1858, Basler, *Collected Works of Abraham Lincoln*, II, 475.

63. (Indianapolis) *Weekly Indiana State Journal*, Jan. 15, 1857; (Springfield) *Illinois Daily Journal*, March 24, 1849.

64. *Daily* (Springfield) *Illinois State Register*, Feb. 6, 1856.

65. *Western Spy and Hamilton Gazette*, Oct. 3, 1804; *Chicago Daily American*, Dec. 4, 1841; *Chicago American*, July 18, 1835.

7. Sectionalism Reborn

1. Samuel Steel to Samuel Galloway, Sept. 4, 1856, folder 5, box 1, Samuel Galloway Papers (Ohio Historical Society, Columbus). On pro-Southern feelings in Indiana, see Morton M. Rosenberg and Dennis V. McClung, *The Politics of Pro-Slavery Sentiment in Indiana, 1816–1861* (Muncie, 1968).

2. *The Congressional Globe*, 31 Cong., 1 sess., pp. 1772, 1764, 1776, 1807, 1837; *Members of Congress since 1789* (Washington, 1977).

3. William H. Herndon to John A. McClernand, Dec. 8, 1859, box 1, John A. McClernand Collection (Illinois State Historical Library, Springfield).

4. William E. Gienapp, *The Origins of the Republican Party, 1852–1856* (New York, 1987), 429-30.

5. *Richmond* (Indiana) *Palladium*, June 18, 1842; Bertram Wyatt-Brown, *Honor and Violence in the Old South* (New York, 1986), 205; James G. Birney to Gerrit Smith, Nov. 11, 1835, Dwight L. Dumond, ed., *Letters of James Gillespie Birney, 1831–1857* (2 vols., Gloucester, Mass., 1966), I, 259; James G. Birney to Lewis Tappan, April 29, 1836, ibid., 319-21; James G. Birney to Lewis Tappan, May 2, 1836, ibid., 324-25; James G. Birney to Lewis Tappan, July 15, 1836, ibid., 342-43; handbill posted in Cincinnati, July 1836, ibid., facing p. 342; James G. Birney to Lewis Tappan, Aug. 10, 1836, ibid., 349; James G. Birney to Lewis Tappan, Feb. 25, 1837, ibid., 375; William Birney to James G. Birney, Aug. 7, 1843, ibid., II, 750-51; Joseph Sullivant to James G. Birney, Sept. 11, 1841, ibid., 632; William Birney to James G. Birney, June 9, 1842, ibid., 697.

6. *Scioto Gazette*, Jan. 8, 1861.

7. Samuel Galloway to John A. Trimble, Jan. 12, 1837, folder 3, box 1, John A. Trimble Papers (Ohio Historical Society, Columbus).

8. Gamaliel Bailey to James G. Birney, May 24, 1838, Dumond, ed., *Letters of James Gillespie Birney*, I, 456-57.

9. George Thomas Palmer, *A Conscientious Turncoat: The Story of John M. Palmer* (New Haven, 1941), 58-59, 24.

10. James G. Birney to Ralph R. Gurley, July 12, 1832, Dumond, ed., *Letters of James Gillespie Birney*, I, 9; Peter Cartwright, *Autobiography of Peter Cartwright* (New York, 1956), 93-94.

11. John Reynolds, *My Own Times: Embracing Also the History of My Life* (Chicago, 1878), 271; *Indiana Daily State Sentinel*, Dec. 15, Dec. 21, 1859; *Daily Scioto Gazette*, Jan. 28, 1857; Samuel Galloway to John S. Galloway, Feb. 9, 1840, folder 1, box 1, Galloway Papers.

12. (Springfield) *Illinois Daily Journal*, Nov. 5, 1850; Godlove S. Orth to Schuyler Colfax, [Jan. 1846], J. Herman Schauinger, ed., "The Letters of Godlove S. Orth, Hoosier Whig," *Indiana Magazine of History*, 39 (Dec. 1943), 365-400, esp. 377; *Indiana Daily State Sentinel*, Feb. 25, 1861.

13. *Indiana Daily State Sentinel*, Dec. 17, 1857.

14. Ibid., Nov. 2, 1859.

15. James M. Lucas to John G. Davis, Dec. 18, 1859, box 5, John Givan Davis Papers (Indiana Historical Society, Indianapolis).

16. (Indianapolis) *Weekly Indiana State Journal,* Dec. 15, 1859.

17. Ibid., Jan. 4, 1851; (Indianapolis) *Indiana State Journal,* Dec. 13, 1850; *Indiana Daily State Sentinel,* July 15, 1857, Sept. 2, 1858.

18. James P. Root to Richard Yates, April 30, 1860, microfilm, Yates Correspondence; Allan Tomlin to Richard Yates, July 21, 1860, ibid.; *Illinois Journal,* Nov. 22, May 14, 1860.

19. (Indianapolis) *Indiana State Journal,* Nov. 29, 1850; William [illegible] to John G. Davis, Feb. 24, 1854, Davis Papers.

20. Carrie Prudence Kofoid, "Puritan Influences in the Formative Years of Illinois History," *Transactions of the Illinois State Historical Society for the Year 1905* (Springfield, 1906), 261-338, esp. 284, 313; William M. Cockrum, *Pioneer History of Indiana including Stories, Incidents and Customs of the Early Settlers* (Oakland City, Ind., 1907), 600; John J. Janney to T. W. Macmahor, Nov. 17, 1860, folder 4, box 1, Janney Family Papers (Ohio State Historical Society, Columbus); S. P. Chase to John T. Trowbridge, March 18, 1844, Stephen Middleton, "Antislavery Litigation in Ohio: The Case-Trowbridge Letters," *Mid-America,* 70 (Oct. 1988), 105-24, esp. 112-14; Cockrum, *Pioneer History of Indiana,* 563-65, 557-58.

21. J. G. Birney to Ralph R. Gurley, June 29, 1833, Dumond, ed., *Letters of James Gillespie Birney,* I, 78-79; James G. Birney to Gerrit Smith, Nov. 14, 1834, ibid., 148; James G. Birney to Ezekial Webb, Thomas Chandler and Darius C. Jackson, Oct. 6, 1836, ibid., 363; James G. Birney to Charles Hammond, Nov. 14, 1835, ibid., 270-71; James G. Birney to Myron Holley, Joshua Leavitt, and Elizur Wright, Jr., May 11, 1840, ibid., 567-71. William W. Freehling, *The Road to Disunion,* vol. I: *Secessionists at Bay, 1776–1854* (New York, 1990), 520, 98-118, 36.

22. (Indianapolis) *Indiana State Journal,* Nov. 23, 1848; (Springfield) *Daily Register,* March 6, 1852; *Daily Illinois State Register,* Nov. 22, 1860.

23. S. S. Marshall to B. P. Hinch, Oct. 25, 1856, folder 2, Benjamin P. Hinch Correspondence (Illinois State Historical Library, Springfield).

24. Jeptha Garrigus to John G. Davis, April 10, 1854, box 2, Davis Papers; Jeptha Garrigus to John G. Davis, April 19, 1858, box 4, ibid.

25. A. Bowen to John G. Davis, Feb. 14, 1858, ibid.; J. B. Turner to Richard Yates, April 8, 1854, box 1, Yates Papers.

26. Allan Tomlin to Richard Yates, July 15, 1856, box 1, Yates Papers; *Daily* (Springfield) *Illinois State Register,* Sept. 20, 1856; *Illinois Journal,* July 2, Aug. 16, Sept. 12, Sept. 28, Dec. 1, 1860; *Indianapolis Daily Journal,* May 25, 1860; Richard J. Jensen, *Illinois: A Bicentennial History* (New York, 1978); Lucretius Lomax to Wm. H. English, May 21, 1860, folder 12, box 3, English Collection.

27. Richard Yates, Speech after the Election of Buchanan, Nov. 1856, box 1, Yates Papers; E. Peck to Lyman Trumbull, Jan. 17, 1856, folder 5, drawer 5, case 26, Trumbull Family Papers.

28. Sam Marshall to John A. McClernand, April 24, 1850, box 1, John A. McClernand Papers (Illinois State Historical Library, Springfield); *Indiana Daily State Sentinel,* July 4, 1860.

29. Robert W. Johannsen, ed., *The Lincoln-Douglas Debates of 1858* (New York, 1965), 157-58.

30. A. M. Puett to John G. Davis, Jan. 29, 1860, box 6, Davis Papers; *Alton Weekly Courier,* Oct. 7, 1858; James Ferguson to John G. Davis, Feb. 3, 1861, box 6, Davis Papers; *Daily Scioto Gazette,* Feb. 14, 1851; Johannsen, ed., *Lincoln-Douglas Debates,* 91; *Indiana Daily State Sentinel,* Aug. 6, 1859.

31. *Daily Illinois State Register,* Aug. 13, 1860; *Indiana Daily State Sentinel,* July 19, 1860.

32. Sidney Breese to Editor & Publisher of the "Reporter," Oct. 28, 1854, SC 165 (Illinois State Historical Library, Springfield); A. Lovering to John G. Davis, May 18, 1858, box 5, Davis Papers.

33. A. Bowen to John G. Davis, Feb. 14, 1858, box 4, Davis Papers; Gordon S. Wood, *The Creation of the American Republic, 1776–1787* (Chapel Hill, 1969); David M. Potter, *The Impending Crisis, 1848–1861* (New York, 1976); Stephen B. Oates, *To Purge This Land with Blood: A Biography of John Brown* (Amherst, 1984); Freehling, *Road to Disunion,* I, 475-76.

34. Potter, *Impending Crisis;* S. A. Douglas to Parmenas Taylor Turnley, Nov. 30, 1852, Robert W. Johannsen, ed., *The Letters of Stephen A. Douglas* (Urbana, 1961), 255-56; S. A. Douglas to the Editor of the Concord, NH, *State Capitol Reporter,* Feb. 16, 1854, Johannsen, ed., *Letters of Stephen A. Douglas,* 285; Speech at Chicago, July 9, 1858, Johannsen, ed., *Lincoln-Douglas Debates of 1858,* 22; S. A. Douglas to John A. McClernand, Nov. 23, 1857, box 1, McClernand Collection.

35. Speech at Chicago, July 9, 1858, Johannsen, ed., *Lincoln-Douglas Debates,* 27-28; F. Gerald Handfield, Jr., "William H. English and the Election of 1880," in *Gentlemen from Indiana: National Party Candidates, 1836–1940,* ed. Ralph D. Gray (Indianapolis, 1977), 83-116; Robert W. Johannsen, *Stephen A. Douglas* (New York, 1973), 439-40.

36. *Congressional Globe,* 33 Cong., 1 sess., p. 1254; *Members of Congress since 1789* (Washington, 1977); Rosenberg and McClung, *Politics of Pro-Slavery Sentiment in Indiana,* 33-38; W. J. Brown to John G. Davis, Feb. 22, 1854, box 2, Davis Papers; D. R. Eckels to J. G. Davis, Feb. 16, 1854, ibid.; Robert W. McCorkle to John G. Davis, March 2, 1854, ibid.; R. S. Hamilton to John G. Davis, Feb. 13, 1854, ibid.

37. (Springfield) *Illinois State Register,* July 10, 1854; Eric Foner, *Free Soil, Free Labor, Free Men: The Ideology of the Republican Party before the Civil War* (New York, 1971), 158; Johannsen, *Stephen A. Douglas,* 448; Paul Selby to Richard Yates, April 8, 1854, box 1, Yates Papers; Geo. Brown to Lyman Trumbull, Jan. 6, 1856, folder 5, drawer 5, case 26, Trumbull Family Papers; Theodore Calvin Pease, *The Story of Illinois* (Chicago, 1925), 228-30; J. W. Osborn to John G. Davis, June 29, 1858, box 5, Davis Papers.

38. W. Utler to John G. Davis, May 24, 1854, box 2, Davis Papers; *Indiana Daily State Sentinel,* Dec. 15, 1857; *Peoria Daily Press,* Aug. 28, 1854; (Springfield) *Illinois State Register,* Aug. 12, Aug. 9, Sept. 27, June 2, Aug. 10, Sept. 6, July 7, 1854.

39. Austin H. Brown to John G. Davis, Dec. 20, 1857, box 3, Davis Papers.

40. *Daily Indiana State Sentinel,* July 17, 1854; W. M. Franklin to J. G. Davis, Feb. 21, 1854, box 2, Davis Papers; W. M. Noel to John Davis, Feb. 23, 1854, ibid.

41. Joseph C. Howell to Richard Yates, March 1, 1854, box 1, Yates Papers; David Davis to Julius Rockwell, July 15, 1854, folder A-23, drawer 1, case 4, David Davis Family Papers (Illinois State Historical Library, Springfield); *Daily Scioto Gazette,* March 20, 1854; Jas. J. Clarkson to Sidney Breese, Sept. 22, 1858, SC 165 (Illinois State Historical Library, Springfield).

42. Johannsen, ed., *Lincoln-Douglas Debates of 1858,* 15; Speech at Peoria, Oct. 16, 1854, Basler, ed., *Collected Works of Abraham Lincoln,* II, 265-66.

43. Speech at Springfield, Illinois, July 17, 1858, ibid., 509; *Weekly Scioto Gazette,* March 23, 1858.

44. Potter, *Impending Crisis,* 354; Speech at Bloomington, Sept. 26, 1854, Basler, ed., *Collected Works of Abraham Lincoln,* II, 239; Speech at Paris, Sept. 7, 1858, ibid., III, 90-91; A. Lincoln to Samuel Galloway, July 28, 1859, ibid., 394-95; Speech at Cincinnati, Sept. 17, 1859, ibid., 447; A. Lincoln to John D. Defrees, Dec. 18, 1860, ibid., IV, 155.
45. *Scioto Gazette,* March 16, 1860; *Daily Scioto Gazette,* Jan. 14, 1856; E. W. Downer to Lyman Trumbull, March 17, 1856, folder 6, drawer 5, case 26, Trumbull Family Papers; Lucas Flattery to John T. Brasee, Nov. 5, 1855, folder 3, box 1, John T. Brasee Papers (Ohio Historical Society, Columbus).
46. Judge John Law to Wm. H. English, June 18, 1860, folder 12, box 3, English Collection.
47. John Cowgill to John G. Davis, Nov. 7, 1859, box 5, Davis Papers; James M. McPherson, *Ordeal by Fire: The Civil War and Reconstruction* (New York, 1982), 124; Potter, *Impending Crisis,* 442-47.

8. Disunion

1. J. B. Otey to John G. Davis, Feb. 25, 1858, box 4, John Givan Davis Papers (Indiana Historical Society, Indianapolis). For the Midwest during the Civil War, see Frank L. Klement, *The Copperheads in the Middle West* (Chicago, 1960); Emma Lou Thornbrough, *Indiana in the Civil War Era, 1850–1880* (Indianapolis, 1965); Kenneth M. Stampp, *Indiana Politics during the Civil War* (Indianapolis, 1949), 13-14, 68, 242-44, 208; G. R. Tredway, *Democratic Opposition to the Lincoln Administration in Indiana* (Indianapolis, 1973).
2. *Indiana Daily State Sentinel,* Jan. 27, 1860.
3. Ibid., Jan. 9, 1861; *Scioto Gazette,* Jan. 8, 1861; O. P. Morton to People of Indiana, printed pamphlet, Oct. 2, 1861, Oliver P. Morton Scrapbook, William R. Holloway Collection (Indiana Historical Society, Indianapolis).
4. T. B. Davis to John G. Davis, Feb. 16, 1861, box 6, Davis Papers; George W. Moore to John G. Davis, Jan. 27, 1861, ibid.
5. For the Crittenden Compromise, see James M. McPherson, *Ordeal by Fire: The Civil War and Reconstruction* (New York, 1982), 135. J. A. Cravens to William English, Jan. 26, 1861, folder 13, box 3, William English Papers (Indiana Historical Society, Indianapolis).
6. *Indiana Daily State Sentinel,* Feb. 22, Feb. 25, Jan. 4, Jan. 5, Jan. 22, 1861; *Illinois Daily State Journal,* Jan. 24, 1861.
7. *Indiana Daily State Sentinel,* Jan. 27, 1860, Jan. 9, 1861; [John M. Palmer], June 18, 1861, box 1, John M. Palmer Papers I (Illinois State Historical Library, Springfield); *Scioto Gazette,* Jan. 22, 1861.
8. *Indiana Daily State Sentinel,* Feb. 22, 1860; C. L. Vallandigham to Dr. J. A. Walters, Jan. 9, 1861, C. L. Vallandigham Correspondence, microfilm, reel 1 (Ohio Historical Society–Western Reserve, Columbus).
9. *Indiana Daily State Sentinel,* April 13, 1861.
10. *Illinois Daily State Journal,* Jan. 24, 1861; *Indianapolis Daily Journal,* Feb. 1, 1861.
11. *Scioto Gazette,* Dec. 18, Nov. 20, 1860.
12. Stampp, *Indiana Politics during the Civil War,* 34-38; Wm. D. Defrees to David Davis, Nov. 26, 1860, folder A-28, drawer 1, case 4, David Davis Family Papers (Illinois State Historical Library, Springfield).
13. John J. Janney to T. B. G., Oct. 24, 1860, folder 3, box 1, Janney Family Papers (Ohio Historical Society, Columbus).

14. *Indianapolis Daily Journal,* Nov. 9, 1860.
15. Governor's Message, *Scioto Gazette,* Jan. 15, 1861.
16. Abraham Lincoln to Horace Greeley, Aug. 22, 1862, in Roy P. Basler, *The Collected Works of Abraham Lincoln* (8 vols., New Brunswick, 1953), V, 388-89; T. B. Davis to John G. Davis, Feb. 16, 1861, box 6, Davis Papers; Eric Foner, *Free Soil, Free Labor, Free Men: The Ideology of the Republican Party before the Civil War* (New York, 1971), 140; Speech at Lafayette, Indiana, Feb. 11, 1861, in Basler, ed., *Collected Works of Abraham Lincoln,* IV, 192; Speech from the Balcony of the Bates House at Indianapolis, Indiana, Feb. 11, 1861, ibid., 194-96.
17. Fragment of Speech Intended for Kentuckians, Feb. 12, 1861, ibid., 200.
18. Ibid.
19. *Scioto Gazette,* Feb. 26, 1861.
20. *Indiana Daily State Sentinel,* Jan. 23, 1861; *Indianapolis Daily Journal,* Jan. 5, 1861; *Indiana Daily State Sentinel,* Jan. 9, 1861.
21. *Scioto Gazette,* April 30, May 21, 1861; Daniel Harmon Brush, *Growing Up with Southern Illinois, 1820 to 1861,* ed. Milo Milton Quaife (Chicago, 1944), 245-48; S. A. McConnell to Richard Yates, April 3, 1861, box 2, Richard Yates Papers (Illinois State Historical Library, Springfield).
22. J. A. Cravens to W. H. English, April 9, 1861, folder 13, box 3, English Papers; *Indianapolis Daily Journal,* Jan. 5, 1861; D. W. Voorhees to [no name], Dec. 12, 1860, folder 3, box 1, Holloway Papers.
23. *Daily State Sentinel,* April 17, April 24, 1861; *Indianapolis Daily Journal,* April 17, April 19, April 22, 1861; *Daily State Sentinel,* April 15, 1861; *Indianapolis Daily Journal,* April 17, 1861; *Daily Illinois State Register,* April 17, 1861; *Illinois Daily State Journal,* April 15, 1861; *Daily Illinois State Register,* April 30, 1861.
24. Ibid., June 21, 1861; *Illinois Daily State Journal,* June 11, 1861; *Daily Illinois State Register,* June 10, 1861; *Illinois Daily State Journal,* June 15, 1861.
25. Ibid., April 30, May 2, May 3, May 11, May 14, June 11, 1861.
26. *Indianapolis Daily Journal,* May 7, May 18, April 29, 1861.

Conclusion

1. John Sherman, *Recollections of Forty Years in the House, Senate and Cabinet* (New York, 1896), 720-21, 738.
2. Meredith Nicholson, *The Valley of Democracy* (New York, 1918), 38. Frank L. Klement, *The Copperheads in the Middle West* (Chicago, 1960); Kenneth M. Stampp, *Indiana Politics during the Civil War* (Indianapolis, 1949); Emma Lou Thornbrough, *Indiana in the Civil War Era, 1850–1880* (Indianapolis, 1965); G. R. Tredway, *Democratic Opposition to the Lincoln Administration in Indiana* (Indianapolis, 1973).
3. Richard Jensen, *The Winning of the Midwest: Social and Political Conflict, 1888–1896* (Chicago, 1971), xv; Paul H. Buck, *The Road to Reunion, 1865–1900* (Boston, 1938), 119-21.
4. Blaine to Harrison, Miller & Elam, Dec. 13, 1884, Albert T. Volwiler, ed., *The Correspondence between Benjamin Harrison and James G. Blaine, 1882–1893* (Philadelphia, 1940), 26-27.
5. Charles Richard Williams, ed., *Diary and Letters of Rutherford Birchard Hayes* (5 vols., Columbus, 1926), V, 1. Robert Haven Schauffler, *Memorial Day: Its Celebration* (New York, 1924) contains a good sampling of Memorial Day

literature. Morton is quoted in Schauffler, 259. For Morton's contribution to bloody-shirt campaigning, see Eric L. McKitrick, *Andrew Johnson and Reconstruction* (Chicago, 1960), 318-19. See David W. Blight, "'For Something beyond the Battlefield': Frederick Douglass and the Struggle for the Memory of the Civil War," in *Memory and American History,* ed. David Thelen (Bloomington, 1990), 27-49, esp. 31 for Frederick Douglass's reaction to this trend in Memorial Day services.

6. Arthur E. Bostwick, *The Different West: As Seen by a Transplanted Easterner* (Chicago, 1913).

7. Nicholson, *Valley of Democracy*, 264.

8. Graham Hutton, *Midwest at Noon* (Chicago, 1946), x-xiii; Sinclair Lewis, *Main Street* (1920, New York, reprint 1948). See the essays in Martin Bucco, *Critical Essays on Sinclair Lewis* (Boston, 1986); David D. Anderson, *Critical Essays on Sherwood Anderson* (Boston, 1981). Andrew R. L. Cayton and Peter Onuf, *The Midwest and the Nation: Rethinking the History of an American Region* (Bloomington, 1990); Lewis Atherton, *Main Street on the Middle Border* (Bloomington, 1954); Robert S. Lynd and Helen Merrell Lynd, *Middletown: A Study in Contemporary American Culture* (New York, 1929), 7-8.

BIBLIOGRAPHY

Manuscript Collections

Alexander S. Boys Papers (Ohio Historical Society, Columbus).
John T. Brasee Papers (Ohio Historical Society, Columbus).
Sidney Breese Papers (Illinois State Historical Library, Springfield).
Orville H. Browning Papers (Illinois State Historical Library, Springfield).
Thomas Corwin, VFM 391 (Ohio Historical Society, Columbus).
David Davis Family Papers (Illinois State Historical Library, Springfield).
John Givan Davis Papers (Indiana Historical Society, Indianapolis).
William H. English Collection (Indiana Historical Society, Indianapolis).
Calvin Fletcher, Bound Volume 1880 (Indiana Historical Society, Indianapolis).
Samuel Galloway Papers (Ohio Historical Society, Columbus).
Governor's Papers, microfilm, reels 12 and 14 (Ohio Historical Society, Columbus).
John Kennedy Graham Papers (Indiana Historical Society, Indianapolis).
William Henry Harrison Collection (Indiana Historical Society, Indianapolis).
Benjamin P. Hinch Correspondence (Illinois State Historical Library, Springfield).
William R. Holloway Collection (Indiana Historical Society, Indianapolis).
Janney Family Papers (Ohio Historical Society, Columbus).
John A. McClernand Papers (Illinois State Historical Library, Springfield).
John M. Palmer Papers I (Illinois State Historical Library, Springfield).
Tammany Society, Chillicothe Wigwam Records, microfilm (Ohio Historical Society, Columbus).
Allen G. Thurman Papers (Ohio Historical Society, Columbus).
John A. Trimble Papers (Ohio Historical Society, Columbus).
Lyman Trumbull Family Papers, microfilm (Illinois State Historical Library, Springfield).
Lyman Trumbull Family Papers (Illinois State Historical Library, Springfield).
C. L. Vallandigham Correspondence, microfilm (Ohio Historical Society–Western Reserve, Columbus).
Vallandigham and Laird Family Papers, microfilm (Ohio Historical Society–Western Reserve, Columbus).
Wallace-Dickey Family Papers (Illinois State Historical Library, Springfield).
Richard Yates Correspondence, microfilm (Illinois State Historical Library, Springfield).
Richard Yates Papers (Illinois State Historical Library, Springfield).

Bibliography

Newspapers

Alton Spectator.
Alton Telegraph & Democratic Review.
Alton Weekly Courier.
Belleville (Illinois) *Advocate* (Also *Weekly Belleville Advocate*).
Charleston (Illinois) *Courier.*
Chester (Illinois) *Herald.*
Chester (Illinois) *Reveille.*
Chicago American (Also *Daily Chicago American*).
Chicago Democrat (Also *Chicago Morning Democrat*).
Chicago Express.
Chicago Weekly Journal (Also *Chicago Daily Journal*).
Chillicothe Supporter.
(Cincinnati) *Cist's Weekly Advertiser.*
Decatur (Illinois) *Daily Chronicle.*
(Connersville, Indiana) *Fayette Observer.*
(Circleville, Ohio) *Fredonian.*
(Lowell, Illinois) *Genius of Liberty.*
(Springfield) *Illinois Daily Journal* (Also *Illinois Journal*).
(Jacksonville) *Illinois Patriot.*
(Kaskaskia) *Illinois Reporter.*
(Springfield) *Illinois State Register* (Also *Illinois Register, Daily Register*).
(Vandalia) *Illinois State Register and People's Advocate* (Also [Vandalia] *Illinois Advocate*).
(Indianapolis) *Indiana Daily State Sentinel.*
(Vincennes) *Indiana Gazette.*
(Charlestown) *Indiana Intelligencer and Farmers' Friend.*
(Indianapolis) *Indiana State Journal* (Also *Indiana Journal, Weekly Indiana State Journal, Tri-Weekly State Journal, Semi-Weekly Journal*).
Joliet (Illinois) *Signal.*
Jonesboro (Illinois) *Gazette.*
(Lawrenceburg, Indiana) *Oracle.*
Peoria Daily Democratic Press (Also *Peoria Daily Press*).
(Connersville, Indiana) *Political Clarion.*
(Kaskaskia, Illinois) *Republican Advocate* (Also *Kaskaskia Republican*).
Richmond (Indiana) *Palladium.*
Richmond (Indiana) *Public Leger.*
(Springfield) *Sangamo Journal.*
Scioto Gazette (Also *Supporter and Scioto Gazette, Scioto Gazette and Independent Whig, Daily Scioto Gazette, Weekly Scioto Gazette, Scioto Gazette and Fredonian Chronicle*).
(Chillicothe) *Supporter.*
(Worthington, Ohio) *Western Intelligencer.*
(Jacksonville, Illinois) *Western Observer.*
(Cincinnati) *Western Spy* (Also *Western Spy and Cincinnati General Advertiser,*

Bibliography

Western Spy and Hamilton Gazette, Western Spy and Miami Gazette, Western Spy and Literary Cadet).
(Vincennes) *Western Sun.*
(Centreville, Indiana) *Western Times.*

Public Documents

Annals of Congress.
Gales & Seaton's Register of Debates in Congress.
Journal of the House of Representatives of the State of Indiana (31st session, Indianapolis, 1846).
Journal of the House of the State of Indiana (20th session, 1835) (Indianapolis, 1836).
Journal of the Senate of the State of Indiana (20th session, Dec. 1835) (Indianapolis, 1835).
Kettleborough, Charles, *Constitution Making in Indiana: A Source Book of Constitutional Documents with Historical Introduction and Critical Notes,* vol. I: *1780–1851* (3 vols., Indianapolis, 1971).
Patterson, Isaac Franklin, *The Constitutions of Ohio* (Cleveland, 1912).
United States Bureau of the Census, *A Century of Population Growth: From the First Census of the United States to the Twelfth, 1790–1900* (Baltimore, 1909, reprint 1970).
———, *Mortality Statistics of the Seventh Census of the United States, 1850* (Washington, D. C., 1855).
———, *Population of the United States in 1860* (Washington, 1864).
———, *The Seventh Census of the United States, 1850* (Washington, 1853).
———, *The Statistical History of the United States: From Colonial Times to the Present* (New York, 1976).
Verlie, Emil Joseph, ed., "Illinois Constitutions," *Collections of the Illinois State Historical Library,* 13 (Springfield, 1919).

Published Primary Sources

Basler, Roy P., ed., *The Collected Works of Abraham Lincoln* (8 vols., New Brunswick, 1953).
Beste, J. Richard, *The Wabash: or Adventures of an English Gentleman's Family in the Interior of America* (2 vols., London, 1855).
Birkbeck, Morris, *Letters from Illinois* (London, 1818, reprint, 1968).
———, "Notes on a Journey in America from the Coast of Virginia to the Territory of Illinois," in *Indiana as Seen by Early Travelers: A Collection of Reprints from Books of Travel, Letters and Diaries Prior to 1830,* ed. Harlow Lindley (Indianapolis, 1916), 171-90.
Blackburn, Glen A., comp., *The John Tipton Papers,* vol. I: *1809–1827* (Indianapolis, 1942).

Blanchard, J., and N. L. Rice, *Debate on Slavery: Held in the City of Cincinnati, on the First, Second, Third, and Sixth Days of October, 1845, upon the Question: Is Slave-Holding in Itself Sinful, and the Relation between Master and Slave, a Sinful Relation?* (Cincinnati, 1846).

Bond, Beverley W., Jr., *The Correspondence of John Cleves Symmes, Founder of the Miami Purchase* (New York, 1926).

Bostwick, Arthur E., *The Different West: As Seen by a Transplanted Easterner* (Chicago, 1913).

Brackenridge, H. M., *Recollections of Persons and Places in the West* (Philadelphia, 1834).

Brush, Daniel Harmon, *Growing Up with Southern Illinois, 1820 to 1861* (Chicago, 1944).

Buckingham, J. H., "Chicago to Springfield and the Towns along the Way," in *Prairie State: Impressions of Illinois, 1673–1967, by Travelers and Other Observers,* ed. Paul M. Angle (Chicago, 1968), 237-53.

Burnet, Jacob, *Notes on the Early Settlement of the North-Western Territory* (New York, 1847).

Burnham, Walter Dean, *Presidential Ballots, 1836–1892* (Baltimore, 1955).

Byrd, William, II, "The History of the Dividing Line betwixt Virginia and North Carolina, Run in the Year of Our Lord 1728," in *Anthology of American Literature,* vol. I: *Colonial through Romantic,* ed. George McMichael (New York, 1985), 216-21.

Caird, Sir James, "A Bird's Eye View of Illinois, Prairie Farming, and the State Capital," in *Prairie State: Impressions of Illinois, 1673–1967, by Travelers and Other Observers,* ed. Paul M. Angle (Chicago, 1968), 313-17.

Carter, Clarence Edwin, comp. and ed., *The Territorial Papers of the United States,* vol. II: *The Territory Northwest of the River Ohio, 1787–1803* (Washington, 1934).

———, comp. and ed., *The Territorial Papers of the United States,* vol. III: *The Territory Northwest of the River Ohio, 1787–1803 Continued* (Washington, 1934).

———, comp. and ed., *The Territorial Papers of the United States,* vol. VII: *The Territory of Indiana, 1800–1810* (Washington, 1939).

———, comp. and ed., *The Territorial Papers of the United States,* vol. VIII: *The Territory of Indiana, 1810–1816 Continued* (Washington, 1939).

———, comp. and ed., *The Territorial Papers of the United States,* vol. XVI: *The Territory of Illinois, 1809–1814* (Washington, 1948).

———, comp. and ed., *The Territorial Papers of the United States,* vol. XVII: *The Territory of Illinois, 1814–1818 Continued* (Washington, 1950).

Cartwright, Peter, *Autobiography of Peter Cartwright* (New York, 1956).

Coffin, Levi, *Reminiscences of Levi Coffin* (Cincinnati, 1880).

Crèvecoeur, Michel-Guillaume-Jean de, "Letters from an American Farmer," in *Anthology of American Literature,* vol. I: *Colonial through Romantic,* ed. George McMichael (New York, 1985), 394-406.

Cuming, F., "Sketches of a Tour to the Western Country, through the States of Ohio and Kentucky; a Voyage down the Ohio and Mississippi Rivers, and a Trip through the Mississippi Territory, and Part of West Florida," in *Early*

Western Travels, 1748–1846, ed. Reuben Gold Thwaites (Cleveland, 1904), IV.

Cutler, William Perkins, and Julia Perkins Cutler, *Life, Journals, and Correspondence of Rev. Manasseh Cutler, LL.D.* (Cincinnati, 1888), II.

Dean, John Candee, ed., "Journal of Thomas Dean: A Voyage to Indiana in 1817," *Indiana Historical Society Publications* (Indianapolis, 1918), VI, no. 2, 271-345.

Dumond, Dwight L., ed., *Letters of James Gillespie Birney, 1831–1857* (2 vols., Gloucester, Mass., 1966).

Dunn, Jacob Piatt, "Slavery Petitions and Papers," *Indiana Historical Society Publications* (Indianapolis, 1894), II, no. 12, 443-529.

Dwight, Margaret Van Horn, *A Journey to Ohio in 1810* (New Haven, 1912).

Esarey, Logan, "The Pioneers of Morgan County: Memoirs of Noah J. Major," *Indiana Historical Society Publications* (Indianapolis, 1915), I, no. 5, 225-516.

Faux, William, "Memorable Days in America; Being a Journal of a Tour to the United States," in *Indiana as Seen by Early Travelers: A Collection of Reprints from Books of Travel, Letters and Diaries Prior to 1830,* ed. Harlow Lindley (Indianapolis, 1916), 291-326.

Finley, James B., *Autobiography of Rev. James B. Finley or, Pioneer Life in the West,* ed. W. P. Strickland (Cincinnati, 1856).

Flint, Timothy, "Recollections of the Last Ten Years, Passed in Occasional Residences and Journeyings in the Valley of the Mississippi," in *Indiana as Seen by Early Travelers: A Collection of Reprints from Books of Travel, Letters and Diaries Prior to 1830,* ed. Harlow Lindley (Indianapolis, 1916), 438-42.

Fordham, Elias Pym, *Personal Narrative of Travels in Virginia, Maryland, Pennsylvania, Ohio, Indiana, Kentucky; and of a Residence in the Illinois Territory: 1817–1818,* ed. Frederic Austin Ogg (Cleveland, 1906).

Glashan, Roy R., *American Governors and Gubernatorial Elections* (Westport, 1979).

Greene, Evarts Boutell, and Clarence Walworth Alvord, "The Governors' Letter-Books, 1818–1834," *Collections of the Illinois State Historical Library,* (Springfield, 1909), IV.

Griffiths, D., Jr., *Two Years in the New Settlements of Ohio* (1835, reprint, Ann Arbor, 1966).

Grimke, Frederick, *The Nature and Tendency of Free Institutions* (Cambridge, Mass., 1968).

Hall, Basil, *Travels in North America, in the Years 1827 and 1828* (Edinburgh, 1829, reprint, 1964), III.

Hamilton, Andrew, James Madison, and John Jay, *The Federalist Papers* (New York, 1961).

Harris, Thaddeus Mason, "The Journal of a Tour into the Territory Northwest of the Allegheny Mountains," in *Early Western Travels, 1748–1846,* ed. Reuben Gold Thwaites (Cleveland, 1904), III.

Howells, William Cooper, *Recollections of Life in Ohio, from 1813 to 1840* (Cincinnati, 1895, reprint, 1963).

Hutton, Graham, *Midwest at Noon* (Chicago, 1946).

Johannsen, Robert W., ed., *The Letters of Stephen A. Douglas* (Urbana, 1961).

———, ed., *The Lincoln-Douglas Debates of 1858* (New York, 1965).

Johnson, Howard, "At Home in the Woods: Oliver Johnson's Reminiscences of Early Marion County," *Indiana Historical Society Publications* (Indianapolis, 1951), XVI, no. 2, 135-234.

Lewis, Sinclair, *Main Street* (1920, New York, reprint, 1948).

Martineau, Harriet, *Society in America* (3 vols., London, 1839).

Massie, Daniel Meade, *Nathaniel Massie, A Pioneer of Ohio: A Sketch of His Life and Selections from His Correspondence* (Cincinnati, 1896).

Michaux, F. A., "Travels to the West of the Allegheny Mountains, in the States of Ohio, Kentucky, and Tennessea, and Back to Charleston, by the Upper Carolinas," in *Early Western Travels, 1748–1856,* ed. Reuben Gold Thwaites (Cleveland, 1904), III, 105-315.

Middleton, Stephen, "Antislavery Litigation in Ohio: The Case-Trowbridge Letters," *Mid-America,* 70 (Oct. 1988), 105-24.

Nicholson, Meredith, *The Valley of Democracy* (New York, 1918).

Ogden, George W., "Letters from the West, Comprising a Tour through the Western Country, and a Residence of Two Summers in the States of Ohio and Kentucky," in *Early Western Travels, 1748–1846,* ed. Reuben Gold Thwaites (Cleveland, 1905), XIX, 21-112.

Oliver, William, *Eight Months in Illinois* (1843, reprint, Ann Arbor, 1966).

Olmsted, Frederick Law, *The Slave States,* ed. Harvey Wish (New York, 1959).

Palmer, George Thomas, *A Conscientious Turncoat: The Story of John M. Palmer* (New Haven, 1941).

Pease, Theodore Calvin, *Illinois Election Returns, 1818–1848* (Springfield, 1923).

Peterson, Svend, *A Statistical History of the American Presidential Election* (Westport, 1981).

Plummer, Mark A., and Michael Maher, eds., "A Newcomer Observes the Climax of the 1858 Lincoln-Douglas Campaign," *Illinois Historical Journal,* 81 (Autumn 1988), 181-90.

Rankin, John, *Letters on American Slavery, Addressed to Mr. Thomas Rankin, Merchant at Middlebrook, Augusta Co., Va.* (1837, reprint, Westport, 1970).

"Report of Lieutenant Fraser," May 4, 1766, in "Documents Relating to the French Settlement on the Wabash," Jacob Piatt Dunn, *Indiana Historical Society Publications* (Indianapolis, 1894), II, no. 11, 408-17.

Report of the Debates and Proceedings of the Convention for the Revision of the Constitution of the State of Ohio, 1850–51 (2 vols., Columbus, 1851).

Reynolds, John, *My Own Times: Embracing Also the History of My Life* (Chicago, 1879).

Robertson, Nellie Armstrong, and Dorothy Riker, comp. and ed., *The John Tipton Papers,* vol. II: *1828–1833* (Indianapolis, 1942).

———, comp. and ed., *The John Tipton Papers,* vol. III: *1834–1839* (Indianapolis, 1942).

Schauffler, Robert Haven, *Memorial Day: Its Celebration* (New York, 1924).

Schauinger, J. Herman, ed., "The Letters of Godlove S. Orth, Hoosier Whig," *Indiana Magazine of History,* 39 (Dec. 1943), 365-400.

Bibliography

Sherman, John, *Recollections of Forty Years in the House, Senate and Cabinet* (New York, 1896).

Smith, William Henry, *The St. Clair Papers* (Cincinnati, 1882), II.

Thomas, David, "Travels through the Western Country in the Summer of 1816," in *Indiana as Seen by Early Travelers: A Collection of Reprints from Books of Travel, Letters and Diaries Prior to 1830,* ed. Harlow Lindley (Indianapolis, 1916), 42-135.

Tillson, Christiana Holmes, *A Woman's Story of Pioneer Illinois* (Chicago, 1919).

Trollope, Frances, *Domestic Manners of the Americans* (London, 1974).

"Unedited Letters of Jonathan Jennings," in *Indiana Historical Society Publications* (Indianapolis, 1933), X, 147-278.

Volwiler, Albert T., ed., *The Correspondence between Benjamin Harrison and James G. Blaine, 1882–1893* (Philadelphia, 1940).

Washburne, E. B., ed., *The Edwards Papers* (Chicago, 1884).

Williams, Charles Richard, ed., *Diary and Letters of Rutherford Birchard Hayes* (5 vols., Columbus, 1926), V.

Woods, John, "Two Years' Residence in the Settlement on the English Prairie," in *Early Western Travels, 1748–1856,* ed. Reuben Gold Thwaites (Cleveland, 1904), X, 171-357.

Wright, Frances, *Views of Society and Manners in America* (Cambridge, Mass., 1963).

Secondary Sources

Abernethy, Thomas P., "Andrew Jackson and the Rise of Southwestern Democracy," *American Historical Review,* 33 (Oct. 1927), 64-77.

Ackerman, W. K., *Early Illinois Railroads* (Chicago, 1884).

Adams, Donald R., Jr., "The Role of Banks in the Economic Development of the Old Northwest," in *Essays in Nineteenth Century Economic History: The Old Northwest,* ed. David C. Klingaman and Richard K. Vedder (Athens, Ohio, 1975), 208-45.

Adams, Willi Paul, *The First American Constitutions: Republican Ideology and the Making of the State Constitutions in the Revolutionary Era,* trans. Rita and Robert Kimber (Chapel Hill, 1980).

Alexander, Thomas B., "The Dimensions of Voter Partisan Constancy in Presidential Elections from 1840 to 1860," in *Essays on American Antebellum Politics, 1840–1860,* ed. Stephen E. Maizlish and John J. Kushma (Arlington, Tex., 1982), 70-121.

———, *Sectional Stress and Party Strength: A Study of Roll-Call Voting Patterns in the United States House of Representatives, 1836–1860* (Nashville, 1967).

Almond, Gabriel A., and Sidney Verba, *Civic Culture: Political Attitudes and Democracy in Five Nations* (Princeton, 1963).

———, "Comparative Political Systems," *Journal of Politics,* 18 (Aug. 1956), 391-409.

———, "The Intellectual History of the Civic Culture Concept," in *The Civic*

Culture Revisited, ed. Gabriel A. Almond and Sidney Verba (Newbury Park, 1989), 1-36.

Alvord, Clarence Walworth, *The Illinois Country, 1673–1818* (Chicago, 1965).

Anderson, David D., *Critical Essays on Sherwood Anderson* (Boston, 1981).

Anderson, Terry L., "The First Privatization Movement," in *Essays on the Economy of the Old Northwest,* ed. David C. Klingaman and Richard K. Vedder (Athens, 1987), 59-75.

Appleby, Joyce, "Republicanism in Old and New Contexts," *William and Mary Quarterly,* 43 (Jan. 1986), 20-34.

Arensberg, Conrad M., and Solon T. Kimball, *Culture and Community* (New York, 1965).

Ashworth, John, *'Agrarians' & 'Aristocrats': Party Political Ideology in the United States, 1837–1846* (London, 1983).

———, "The Democratic Republicans before the Civil War: Political Ideology and Economic Change," *Journal of American Studies,* 20 (Dec. 1986), 375-90.

———, "The Jacksonian as Leveler," *Journal of American Studies,* 14 (Dec. 1980), 407-21.

Atack, Jeremy, and Fred Bateman, "Yankee Farming and Settlement in the Old Northwest: A Comparative Analysis," in *Essays in the Economy of the Old Northwest,* ed. David C. Klingaman and Richard K. Vedder (Athens, 1987), 77-102.

Atherton, Lewis, *Main Street on the Middle Border* (Bloomington, 1954).

Ayers, Edward L., *Vengeance and Justice: Crime and Punishment in the 19th-Century American South* (New York, 1984).

Bailyn, Bernard, *The Ideological Origins of the American Revolution* (Cambridge, Mass., 1967).

Baker, Jean H., *Affairs of Party: The Political Culture of Northern Democrats in the Mid-Nineteenth Century* (Ithaca, 1983).

———, "From Belief into Culture: Republicanism in the Antebellum North," *American Quarterly,* 37 (Fall 1985), 532-50.

———, *"Not Much of Me": Abraham Lincoln as a Typical American* (Fort Wayne, 1988).

Banning, Lance, "Jeffersonian Ideology Revisited: Liberal and Classical Ideals in the New American Republic," *William and Mary Quarterly,* 43 (Jan. 1986), 3-19.

———, *The Jeffersonian Persuasion: Evolution of a Party Ideology* (Ithaca, 1978).

Barkan, Elliott R., "The Emergence of a Whig Persuasion: Conservatism, Democratism, and the New York State Whigs," *New York History,* 52 (Oct. 1971), 367-95.

Barney, William, *The Road to Secession: A New Perspective on the Old South* (New York, 1972).

———, *The Secessionist Impulse: Alabama and Mississippi in 1860* (Princeton, 1974).

Barnhart, John D., and Donald F. Carmony, *Indiana from Frontier to Industrial Commonwealth* (4 vols., New York, 1954), I.

Bibliography

———, "The Migration of Kentuckians across the Ohio River," *Filson Club Historical Quarterly,* 25 (Jan. 1951), 24-32.

———, "Sources of Southern Migration into the Old Northwest," *Mississippi Valley Historical Review,* 22 (June 1935), 49-62.

———, "Southern Contributions to the Social Order of the Old Northwest," *North Carolina Historical Review,* 17 (July 1940), 237-48.

———, "The Southern Element in the Leadership of the Old Northwest," *Journal of Southern History,* 1 (May 1935), 186-97.

———, "The Southern Influence in the Formation of Indiana," *Indiana Magazine of History,* 33 (Sept. 1937), 261-76.

———, *Valley of Democracy: The Frontier versus the Plantation in the Ohio Valley, 1775–1818* (Bloomington, 1953).

Barnwell, John, *Love of Order: South Carolina's First Secession Crisis* (Chapel Hill, 1982).

Barron, Hal S., "Rediscovering the Majority: The New Rural History of the Nineteenth-Century North," *Historical Methods,* 19 (Fall 1986), 141-52.

———, "Staying Down on the Farm: Social Processes of Settled Rural Life in the Nineteenth-Century North," in *The Countryside in the Age of Capitalist Transformation: Essays in the Social History of Rural America,* ed. Steven Hahn and Jonathan Prude (Chapel Hill, 1985), 327-43.

Beard, Charles A., and Mary R. Beard, *The Rise of American Civilization* (2 vols., New York, 1927), II.

Bergquist, James M., "Tracing the Origins of a Midwestern Culture: The Case of Central Indiana," *Indiana Magazine of History,* 77 (March 1981), 1-32.

Berthoff, Rowland, "Conventional Mentality: Free Blacks, Women, and Business Corporations as Unequal Persons, 1820–1870," *Journal of American History,* 76 (Dec. 1989), 653-84.

———, "Independence and Attachment, Virtue and Interest: From Republican Citizen to Free Enterpriser, 1787–1837," in *Uprooted Americans: Essays to Honor Oscar Handlin,* ed. Richard L. Bushman et al. (Boston, 1979), 97-124.

Berwanger, Eugene H., *The Frontier against Slavery: Western Anti-Negro Prejudice and the Slavery Extension Controversy* (Urbana, 1967).

Billington, Ray A., "The Frontier in Illinois History," *Journal of the Illinois State Historical Society,* 43 (Spring 1950), 28-45.

———, *Westward Expansion: A History of the American Frontier* (New York, 1960).

Binder, Frederick M., *The Age of the Common School, 1830–1865* (New York, 1974).

Blight, David W., "'For Something beyond the Battlefield': Frederick Douglass and the Struggle for the Memory of the Civil War," in *Memory and American History,* ed. David Thelen (Bloomington, 1990), 27-49.

Bodnar, John, *Remaking America: Public Memory, Commemoration, and Patriotism in the Twentieth Century* (Princeton, 1992).

Boggess, Arthur Clinton, *The Settlement of Illinois, 1778–1830* (Chicago, 1908).

Bogue, Allan G., *From Prairie to Corn Belt: Farming on the Illinois and Iowa Prairies in the Nineteenth Century* (Chicago, 1963).

Bond, Beverley W., Jr., *The Civilization of the Old Northwest: A Study of*

Political, Social, and Economic Development, 1788–1812 (New York, 1934).

——, *The Foundations of Ohio* (Columbus, 1941).

Brauer, Jerald C., "Regionalism and Religion in America," *Church History,* 54 (Sept. 1985), 366-78.

Brown, Jeffrey Paul, "Frontier Politics: The Evolution of a Political Society in Ohio, 1788–1814" (Ph.D. diss., University of Illinois, Urbana-Champaign, 1979).

——, "The Ohio Federalists, 1803–1815," *Journal of the Early Republic,* 2 (Fall 1982), 261-82.

Brown, Jeffrey Paul, and Andrew R. L. Cayton, eds., *The Pursuit of Public Power: Political Culture in Ohio, 1787–1861* (Kent, 1994).

Brown, Lloyd Arnold, *Early Maps of the Ohio Valley: A Selection of Maps, Plans, and Views Made by Indians and Colonials from 1673 to 1783* (Pittsburgh, 1959).

Brown, Thomas, *Politics and Statesmanship: Essays on the American Whig Party* (New York, 1985).

Bruce, Dickson D., Jr., *And They All Sang Hallelujah: Plain-Folk Camp-Meeting Religion, 1800–1845* (Knoxville, 1974).

——, "Religion, Society and Culture in the Old South: A Comparative View," *American Quarterly,* 26 (Oct. 1974), 399-416.

——, *Violence and Culture in the Antebellum South* (Austin, 1979).

Bucco, Martin, *Critical Essays on Sinclair Lewis* (Boston, 1986).

Buck, Paul H., *The Road to Reunion, 1865–1900* (Boston, 1938).

Buley, R. Carlyle, *The Old Northwest: Pioneer Period, 1815–1840* (2 vols., Indianapolis, 1950).

Bushman, Richard L., and Claudia L. Bushman, "The Early History of Cleanliness in America," *Journal of American History,* 74 (March 1988), 1213-38.

Cady, Edwin Harrison, *The Gentleman in America: A Literary Study in American Culture* (Syracuse, 1949).

Campbell, John C., *The Southern Highlander and His Homeland* (New York, 1921).

Canup, Charles E., "Temperance Movements and Legislation in Indiana," *Indiana Magazine of History,* 16 (March 1920), 3-37.

Cardwell, Guy A., "The Duel in the Old South: Crux of a Concept," *South Atlantic Quarterly,* 64 (Winter 1967), 50-69.

Carnes, Mark C., and Clyde Griffen, eds., *Meanings for Manhood: Constructions of Masculinity in Victorian America* (Chicago, 1990).

——, *Secret Ritual and Manhood in Victorian America* (New Haven, 1989).

Carney, George O., "Music and Dance," in *This Remarkable Continent: An Atlas of United States and Canadian Society and Culture,* ed. John F. Rooney, Wilbur Zelinsky, and Dean R. Louder (College Station, Tex., 1982), 234-53.

Carpenter, Jesse T., *The South as a Conscious Minority, 1789–1861* (New York, 1930).

Carter, Kit Carson, III, "Indiana Voters during the Second American Party System, 1836–1860: A Study in Social, Economic, and Demographic Distinctions and in Voter Constancy" (Ph.D. diss., University of Alabama, 1975).

Bibliography

Caruso, John Anthony, *The Great Lakes Frontier: An Epic of the Old Northwest* (Indianapolis, 1961).

Cash, W. J., *The Mind of the South* (New York, 1965).

Cayton, Andrew R. L., *The Frontier Republic: Ideology and Politics in the Ohio Country, 1780–1815* (Kent, 1986).

———, "Land, Power, and Reputation: The Cultural Dimensions of Politics in the Ohio Country," *William and Mary Quarterly*, 47 (April 1990), 266-86.

———, "Marietta and the Ohio Company," in *Appalachian Frontiers: Settlement, Society, & Development in the Preindustrial Era*, ed. Robert D. Mitchell (Lexington, 1990), 187-200.

———, "'Separate Interests' and the Nation-State: The Washington Administration and the Origins of Regionalism in the Trans-Appalachian West," *Journal of American History*, 79 (June 1992), 39-67.

———, "The Origins of Politics in the Old Northwest," in *Pathways to the Old Northwest: An Observance of the Bicentennial of the Northwest Ordinance* (Indianapolis, 1988), 59-69.

Cayton, Andrew R. L., and Peter S. Onuf, *The Midwest and the Nation: Rethinking the History of an American Region* (Bloomington, 1990).

Cecil-Fronsman, Bill, *Common Whites: Class and Culture in Antebellum North Carolina* (Lexington, 1992).

Chambers, William N., and Philip C. Davis, "Party, Competition, and Mass Participation: The Case of the Democratizing Party System, 1824–1852," in *The History of American Electoral Behavior*, ed. Joel H. Silbey, Allan G. Bogue, and William H. Flanigan (Princeton, 1978), 174-97.

Channing, Steven A., *Crisis of Fear: Secession in South Carolina* (New York, 1970).

Chase, James Stanton, "Jacksonian Democracy and the Rise of the Nominating Convention," *Mid-America*, 45 (Oct. 1963), 229-49.

Church, Charles A., *History of the Republican Party in Illinois, 1854–1912* (Rockford, Ill., 1912).

Clark, Christopher, "Household Economy, Market Exchange and the Rise of Capitalism in the Connecticut Valley, 1800–1860," *Journal of Social History*, 13 (Winter 1979), 169-89.

Clark, Thomas D., *The Rampaging Frontier: Manners and Humors of Pioneer Days in the South and the Middle West* (Indianapolis, 1939).

Cockrum, William M., *Pioneer History of Indiana including Stories, Incidents and Customs of the Early Settlers* (Oakland City, Ind., 1907).

Coggeshall, John M., "Carbon-Copy Towns? The Regionalization of Ethnic Folklife in Southern Illinois's Egypt," in *Sense of Place: American Regional Cultures*, ed. Barbara Allen and Thomas J. Schlereth (Lexington, 1990), 103-19.

Colbourn, H. Trevor, *The Lamp of Experience: Whig History and the Intellectual Origins of the American Revolution* (Chapel Hill, 1965).

Converse, Philip E., "The Nature of Belief Systems in Mass Publics," in *Ideology and Discontent*, ed. David Apter (New York, 1969), 206-61.

Cooper, William J., Jr., *Liberty and Slavery: Southern Politics to 1860* (New York, 1983).

———, *The South and the Politics of Slavery, 1828–1856* (Baton Rouge, 1978).

Cott, Nancy F., "On Men's History and Women's History," in *Meanings for Manhood: Constructions of Masculinity in Victorian America,* ed. Mark C. Carnes and Clyde Griffen (Chicago, 1990), 205-11.

Craven, Avery, *The Coming of the Civil War* (Chicago, 1953).

Curtis, Henry B., "Pioneer Days in Central Ohio," *Ohio Archaeological and Historical Publications,* 1 (1888), 243-54.

Cutler, Julia Perkins, *Life and Times of Ephraim Cutler* (Cincinnati, 1890).

Dannenbaum, Jed, "The Crusader: Samuel Cary and Cincinnati Temperance," *Cincinnati Historical Society Bulletin,* 33 (Summer 1975), 137-51.

Davis, Cullom, "Illinois: Crossroads and Cross Section," in *Heartland: Comparative Histories of the Midwestern States,* ed. James H. Madison (Bloomington, 1988), 127-57.

Davis, Harold E., "Economic Basis of Ohio Politics, 1820–1840," *Ohio State Archaeological and Historical Quarterly,* 47 (Oct. 1938), 288-318.

Davis, James E., *Frontier America, 1800–1840: A Comparative Demographic Analysis of the Settlement Process* (Glendale, Calif., 1977).

——— "'New Aspects of Men and New Forms of Society': The Old Northwest, 1790–1820," *Journal of the Illinois State Historical Society,* 69 (Aug. 1976), 164-72.

Davis, Joseph L., *Sectionalism in American Politics, 1774–1787* (Madison, 1977).

Davis, Rodney O., "Partisanship in Jacksonian State Politics: Party Divisions in the Illinois Legislature, 1834–1841," in *Quantification in American History: Theory and Research,* ed. Robert P. Swierenga (New York, 1970), 149-62.

Degler, Carl N., *Place Over Time: The Continuity of Southern Distinctiveness* (Baton Rouge, 1977).

Devine, Donald J., *The Political Culture of the United States: The Influence of Member Values on Regime Maintenance* (Boston, 1972).

Dick, Everett, *The Dixie Frontier: A Social History of the Southern Frontier from the First Transmontane Beginnings to the Civil War* (New York, 1948).

Douglas, Ann, *The Feminization of American Culture* (New York, 1977).

Downes, Randolph Chandler, *Frontier Ohio, 1788–1803* (Columbus, 1935).

Duncan, Robert B., "Old Settlers," *Indiana Historical Society Publications* (Indianapolis, 1894), II, no. 10, 375-402.

Dunn, Durwood, *Cades Cove: The Life and Death of a Southern Appalachian Community, 1818–1937* (Knoxville, 1988).

Dunn, J. P., Jr., *Indiana: A Redemption from Slavery* (Boston, 1888, reprint, 1905).

Eaton, Clement, *The Growth of Southern Civilization, 1790–1860* (New York, 1861).

———, *The Mind of the Old South* (Baton Rouge, 1964).

———, "The Role of Honor in Southern Society," *Southern Humanities Review,* 10 (Bicentennial Issue, 1976), 47-58.

Eblen, Jack Ericson, *The First and Second United States Empires: Governors and Territorial Government, 1784–1912* (Pittsburgh, 1968).

Elazar, Daniel J., *Cities of the Prairie: The Metropolitan Frontier and American Politics* (New York, 1970).

Elias, Norbert, *The Civilizing Process: A History of Manners,* trans. Edmund Jephcott (New York, 1978).

Elkins, Stanley, and Eric McKitrick, "A Meaning for Turner's Frontier. Part I: Democracy in the Old Northwest," *Political Science Quarterly,* 69 (Sept. 1954), 321-53.

———, "A Meaning for Turner's Frontier. Part II: The Southwest Frontier and New England," *Political Science Quarterly,* 69 (Dec. 1954), 565-602.

Erickson, Leonard, "Politics and the Repeal of Ohio's Black Laws, 1837–1849," *Ohio History,* 82 (Summer-Autumn 1973), 154-75.

Ershkowitz, Herbert, and William G. Shade, "Consensus or Conflict? Political Behavior in the State Legislatures during the Jacksonian Era," *Journal of American History,* 58 (Dec. 1971), 591-621.

Esarey, Logan, *A History of Indiana from Its Exploration to 1850* (Indianapolis, 1970).

———, "The Organization of the Jacksonian Party in Indiana," *Proceedings of the Mississippi Valley Historical Association* (1914), VII, 220-43.

Escott, Paul D., and Jeffrey J. Crow, "The Social Order and Violent Disorder: An Analysis of North Carolina in the Revolution and the Civil War," *Journal of Southern History,* 52 (Aug. 1986), 373-402.

Ewbank, Lewis B., "A Real Pioneer," *Indiana Magazine of History,* 38 (June 1942), 143-64.

Faragher, John Mack, "Open-Country Community: Sugar Creek, Illinois, 1820–1850," in *The Countryside in the Age of Capitalist Transformation: Essays in the Social History of Rural America,* ed. Steven Hahn and Jonathan Prude (Chapel Hill, 1985), 233-58.

———, *Sugar Creek: Life on the Illinois Prairie* (New Haven, 1986).

Fehrenbacher, Don E., *The Era of Expansion: 1800–1848* (New York, 1969).

Fenton, John H., *Midwest Politics* (New York, 1966).

Finkelman, Paul, "Evading the Ordinance: The Persistence of Bondage in Indiana and Illinois," *Journal of the Early Republic,* 9 (Spring 1989), 21-51.

———, "Slavery and the Northwest Ordinance: A Study in Ambiguity," *Journal of the Early Republic,* 6 (Winter 1986), 343-70.

Finnie, Gordon E., "The Antislavery Movement in the Upper South before 1840," *Journal of Southern History,* 35 (Aug. 1969), 319-42.

Flinn, Thomas A., "Continuity and Change in Ohio Politics," *Journal of Politics,* 24 (Aug. 1962), 521-44.

Floan, Howard R., *The South in Northern Eyes, 1831 to 1861* (Austin, 1958).

Foner, Eric, *Free Soil, Free Labor, Free Men: The Ideology of the Republican Party before the Civil War* (New York, 1971).

Ford, Henry A., and Kate B. Ford, *History of Hamilton County, Ohio* (Cleveland, 1881).

Ford, Lacy K., "Yeoman Farmers in the South Carolina Upcountry: Changing Production Patterns in the Late Antebellum Era," *Agricultural History,* 60 (Fall 1986), 17-37.

Formisano, Ronald P., "Deferential-Participant Politics: The Early Republic's Political Culture, 1789–1840," *American Political Science Review,* 68 (June 1974), 473-87.

———, "Political Character, Antipartyism and the Second Party System," *American Quarterly*, 21 (Winter 1969), 683-709.

———, "Toward a Reorientation of Jacksonian Politics: A Review of the Literature, 1959–1975," *Journal of American History*, 63 (June 1976), 42-65.

———, *The Transformation of Political Culture, 1790s–1840s* (New York, 1983).

Fox, Stephen C., "The Bank Wars, the Idea of 'Party,' and the Division of the Electorate in Jacksonian Ohio," *Ohio History*, 88 (Summer 1979), 253-76.

Franklin, John Hope, *The Militant South, 1800–1861* (Cambridge, Mass., 1956).

Fraser, John, *America and the Patterns of Chivalry* (Cambridge, Eng., 1982).

Fredrickson, George M., *The Black Image in the White Mind: The Debate on Afro-American Character and Destiny, 1817–1914* (Middletown, 1987).

Freehling, William W., *The Road to Disunion*, vol. I: *Secessionists at Bay, 1776–1854* (New York, 1990).

Friedman, Bernard, "William Henry Harrison: The People against the Parties," in *Gentlemen from Indiana: National Party Candidates, 1836–1940*, ed. Ralph D. Gray (Indianapolis, 1977), 1-28.

Fuller, Wayne E., *The Old Country School: The Story of Rural Education in the Middle West* (Chicago, 1982).

Furlong, Patrick J., and Gerald E. Hartdagen, "Schuyler Colfax: A Reputation Tarnished," in *Gentlemen from Indiana: National Party Candidates, 1836–1940*, ed. Ralph D. Gray (Indianapolis, 1977), 55-82.

Garraty, John, *The New Commonwealth, 1877–1890* (New York, 1968).

Gastil, Raymond D., "Homicide and a Regional Culture of Violence," *American Sociological Review*, 36 (June 1971), 412-27.

Gaustad, Edwin Scott, *Historical Atlas of Religion in America* (New York, 1962).

Geertz, Clifford, *The Interpretation of Cultures* (New York, 1973).

Genovese, Eugene D., *The Political Economy of Slavery: Studies in the Economy and Society of the Slave South* (New York, 1967).

———, *The World the Slaveholders Made: Two Essays in Interpretation* (Middletown, 1988).

———, "Yeomen Farmers in a Slaveholders' Democracy," *Agricultural History*, 49 (April 1975), 331-42.

Gerzon, Mark, *A Choice of Heroes: The Changing Faces of American Manhood* (Boston, 1992).

Gienapp, William E., *The Origins of the Republican Party, 1852–1856* (New York, 1987).

———, "'Politics Seem To Enter into Everything': Political Culture in the North, 1840–1860," in *Essays on American Antebellum Politics, 1840–1860*, ed. Stephen E. Maizlish and John J. Kushma (Arlington, Tex., 1982), 14-69.

Gilmore, David D., *Manhood in the Making: Cultural Concepts of Masculinity* (New Haven, 1990).

Glassie, Henry, *Pattern in the Material Folk Culture of the Eastern United States* (Philadelphia, 1968).

Goodman, Paul, "The Social Basis of New England Politics in Jacksonian America," *Journal of the Early Republic*, 6 (Spring 1986), 23-58.

Goodrich, Carter, *Government Promotion of American Canals and Railroads, 1800–1890* (New York, 1960).

Gorn, Elliott J., "'Gouge and Bite, Pull Hair and Scratch': The Social Significance of Fighting in the Southern Backcountry," *American Historical Review*, 90 (Feb. 1985), 18-43.

Govan, Thomas P., "Was the Old South Different?" *Journal of Southern History*, 21 (Nov. 1955), 447-55.

Gray, Ralph D., "The Canal Era in Indiana," in *Transportation and the Early Nation: Papers Presented at an Indiana American Revolution Bicentennial Symposium* (Indianapolis, 1982), 113-34.

Green, Fletcher M., "Democracy in the Old South," *Journal of Southern History*, 12 (Feb. 1956), 3-23.

Greenberg, Kenneth S., *Masters and Statesmen: The Political Culture of American Slavery* (Baltimore, 1985).

Griffen, Clyde, "Reconstructing Masculinity from the Evangelical Revival to the Waning of Progressivism: A Speculative Synthesis," in *Meanings for Manhood: Constructions of Masculinity in Victorian America*, ed. Mark C. Carnes and Clyde Griffen (Chicago, 1990), 183-204.

Gusfield, Joseph R., *Symbolic Crusade: Status Politics and the American Temperance Movement* (Urbana, 1986).

Hackney, Sheldon, "Southern Violence," *American Historical Review*, 74 (Feb. 1969), 906-25.

Hahn, Steven, *The Roots of Southern Populism: Yeoman Farmers and the Transformation of the Georgia Upcountry, 1850–1890* (New York, 1983).

——, "The 'Unmaking' of the Southern Yeomanry: The Transformation of the Georgia Upcountry, 1850–1890," in *The Countryside in the Age of Capitalist Transformation: Essays in the Social History of Rural America*, ed. Steven Hahn and Jonathan Prude (Chapel Hill, 1985), 179-203.

——, "The Yeomanry of the Nonplantation South: Upper Piedmont Georgia, 1850–1860," in *Class, Conflict, and Consensus: Antebellum Southern Community Studies*, ed. Orville Vernon Burton and Robert C. McMath, Jr. (Westport, 1982), 29-56.

Handfield, F. Gerald, Jr., "William H. English and the Election of 1880," in *Gentlemen from Indiana: National Party Candidates, 1836–1940*, ed. Ralph D. Gray (Indianapolis, 1977), 83-116.

Hansen, Stephen L., *The Making of the Third Party System: Voters and Parties in Illinois, 1850–1876* (Ann Arbor, 1980).

Harrold, Stanley, *Gamaliel Bailey and Antislavery Union* (Kent, 1986).

Harstad, Peter T., "Indiana and the Art of Adjustment," in *Heartland: Comparative Histories of the Midwestern States*, ed. James H. Madison (Bloomington, 1988), 158-85.

Henretta, James A., "Families and Farms: *Mentalité* in Pre-Industrial America," *William and Mary Quarterly*, 35 (Jan. 1978), 4-32.

Hofstadter, Richard, *The Idea of a Party System: The Rise of Legitimate Opposition in the United States, 1780–1840* (Berkeley, 1969).

Hofstra, Warren R., "'A Parcel of Barbarians and an Uncooth Set of People': Settlers and Settlements of the Shenandoah Valley" (presented at the conference "George Washington and the Virginia Backcountry," April 21-22, 1989, Shenandoah College, Winchester, Va., copy in Nicole Etcheson's possession).

Bibliography

Hollinger, David A., "How Wide the Circle of 'We'? American Intellectuals and the Problem of the Ethnos since World War II," *American Historical Review,* 98 (April 1993), 317-37.

Holt, Michael F., *The Political Crisis of the 1850s* (New York, 1978).

———, "Winding Roads to Recovery: The Whig Party from 1844 to 1848," in *Essays on American Antebellum Politics, 1840–1860,* ed. Stephen E. Maizlish and John J. Kushma (Arlington, Tex., 1982), 122-65.

Horsman, Reginald, "The Dimensions of an 'Empire for Liberty': Expansion and Republicanism, 1775–1825," *Journal of the Early Republic,* 9 (Spring 1989), 1-20.

Horton, John J., *The Jonathan Hale Farm: A Chronicle of the Cuyahoga Valley* (Cleveland, 1961).

Howard, Robert P., *Illinois: A History of the Prairie State* (Grand Rapids, 1972).

Howe, Daniel Wait, "Making a Capital in the Wilderness," *Indiana Historical Society Publications* (Indianapolis, 1908), IV, no. 4, 199-338.

Howe, Daniel Walker, "American Victorianism as a Culture," *American Quarterly,* 27 (Dec. 1975), 507-32.

———, *The Political Culture of the American Whigs* (Chicago, 1979).

Howe, John R., "Republican Thought and the Political Violence of the 1790s," *American Quarterly,* 19 (Summer 1967), 147-65.

Hubbart, Henry Clyde, "'Pro-Southern' Influences in the Free West, 1840–1865," *Mississippi Valley Historical Review,* 20 (June 1933), 45-62.

Hurt, R. Douglas, "Ohio: Gateway to the Midwest," in *Heartland: Comparative Histories of the Midwestern States,* ed. James H. Madison (Bloomington, 1988), 206-25.

Hutslar, Donald A., *The Architecture of Migration: Log Construction in the Ohio Country, 1750–1850* (Athens, Ohio, 1986).

"The Illinois Constitutional Convention of 1818," *Journal of the Illinois State Historical Society,* 6 (Oct. 1913), 327-424.

Inscoe, John C., *Mountain Masters: Slavery and the Sectional Crisis in Western North Carolina* (Knoxville, 1989).

Jensen, Richard J., *Illinois: A Bicentennial History* (New York, 1978).

———, *The Winning of the Midwest: Social and Political Conflict, 1888–1896* (Chicago, 1971).

Johannsen, Robert W., *Stephen A. Douglas* (New York, 1973).

Johnson, Hildegard Binder, *Order upon the Land: The U.S. Rectangular Land Survey and the Upper Mississippi Country* (New York, 1976).

Johnson, Michael P., "Planters and Patriarchy: Charleston, 1800–1860," *Journal of Southern History,* 46 (Feb. 1980), 45-22.

———, *Toward a Patriarchal Republic: The Secession of Georgia* (Baton Rouge, 1977).

Jordan, Terry G., and Matti Kaups, *The American Backwoods Frontier: An Ethnic and Ecological Interpretation* (Baltimore, 1989).

———, "Division of the Land," in *This Remarkable Continent: An Atlas of United States and Canadian Society and Culture,* ed. John F. Rooney, Jr., Wilbur Zelinsky, and Dean R. Louder (College Station, Tex., 1982), 43-70.

Bibliography

Kammen, Michael, *Mystic Chords of Memory: The Transformation of Tradition in American Culture* (New York, 1991).

Kasson, John F., *Rudeness & Civility: Manners in Nineteenth-Century Urban America* (New York, 1990).

Katz, Michael B., "The Origins of Public Education: A Reassessment," in *The Social History of American Education*, ed. B. Edward McClellan and William J. Reese (Urbana, 1988), 91-117.

Kelley, Robert, "Ideology and Political Culture from Jefferson to Nixon," *American Historical Review*, 82 (June 1977), 531-62.

Kenzer, Robert C., "Family, Kinship, and Neighborhood in an Antebellum Southern Community," in *A Master's Due: Essays in Honor of David Herbert Donald*, ed. William J. Cooper, Jr., Michael F. Holt, and John McCardell (Baton Rouge, 1985), 138-60.

Klein, Rachel N., *Unification of a Slave State: The Rise of the Planter Class in the South Carolina Backcountry, 1760–1808* (Chapel Hill, 1990).

Klement, Frank L., *The Copperheads in the Middle West* (Chicago, 1960).

Kleppner, Paul, *The Third Electoral System, 1853–1892: Parties, Voters, and Political Cultures* (Chapel Hill, 1979).

Kloppenberg, James T., "The Virtues of Liberalism: Christianity, Republicanism and Ethics in Early American Political Discourse," *Journal of American History*, 74 (June 1987), 9-33.

Kniffen, Fred, and Henry Glassie, "Building in Wood in the Eastern United States: A Time-Place Perspective," *Geographical Review*, 56 (Jan. 1966), 40-66.

Knollenberg, Bernhard, "Pioneer Sketches of the Upper Whitewater Valley: Quaker Stronghold of the West," *Indiana Historical Society Publications* (Indianapolis, 1945), IV, no. 1.

Kofoid, Carrie Prudence, "Puritan Influences in the Formative Years of Illinois History," *Transactions of the Illinois State Historical Society for the Year 1905* (Springfield, 1906), 261-338.

Kolodny, Annette, *The Land Before Her: Fantasy and Experience of the American Frontiers, 1630–1860* (Chapel Hill, 1984).

Kramnick, Isaac, *Republicanism and Bourgeois Radicalism: Political Ideology in Late Eighteenth-Century England and America* (Ithaca, 1990).

Kruman, Marc W., "The Second American Party System and the Transformation of Revolutionary Republicanism," *Journal of the Early Republic*, 12 (Winter 1992), 509-27.

Lang, Elfrieda, "An Analysis of Northern Indiana's Population in 1850," *Indiana Magazine of History*, 49 (March 1953), 17-60.

———, "Southern Migration to Northern Indiana before 1850," *Indiana Magazine of History*, 50 (Dec. 1954), 349-56.

Latner, Richard B., and Peter Levine, "Perspectives on Antebellum Pietistic Politics," *Reviews in American History*, 4 (March 1976), 15-24.

Lawlis, Chelsea L., "Settlement of the Whitewater Valley, 1790–1810," *Indiana Magazine of History*, 43 (March 1947), 23-40.

Lawson, Hughie G., "Geographical Origins of White Migrants to Trigg and Calloway Counties in the Ante-Bellum Period," *Filson Club History Quarterly*, 57 (July 1983), 286-304.

Lebergott, Stanley, "'O Pioneers': Land Speculation and the Growth of the Midwest," in *Essays on the Economy of the Old Northwest,* ed. David C. Klingaman and Richard K. Vedder (Athens, 1987), 37-57.

Leverenz, David, *Manhood and the American Renaissance* (Ithaca, 1989).

Limerick, Patricia Nelson, *The Legacy of Conquest: The Unbroken Past of the American West* (New York, 1987).

Litwack, Leon F., *North of Slavery: The Negro in the Free States, 1790–1860* (Chicago, 1961).

Lynch, William O., "The Westward Flow of Southern Colonists before 1861," *Journal of Southern History,* 9 (Aug. 1943), 303-27.

Lynd, Robert S., and Helen Merrell Lynd, *Middletown: A Study in Contemporary American Culture* (New York, 1929).

McCardell, John, *The Idea of a Southern Nation: Southern Nationalists and Southern Nationalism, 1830–1860* (New York, 1979).

McColley, Robert, *Slavery and Jeffersonian Virginia* (Urbana, 1973).

McCormick, Richard C., "Ethno-Cultural Interpretations of Nineteenth-Century American Voting Behavior," *Political Science Quarterly,* 89 (June 1974), 351-77.

——, "Political Development and the Second Party System," in *The American Party Systems: Stages of Political Development,* ed. William Nisbet Chambers and Walter Dean Burnham (New York, 1967), 90-116.

——, *The Second American Party System: Party Formation in the Jacksonian Era* (Chapel Hill, 1966).

McCoy, Drew R., *The Elusive Republic: Political Economy in Jeffersonian America* (Chapel Hill, 1980).

McDonald, Forrest, and Grady McWhiney, "The South from Self-Sufficiency to Peonage: An Interpretation," *American Historical Review,* 85 (Dec. 1980), 1095-1118.

McKitrick, Eric L., *Andrew Johnson and Reconstruction* (Chicago, 1960).

McPherson, James M., *Ordeal by Fire: The Civil War and Reconstruction* (New York, 1982).

McWhiney, Grady, *Cracker Culture: Celtic Ways in the Old South* (Tuscaloosa, 1988).

——, "Ethnic Roots of Southern Violence," in *A Master's Due: Essays in Honor of David Herbert Donald,* ed. William J. Cooper, Jr., Michael F. Holt, and John McCardell (Baton Rouge, 1985), 112-37.

Madison, James H., *The Indiana Way: A State History* (Bloomington, 1986).

Maizlish, Stephen E., "The Meaning of Nativism and the Crisis of the Union: The Know-Nothing Movement in the Antebellum North," in *Essays on American Antebellum Politics, 1840–1860,* ed. Stephen E. Maizlish and John J. Kushma (Arlington, Tex., 1982), 166-98.

Marshall, Lynn L., "The Genesis of Grass-Roots Democracy in Kentucky," *Mid-America,* 47 (Oct. 1965), 269-87.

Mason, Edward G., *Early Chicago and Illinois* (Chicago, 1890).

Mathews, Donald G., *Religion in the Old South* (Chicago, 1977).

Meinig, D. W., "The Continuous Shaping of America: A Prospectus for Geographers and Historians," *American Historical Review,* 83 (Dec. 1978), 1186-1205.

Bibliography

———, *The Shaping of America: A Geographical Perspective on 500 Years of History,* vol. I: *Atlantic America, 1492–1800* (New Haven, 1986).

"Members of the Indiana Constitutional Convention of 1816," *Indiana Magazine of History,* 26 (June 1930), 147-51.

Merrill, Michael, "Cash Is Good to Eat: Self-Sufficiency and Exchange in the Rural Economy of the United States," *Radical History Review,* 4 (Winter 1977), 42-71.

Moore, Arthur K., *The Frontier Mind: A Cultural Analysis of the Kentucky Frontiersman* (Lexington, 1957).

Moores, Charles, *Caleb Mills and the Indiana School System* (Indianapolis, 1905).

Morgan, Edmund S., *American Slavery, American Freedom: The Ordeal of Colonial Virginia* (New York, 1975).

Murdock, George Peter, "How Culture Changes," in *Man, Culture, and Society,* ed. Harry L. Shapiro (New York, 1960), 247-60.

Nichols, Roy F., *The Disruption of American Democracy* (New York, 1968).

———, *The Invention of the American Political Parties* (New York, 1967).

Norton, Anne, *Alternative Americas: A Reading of Antebellum Political Culture* (Chicago, 1986).

Oates, Stephen B., *To Purge This Land with Blood: A Biography of John Brown* (Amherst, 1984).

———, *With Malice toward None: The Life of Abraham Lincoln* (New York, 1978).

O'Connor, Thomas H., *Lords of the Loom: The Cotton Whigs and the Coming of the Civil War* (New York, 1968).

Onuf, Peter S., *Statehood and Union: A History of the Northwest Ordinance* (Bloomington, 1987).

Otto, John Solomon, "The Migration of the Southern Plain Folk: An Interdisciplinary Synthesis," *Journal of Southern History,* 51 (May 1985), 183-200.

Ownby, Ted, *Subduing Satan: Religion, Recreation, and Manhood in the Rural South, 1865–1920* (Chapel Hill, 1990).

Owsley, Frank L., "The Pattern of Migration and Settlement on the Southern Frontier," *Journal of Southern History,* 11 (May 1945), 147-76.

———, *Plain Folk of the Old South* (Baton Rouge, 1949).

Paludan, Phillip S., *Victims: A True Story of the Civil War* (Knoxville, 1981).

Pangle, Thomas L., *The Spirit of Modern Republicanism: The Moral Vision of the American Founders and the Philosophy of Locke* (Chicago, 1988).

Paxson, Frederic L., *History of the American Frontier, 1763–1893* (Boston, 1924).

Pease, Theodore Calvin, *The Story of Illinois* (Chicago, 1925).

Peristiany, J. G., and Julian Pitt-Rivers, eds., *Honor and Grace in Anthropology* (Cambridge, Eng., 1992).

Persons, Stow, *The Decline of American Gentility* (New York, 1973).

Pessen, Edward, "How Different from Each Other Were the Antebellum North and South?" *American Historical Review,* 85 (Dec. 1980), 119-49.

———, *Jacksonian America: Society, Personality, and Politics* (Urbana, 1985).

Pierce, Merrily, "Luke Decker and Slavery: His Cases with Bob and Anthony, 1817–1822," *Indiana Magazine of History,* 85 (March 1989), 31-49.

Pitt-Rivers, Julian, "Honor," in *International Encyclopedia of the Social Sciences,* ed. David L. Sills (New York, 1968), VI, 503-11.

———, "Honour and Social Status," in *Honour and Shame: The Values of Mediterranean Society,* ed. J. G. Peristiany (Chicago, 1966), 19-77.

Pocock, J. G. A., *Virtue, Commerce, and History: Essays in Political Thought and History, Chiefly in the Eighteenth Century* (Cambridge, Eng., 1985).

Pole, J. R., "Historians and the Problem of Early American Democracy," *American Historical Review,* 67 (April 1962), 626-46.

Potter, David M., *The Impending Crisis, 1848–1861* (New York, 1976).

Power, Richard Lyle, "The Hoosier as an American Folk-Type," *Indiana Magazine of History,* 38 (June 1942), 107-22.

———, *Planting Corn Belt Culture: The Impress of Upland Southerner and Yankee in the Old Northwest* (Indianapolis, 1953).

———, "Wet Lands and the Hoosier Stereotype," *Mississippi Valley Historical Review,* 32 (June 1935), 33-48.

Putnam, Jackson K., "The Turner Thesis and the Westward Movement: A Reappraisal," *Western Historical Quarterly,* 7 (Oct. 1976), 377-404.

Pye, Lucian W., "Introduction: Political Culture and Political Development," in *Political Culture and Political Development,* ed. Lucian W. Pye and Sidney Verba (Princeton, 1965), 3-26.

Raitz, Karl B., "Settlement," in *This Remarkable Continent: An Atlas of United States and Canadian Society and Culture,* ed. John F. Rooney, Jr., Wilbur Zelinsky, and Dean R. Louder (College Station, Tex., 1982), 25-53.

Ransom, Roger L., "Public Canal Investment and the Opening of the Old Northwest," in *Essays in Nineteenth Century Economic History: The Old Northwest,* ed. David C. Klingaman and Richard K. Vedder (Athens, Ohio, 1975), 246-68.

Ratcliffe, Donald J., "The Experience of Revolution and the Beginnings of Party Politics in Ohio, 1776–1816," *Ohio History,* 85 (Summer 1976), 186-230.

———, "Politics in Jacksonian Ohio: Reflections on the Ethnocultural Interpretation," *Ohio History,* 88 (Winter 1979), 5-36.

———, "The Role of Voters and Issues in Party Formation: Ohio, 1824," *Journal of American History,* 59 (March 1973), 847-70.

Reed, John Shelton, *One South: An Ethnic Approach to Regional Culture* (Baton Rouge, 1982), 139-53.

———, *Southerners: The Social Psychology of Sectionalism* (Chapel Hill, 1983).

Reynolds, David S., "The Feminization Controversy: Sexual Stereotypes and the Paradoxes of Piety in Nineteenth-Century America," *New England Quarterly,* 53 (March 1980), 96-106.

Riddleberger, Patrick W., *George Washington Julian, Radical Republican: A Study in Nineteenth-Century Politics and Reform* (Indianapolis, 1966).

Robbins, Caroline, *The Eighteenth-Century Commonwealthmen: Studies in the Transmission, Development and Circumstance of English Liberal Thought from the Restoration of Charles II until the War with the Thirteen Colonies* (Cambridge, Mass., 1959).

Rodgers, Daniel T., "Republicanism: The Career of a Concept," *Journal of American History*, 79 (June 1992), 12-38.

Rodgers, Thomas Earl, "Northern Political Ideologies in the Civil War Era: West-Central Indiana, 1860–1866" (Ph.D. diss., Indiana University, 1991).

Rohrbough, Malcolm J., "Diversity and Unity in the Old Northwest, 1790–1850: Several Peoples Fashion a Single Region," in *Pathways to the Old Northwest: An Observance of the Bicentennial of the Northwest Ordinance* (Indianapolis, 1988), 71-87.

——, *The Land Office Business: The Settlement and Administration of American Public Lands, 1789–1837* (Belmont, 1990).

——, *The Trans-Appalachian Frontier: People, Societies, and Institutions, 1775–1850* (New York, 1978).

Rorabough, W. J., *The Alcoholic Republic: An American Tradition* (New York, 1979).

Rose, Gregory S., "Hoosier Origins: The Nativity of Indiana's United States–Born Population in 1850," *Indiana Magazine of History*, 81 (Sept. 1985), 201-32.

——, "Upland Southerners: The County Origins of Southern Migrants to Indiana by 1850," *Indiana Magazine of History*, 82 (Sept. 1986), 242-63.

Roseboom, Eugene Holloway, *The Civil War Era, 1850–1873* (Columbus, 1944).

——, "Salmon P. Chase and the Know Nothings," *Mississippi Valley Historical Review*, 25 (Dec. 1938), 335-50.

Roseboom, Eugene Holloway, and Francis Phelps Weisenburger, *A History of Ohio* (New York, 1934).

Rosenbaum, Walter A., *Political Culture* (New York, 1975).

Rosenberg, Morton M., and Dennis V. McClung, *The Politics of Pro-Slavery Sentiment in Indiana, 1816–1861* (Muncie, Ind., 1968).

Rotundo, E. Anthony, *American Manhood: Transformations in Masculinity from the Revolution to the Modern Era* (New York, 1993).

——, "Romantic Friendship: Male Intimacy and Middle-Class Youth in the Northern United States, 1800–1900," *Journal of Social History*, 23 (Fall 1989), 1-25.

Rozett, John Michael, "The Social Bases of Party Conflict in the Age of Jackson: Individual Voting Behavior in Greene County, Illinois, 1838–1848" (Ph.D. diss., University of Michigan, 1974).

Rudolph, L. C., *Hoosier Zion: The Presbyterians in Early Indiana* (New Haven, 1963).

Russo, David J., "The Major Political Issues of the Jacksonian Period and the Development of Party Loyalty in Congress, 1830–1840," *Transactions of the American Philosophical Society*, 62 (May 1972), 1-51.

Scheiber, Harry N., *Ohio Canal Era: A Case Study of Government and the Economy, 1820–1861* (Athens, Ohio, 1969).

Schlotterbeck, John T., "The 'Social Economy' of an Upper South Community: Orange and Greene Counties, Virginia, 1815–1860," in *Class, Conflict, and Consensus: Antebellum Southern Community Studies*, ed. Orville Vernon Burton and Robert C. McMath, Jr. (Westport, 1982), 3-28.

Schob, David E., *Hired Hands and Plowboys: Farm Labor in the Midwest, 1815–60* (Urbana, 1975).

Schwartz, Seymour I., and Ralph Ehrenberg, *The Mapping of America* (New York, 1980).

Sears, Alfred Byron, *Thomas Worthington, Father of Ohio Statehood* (Columbus, 1958).

Seldon, Mary Elizabeth, "George W. Julian: A Political Independent," in *Gentlemen from Indiana: National Party Candidates, 1836–1940,* ed. Ralph D. Gray (Indianapolis, 1977), 29-54.

Sellers, Charles Grier, Jr., "Who Were the Southern Whigs?" *American Historical Review,* 59 (Jan. 1954), 335-46.

Shade, William G., *Banks or No Banks: The Money Issue in Western Politics, 1832–1865* (Detroit, 1972).

———, "Pennsylvania Politics in the Jacksonian Period: A Case Study, Northampton County, 1824–1844," *Pennsylvania History,* 39 (July 1972), 313-33.

———, "Politics and Parties in Jacksonian America," *Pennsylvania Magazine of History and Biography,* 110 (Oct. 1986), 483-507.

———, "Society and Politics in Antebellum Virginia's Southside," *Journal of Southern History,* 53 (May 1987), 163-93.

Shalhope, Robert E., "Jacksonian Politics in Missouri: A Comment on the McCormick Thesis," *Civil War History,* 15 (Sept. 1969), 210-25.

———, "Republicanism and Early American Historiography," *William and Mary Quarterly,* 39 (April 1982), 334-56.

———, "Toward a Republican Synthesis: The Emergence of an Understanding of Republicanism in American Historiography," *William and Mary Quarterly,* 29 (Jan. 1972).

Sharp, James Roger, *The Jacksonians versus the Banks: Politics in the States after the Panic of 1837* (New York, 1970).

Shaw, Ronald E., "The Canal Era in the Old Northwest," in *Transportation and the Early Nation: Papers Presented at an Indiana American Revolution Bicentennial Symposium* (Indianapolis, 1982), 89-112.

Shortridge, James R., *The Middle West: Its Meaning in American Culture* (Lawrence, 1989).

Silbey, Joel, *A Respectable Minority: The Democratic Party in the Civil War Era, 1860–1868* (New York, 1977).

———, *The Shrine of Party: Congressional Voting Behavior, 1841–1852* (Pittsburgh, 1967).

———, "The Surge of Republican Power: Partisan Antipathy, American Social Conflict, and the Coming of the Civil War," in *Essays on American Antebellum Politics, 1840–1860,* ed. Stephen E. Maizlish and John J. Kushma (Arlington, Tex., 1982), 199-229.

Slotkin, Richard M., *The Fatal Environment: The Myth of the Frontier in the Age of Industrialization, 1800–1890* (New York, 1985).

———, *Regeneration through Violence: The Mythology of the American Frontier, 1600–1860* (Middletown, 1973).

Smith, Henry Nash, *Virgin Land: The American West as Symbol and Myth* (Cambridge, Mass., 1978).

Bibliography

Sorauf, Frank J., "Political Parties and Political Analysis," in *The American Party Systems: Stages of Political Development*, ed. William Nisbet Chambers and Walter Dean Burnham (New York, 1967), 33-55.

Sosin, Jack M., *The Revolutionary Frontier, 1763–1783* (New York, 1967).

Stampp, Kenneth M., *America in 1857: A Nation on the Brink* (New York, 1990).

———, *Indiana Politics during the Civil War* (Indianapolis, 1949).

Stearns, Peter N., *Be a Man! Males in Modern Society* (New York, 1979).

Stevens, Edward W., Jr., "Structural and Ideological Dimensions of Literacy and Education in the Old Northwest," in *Essays on the Economy of the Old Northwest*, ed. David C. Klingaman and Richard K. Vedder (Athens, 1987), 157-85.

Stevens, Harry R., *The Early Jackson Party in Ohio* (Durham, 1957).

Stilgoe, John R., *Common Landscape of America, 1580–1845* (New Haven, 1982).

Stourzh, Gerald, *Alexander Hamilton and the Idea of Republican Government* (Stanford, 1970).

Stover, John F., "Iron Roads in the Old Northwest: The Railroads and the Growing Nation," in *Transportation and the Early Nation: Papers Presented at an Indiana American Revolution Bicentennial Symposium* (Indianapolis, 1982), 135-56.

Stowe, Steven M., *Intimacy and Power in the Old South: Ritual in the Lives of the Planters* (Baltimore, 1987).

Swierenga, Robert P., "The Settlement of the Old Northwest: Ethnic Pluralism in a Featureless Plain," *Journal of the Early Republic*, 9 (Spring 1989), 73-105.

Taylor, William R., *Cavalier and Yankee: The Old South and American National Character* (Cambridge, 1979).

Thornbrough, Emma Lou, *Indiana in the Civil War Era, 1850–1880* (Indianapolis, 1965).

———, *The Negro in Indiana: A Study of a Minority* (Indianapolis, 1957).

Thornton, J. Mills, III, *Politics and Power in a Slave Society: Alabama, 1800–1860* (Baton Rouge, 1978).

Thurston, Helen M., "The 1802 Constitutional Convention and Status of the Negro," *Ohio History*, 81 (Winter 1972), 15-37.

Tillson, Albert H., Jr., *Gentry and Common Folk: Political Culture on a Virginia Frontier, 1740–1789* (Lexington, 1991).

———, "The Localist Roots of Backcountry Loyalism: An Examination of Popular Political Culture in Virginia's New River Valley," *Journal of Southern History*, 54 (Aug. 1988), 387-404.

Tredway, G. R., *Democratic Opposition to the Lincoln Administration in Indiana* (Indianapolis, 1973).

Turner, Frederick Jackson, *The Significance of Sections in American History* (Gloucester, Mass., 1959).

———, "The Significance of the Frontier in American History," *Proceedings of the Forty-First Annual Meeting of the State Historical Society of Wisconsin* (Madison, 1894), 79-112.

196

Bibliography

Tyrrell, Ian R., "Drink and Temperance in the Antebellum South: An Overview and Interpretation," *Journal of Southern History*, 48 (Nov. 1982), 485-510.

———, *Sobering Up: From Temperance to Prohibition in Antebellum America, 1800–1860* (Westport, 1979).

Utter, William T., *The Frontier State, 1803–1825* (Columbus, 1942).

Van Bolt, Roger H., "The Hoosier Politician of the 1840's," *Indiana Magazine of History*, 48 (March 1952), 23-36.

Verba, Sidney, "Comparative Political Culture," in *Political Culture and Political Development*, ed. Lucian W. Pye and Sidney Verba (Princeton, 1965), 512-60.

Vetterli, Richard, and Gary Bryner, *In Search of the Republic: Public Virtue and the Roots of American Government* (Totowa, 1987).

Volpe, Vernon L., *Forlorn Hope of Freedom: The Liberty Party in the Old Northwest, 1838–1848* (Kent, 1990).

Wade, Richard C., *The Urban Frontier: The Rise of Western Cities, 1790–1830* (Cambridge, Mass., 1959).

Walters, Ronald G., "The Erotic South: Civilization and Sexuality in American Abolitionism," *American Quarterly*, 25 (May 1973), 177-201.

Washburne, E. B., *Sketch of Edward Coles, Second Governor of Illinois, and of the Slavery Struggle of 1823–4* (Chicago, 1882).

Watson, Harry L., "Conflict and Collaboration: Yeomen, Slaveholders, and Politics in the Antebellum South," *Social History*, 20 (Oct. 1985), 273-98.

———, *Jacksonian Politics and Community Conflict: The Emergence of the Second American Party System in Cumberland County North Carolina* (Baton Rouge, 1981).

Watts, Steven, *The Republic Reborn: War and the Making of Liberal America, 1790–1820* (Baltimore, 1987).

Wilentz, Sean, *Chants Democratic: New York City & the Rise of the American Working Class, 1788–1850* (New York, 1984).

———, "On Class and Politics in Jacksonian America," *Reviews in American History*, 10 (Dec. 1982), 45-63.

Williams, Jack K., *Dueling in the Old South: Vignettes of Social History* (College Station, Tex., 1980).

———, *Vogues in Villainy: Crime and Retribution in Ante-Bellum South Carolina* (Columbia, 1959).

Wilson, Major L., *Space, Time and Freedom: The Quest for Nationality and the Irrepressible Conflict, 1815–1861* (Westport, 1974).

Winkle, Kenneth J., *The Politics of Community: Migration and Politics in Antebellum Ohio* (Cambridge, Eng., 1988).

Winkler, Allan M., "Drinking on the American Frontier," *Quarterly Journal of Studies on Alcohol*, 29 (June 1968), 413-45.

Wittke, Carl, "The Germans of Cincinnati," *Bulletin of the Historical and Philosophical Society of Ohio*, 20 (Jan. 1962), 3-14.

Wood, Gordon S., "Conspiracy and the Paranoid Style: Causality and Deceit in the Eighteenth Century," *William and Mary Quarterly*, 39 (July 1982), 401-41.

———, *The Creation of the American Republic, 1776–1787* (Chapel Hill, 1969).

Woods, James., *Rebellion and Realignment: Arkansas's Road to Secession* (Fayetteville, 1987).

Woodward, C. Vann, "The Irony of Southern History," *Journal of Southern History,* 19 (Feb. 1953), 3-19.

Wooster, Ralph A., *Politicians, Planters and Plain Folk: Courthouse and State-house in the Upper South, 1850–1860* (Knoxville, 1975).

Wyatt-Brown, Bertram, *Southern Honor: Ethics and Behavior in the Old South* (Oxford, 1982).

Zelinsky, Wilbur, "General Cultural and Popular Regions," in *This Remarkable Continent: An Atlas of United States and Canadian Society and Culture,* ed. John F. Rooney, Jr., Wilbur Zelinsky, and Dean R. Louder (College Station, Tex., 1982), 3-24.

———, "Where the South Begins: The Northern Limit of the Cis-Appalachian South in Terms of Settlement Landscape," *Social Forces,* 30 (Dec. 1951), 172-78.

INDEX

Index

NICOLE ETCHESON is Assistant Professor of history at the University of South Dakota.